A View from Two Benches

A View from Two Benches

Bob Thomas in Football and the Law

Doug Feldmann

with foreword by Mike Ditka

Northern Illinois University Press
an imprint of Cornell University Press
Ithaca and London

First published 2020 by Cornell University Press

Printed in the United States of America

Library of Congress Cataloging-in-Publication Data

Names: Feldmann, Doug, 1970– author. | Ditka, Mike,
    writer of foreword.
Title: A view from two benches : Bob Thomas in football and the law /
    Doug Feldmann ; with foreword by Mike Ditka.
Description: Ithaca : Northern Illinois University Press, an imprint
    of Cornell University Press, 2020. | Includes bibliographical references
    and index.
Identifiers: LCCN 2019037779 (print) | LCCN 2019037780 (ebook) |
    ISBN 9781501749988 (hardcover) | ISBN 9781501750007 (pdf) |
    ISBN 9781501749995 (ebook)
Subjects: LCSH: Thomas, Bob, 1952– | Chicago Bears (Football team) |
    Illinois. Supreme Court. | Football players—United States—Biography. |
    Judges—Illinois—Biography.
Classification: LCC GV939.T454 .F44 2020 (print) |
    LCC GV939.T454 (ebook) | DDC 796.332092 [B]—dc23
LC record available at https://lccn.loc.gov/2019037779
LC ebook record available at https://lccn.loc.gov/2019037780

To August and Anne Thomas

Nobody told me
The road would be easy
And I don't believe He's brought me this far
To leave me.

Contents

Foreword

Mike Ditka

Coming out of Notre Dame, the Bears knew they were getting a Christian young man in Bob Thomas. But being a Christian isn't necessarily about just going to church; it's about how you live your life. It's the way you communicate with people, the way you talk to people, and the way you treat people. To me, that's how you show your Christianity, and that's how Bob is. Everyone on the Bears loved him from day one.

When I got to the Bears, the cupboard was not bare. Some changes needed to be made, but there were a lot of talented players. I inherited a pretty darn good football team—we had Dan Hampton, Steve McMichael, Mike Singletary, Walter Payton, and all those guys, and Bob was part of that tremendous group that was already there. He always did a great job for us. We ultimately drafted another kicker in Kevin Butler, but Bob's a guy I really remember from those teams, mainly because of the outstanding person he was—and continues to be.

The first thing I told the team in 1982 was that it is important to set goals—but you also need to have methods to execute and reach those goals.

Bob exemplified this pursuit; he was a great goal-setter in wanting to improve himself as a kicker, to go to law school, and to accomplish other things. But unlike many people, he made certain he went out and *achieved* the goals he set.

Along the way, Bob has also shown a tremendous sense of humor. The Bears of the 1980s worked hard at practice—no one worked any harder than us—but we also had a lot of fun. I think it's important to mix those two things. If you make practice drudgery for your football team, they're not going to respond. Bob and some of the other guys would sometimes pull pranks on me, but it was OK—I actually enjoyed it because I knew we were bonding as a team. And every time I looked around, Bob was at the center of that bond.

Enjoy Doug's story of Bob's remarkable life.

PREFACE

I first met Bob Thomas when I was six years old. We did not cross paths again until I was forty-six. Naturally, much happened in each of our lives in the intervening four decades. Nonetheless, I discovered at our reunion that his moral core had not changed. "He remained true through the years," as Chicago Bulls announcer Chuck Swirsky told me about Bob. "Not the *same*, but *true*."

The story began for me as a kindergartner in the northwest Chicago suburb of Algonquin in 1975, the year I started following the Bulls, Cubs, White Sox, Blackhawks, and Bears. In those days, the easiest way for a kid learn about the teams was to get a pack of sports cards at the local White Hen convenience store, a courtesy permitted by my mother when I accompanied her on errands.

It was an interesting time for a child—or anyone, for that matter—to begin watching the Bears. The team did not simply *press* the reset button in 1975; they pounded it in frustration. Owner George Halas hired a new general manager when the previous season had ended, a new coach by January, and thirty-four new players come September. The 1975 Bears were laden with a bevy of rookies—Walter Payton, Mike Hartenstine, Virgil Livers, Bob Thomas, Revie Sorey, Bob Avellini, Tom Hicks, Roger Stillwell, Doug Plank, Roland Harper, and seven other first-year players—in addition to seventeen veteran free agents or trade acquisitions who also made the club.

The inevitable struggle ensued. After the running back Payton netted zero rushing yards on eight carries in his opening-day debut (which prompted me to ask my kindergarten teacher whether she thought the Bears should keep him), I agonized as the young team took regular beatings week after week. If enough diehards had pushed through the turnstiles at Soldier Field to keep a home game from being blacked out on television, I peeked at the screen through my hands, yearning to one day join the Bears and help them—although I confessed to my parents the fear of being tackled by Jack Lambert of the Pittsburgh Steelers. My parents soothed me as they always did, pointing out that Mr. Lambert would likely not be playing in the National Football League by the time I got there.

Things got a little better in 1976 as I reached grade school. That October, I went to the nearby Crystal Point Mall to get autographed photos from backup quarterback Virgil Carter and the kicker Thomas. With a smile, Mr. Thomas assured me that the Bears were indeed getting better and suggested I come out and see them play in person sometime.

With each passing year through childhood, my surveillance of Chicago sports teams grew into a daily, incessant scrutiny—bordering on the pathological.

Summer days were spent at the Algonquin Pool and its adjoining baseball fields, located just a few blocks from my house on the old east side of town. My friends and I played pickup baseball games in the mornings so that by 1 p.m. we could get to the pool—where the lifeguard grew tired of my regular requests to turn up the volume on the Cubs' WGN broadcast emanating from the snack bar. Later in the afternoon, as soon as Vince Lloyd told me that Frank Taveras had grounded out to end the Pirates' half of the fifth inning, I grabbed my towel, hopped on my bike, and sped home to make sure I saw the first pitch to Manny Trillo in the bottom of the fifth.

In the evening it was time for the White Sox. Via the "secret" radio under my bed (which my parents actually knew about), a late-night bonus was presented if the team was playing on the West Coast. The exciting stories in the dark continued during the wintertime, as I was levitated off to the Pacific shore when Bulls' broadcaster Jim Durham announced, "Wilbur Holland just hit one from the Twilight Zone!" against the Lakers in Los Angeles.

With major-league baseball games televised daily in the Chicago area, I took them for granted when I was a kid. I even occasionally missed a few. But I *never* missed a Bears game.

I can honestly attest that from 1975 until I left for college thirteen years later, there was only one Bears contest I did not follow on TV or radio. The date was December 4, 1983, when I begrudgingly attended my church's youth group retreat for eighth graders. The staff at St. Margaret Mary School made it clear we would have no recreational connection to the outside world over the weekend, thus preventing me from catching even a glimpse of the Bears' game at Green Bay.

Considering the fanaticism I've just described, one might assume my greatest day as a young Bears fan occurred just over two years later, on January 26, 1986. It did not. I simply expected another triumph on that date, as on every Sunday for the previous four months. A coronation took place that day in New Orleans—not a Super Bowl.

Instead, my greatest Bears day was December 18, 1977.

Joining my second-grade class at St. Margaret's that fall was a boy named Jeff Mitchell. Before long, Jeff and I were debating pro football with an intensity rivaling the pre-game shows on television. Waiting until the teacher had turned toward the chalkboard, we pulled out our copies of *All-Pro Football Stars 1977*—obtained through our classroom's Scholastic Book Club program—to locate our next talking points.

The weeklong arguments Jeff and I conducted over players, teams, and games served as our simmering prelude to Sunday, when the rest of my family joined me at St. Margaret's for 11 a.m. mass. I tried to pay attention during the homily, but my mind drifted—wondering how Payton, Avellini, and Thomas would perform when the clock struck 1 p.m.

Having moved to Algonquin from Pittsburgh, Jeff extolled the toughness of Lambert and the rest of the powerful Steelers (I never, of course, revealed my fear of the linebacker to him—until now). Already a veteran of two Super Bowl titles with the Steelers by the age of seven, Jeff teased me regularly about my struggling Chicago team.

Eight weeks into the 1977 campaign, the Bears appeared destined for another disappointing year as their record stood at 3–5, with any remote postseason hopes flickering. But like a Payton cutback run, the season turned on a dime in November.

A startling comeback victory was pulled from the fire against the Kansas City Chiefs on November 13. On a cold, rainy Chicago afternoon a week later—a couple of hours after I made my first communion at St. Margaret's—Payton shattered the single-game rushing record as the Minnesota Vikings were next to fall. Tim Ryan and Johnny Morris were usually at the CBS microphone for Chicago games back then, and when the Bears snapped the ball on offense the gifted Ryan, in his high-pitched voice, would usually just say "Payton"—letting the TV screen do the talking as the runner darted through the defense with amazing elusiveness.

More victories followed. I celebrated the arrival of Christmas break with the close of school on Friday, December 16, with the possibility of an early gift beyond my wildest dreams—a playoff appearance for the Bears if they could beat the New York Giants on the road on Sunday.

While seeing the ice-covered playing surface of the Meadowlands on television from the warmth of my home merely added to my excitement, the conditions were brutal for the players. Late in the second quarter, the score was tied 3–3 after Thomas and Giants kicker Joe Danelo each managed to drive a field goal through the howling sleet. At halftime, I hopped out into our snow-filled front yard and decided to boot a few myself.

I pretended to be Thomas, the nice man who had smiled and signed the autographed photo for me a year earlier in Crystal Lake. Flexing my lower right leg a few times just as the Bears kicker did in readying himself, I stared down at the spot where my brother—pretending to be holder Brian Baschnagel—gently set his finger upon the orange Nerf football (which had the obligatory hole dug into it where the thumb rested). After my field goal sailed successfully over the basketball hoop, I jogged off the "field" in a nonchalant manner (like Thomas) while my brother triumphantly thrust his index fingers into the air (like Baschnagel). I then scurried back inside to watch the conclusion of the Meadowlands story.

As I grew older and continued to watch every Bears game through my middle-school and high-school years, I regularly noticed there was something distinctive about Thomas. Something cerebral . . . something thoughtful. This distinctiveness manifested itself in a crucial battle late in the 1984 season against the Detroit Lions at Soldier Field.

With mere seconds remaining, Thomas kicked his third field goal of the day for a 16–14 Chicago win. Yet, when interviewed afterward on TV, he did not bask in his own glory. Rather, he reserved his appreciation for another: his longtime and normally sure-handed partner Baschnagel, who had dropped two snaps on two other field goal attempts that afternoon. "I'm happy for the opportunity Brian had to get out there and put another one down," Thomas said of the game winner. "He's a great holder, and he'll be out there next week with me. He's never made those mistakes before, and I'm sure he won't again."

The empathy reminded me of the kind man I had met in Crystal Lake as a six-year-old. Nearly a half century later, I found that his concern for others had not changed.

When I met with him in late 2016 to discuss this book project, Justice Thomas displayed the same friendliness as he had at our first meeting forty years earlier at the Crystal Point Mall. Instead of talking about himself, he was more interested in asking about *me*. He listened intently as I sat across from him at his desk, leaning forward with his hands folded across his chin. With each topic of life we discussed, we discovered we had more in common: my emulation of him was a prelude to my nondescript career as a walk-on player at Northern Illinois, but, most important, our Christian faiths had permitted our families to grow and prosper.

At the age of five, one's sports heroes are indomitable pillars of strength—but they are also monolithic. Don Kessinger was a hero of mine because he played a smooth shortstop for the Cubs. Keith Magnuson was a hero of mine because he was fighter for the Blackhawks. Bob Thomas was a hero of mine because he kicked field goals for the Bears, while Walter Payton dazzled me with his breathtaking runs.

Then you grow up. You discover your sports heroes are neither indomitable nor monolithic. They face challenges and setbacks in life, just like the rest of us. And like the rest of us, they either overcome these challenges or succumb to them.

The running back Payton was the embodiment of indestructibility, while Thomas was the embodiment of dependability. Yet, unknown to my admiring grade-school self at the time, they were simply mortal young men. They had breadth and depth. They had feelings, sensitivities, and vulnerabilities.

They had goals and dreams off the field. They were human beings who, out-side the public eye, occasionally needed the support of others—long before athletes had every second of their lives scrutinized on the internet and social media

Thomas and Payton—two men who, when I was a child, I was convinced were impervious to any semblance of pain or difficulty—leaned on one an-other in the tough times. One literally leaned on the other when the end of his football career was imminent; a decade later, the roles were reversed as the other's *death* was imminent. But through the peaks and valleys of life, the common thread throughout it all was trust in Providence. Both men achieved fame in reaching the top of their profession, and one of them would reach the top of a second profession as well. But in the end, each discovered—in different ways—that trusting in God was what remained when the cheers faded.

Perhaps in a perfect world for Bob Thomas, the Super Bowl played on Jan-uary 26, 1986, would have been tied 0–0 with ten seconds left. At that point, Payton would have made the most brilliant run of his career: breaking three tackles at midfield and eluding four more, sprinting down the sideline at the Superdome before being corralled by the last New England defender on the Patriots' twenty-three-yard line. The Bears would have called a time-out, with Thomas entering the game for a forty-yard field goal to decide it all.

But as Thomas knows well, it is not a perfect world. It is wrought with hardship, injustice, challenges, and purging trials.

Yet, if a strong faith is coupled with an undaunted resilience, anything is possible, as Bob has shown. His pioneering parents proved it before him—and they proved it *for* Bob and his brother, Rick.

After all, as John Lennon said, life is what happens to you while you're busy making other plans.

Doug Feldmann

Acknowledgments

While any author understands the monumental effort necessary to write a book, it hardly feels like work when one has privilege of becoming acquainted with so many fascinating people along the way.

Illinois Supreme Court Justice Robert R. Thomas graciously allowed me to pepper him weekly—and sometimes *daily*—with hundreds of questions over the past two and a half years, and the conversations were always a pleasure. In the process of getting to know Bob, I also developed a deep admiration for his family—Maggie, Brendan, Jonathan, Jessica, their children, and Bob's brother, Rick, as well as Anne and Augie, Bob's parents, who made this story possible with their courage to bring dreams to a new shore.

Invaluable perspectives on Bob were offered by his many friends, family members, former teammates, newspaper reporters, and legal associates whom I enjoyed interviewing for this book, including Joe Alvarado, Bob Avellini, Brian Baschnagel, Rolf Benirschke, Illinois Supreme Court Justice Anne Burke, Dave Casper, Paul Coffman, Mike Ditka, Brian Doherty, Robin Earl, the Reverend Joe Ehrmann, Illinois Supreme Court Justice Rita Garman,

Gary Gianforti, Dr. John Grieco, Mike Grieco, Gary Huff, Dr. Charlie Ireland, John James, Illinois Supreme Court Justice Lloyd Karmeier, Illinois Supreme Court Justice Thomas Kilbride, the Reverend Patrick King, Eddie Murray, Dan Neal, the late Ara Parseghian, Bob Parsons, Mickey Penosky, Don Pierson, Doug Plank, Joe Power, Terry Schmidt, Steve Schubert, John Skibinski, Tom Skladany, Chuck Swirsky, Illinois Supreme Court Justice Mary Jane Theis, Cook County Circuit Court Judge Debra Walker, and Jim Zloch.

Thanks are also in order for Matt Simeone, Adam Widman, and Meghan Bower from the Media Relations Office of the Chicago Bears, as well as for Chris and Kandace Brown for their assistance with research. Finally, a note of appreciation to my acquisitions editor Amy Farranto, who generously and expertly spent much time in consultation with me on the manuscript, as did production editor Michelle Witkowski.

A View from Two Benches

Chapter 1

A Ride to Freedom

Most of my friends played catch with their fathers after supper.
I kicked a soccer ball with mine.

—Bob Thomas, reflecting on his childhood in Rochester,
New York

Forty-six years after kicking the winning field goal in the 1973 Sugar Bowl for Notre Dame over the University of Alabama, Illinois Supreme Court Justice Robert Thomas thought back on his life in football and the law. "I've had two great careers, so I've been really blessed," Bob said with a faith-fueled gratitude. "In each case, you could say that I've always had the best view from the bench."

The football field was his first view, of course. After Notre Dame, Bob had become a kicker in the National Football League—first and most significantly with the Chicago Bears (1975–1982 and 1983–1984), a season each with the Detroit Lions (1982) and the San Diego Chargers (1985), and a brief stint with the New York Giants (1986). The year he was elected to the Illinois Appellate Court, Second District (1994), he acknowledged the big part sports had played in his life: "I probably wouldn't be here at all—I would never have existed—if it hadn't been for the role sports played in my family heritage." For a view of that role, Bob looks back to a time before he was born.

It was 1937 in Milan, Italy, when a train carrying a group of soccer-playing French teenagers pulled into Stazione Milano Centrale. Italian dictator Benito Mussolini, who had seized unilateral power in 1925, had become enamored with the idea of sports achievement as a way of advancing Italy's stature in the international community. He staged elaborate and highly publicized soccer exhibitions as a vehicle to accomplish this goal, pitting Italian youth clubs against teams from other countries and ordering massive stadiums to be built in Milan, Rome, Bari, Bologna, Turin, Florence, Livorno, and elsewhere. The venues were constructed to serve as monuments to fascist pride, and selection committees impressed with the stadiums' opulence chose Italy to host the 1933 World University Games and the 1934 World Cup.

The arriving French team had been invited to Milan to play against one of the local "schools," institutions created by Mussolini's government for children across the country. But rather than being devoted to adolescent development, the schools were de facto military training camps, organized to indoctrinate Italian boys and girls into strict allegiance to the leader. Upon reaching the "graduation" age of twenty, boys were sent into compulsory service in the regular army, while the sole duty of Italian girls was to grow into women who would give birth to future soldiers.

Draconian in both design and operation, the camps relied on harsh discipline and a rigorous daily schedule. As punishment for even minor offenses, students were locked in closets measuring only a few inches taller and wider than the average student's size. And if Il Duce himself visited, all in the camp were forced to stand motionless at attention for hours in the hot sun.

While the girls were afforded little recreation amid the unrelenting misery, among the few moments of joy that existed for the boys was the chance to play soccer. After their dismissal from the dinner hall, the boys hurried outside to take advantage of their brief free time and divided themselves into sides. The winning team stayed on the field until beaten by a challenger, with the last game halted by a curfew bell that sounded at dusk.

The very best players were chosen for Mussolini's carefully orchestrated international competitions, such as the one taking place against the team from France. Always selected from the Milan school were a pair of skilled brothers named Louis and August Tomasso, known to their friends as "Louie" and "Augie," aged nineteen and seventeen, respectively. Having endured the camp for ten long years, the brothers had learned to secure a few extra privileges through their soccer abilities; because of Mussolini's new focus upon competitive athletics, those who excelled enjoyed small measures of relief. "I remember our team getting oranges to eat. It was the first time I had ever seen or tasted the fruit," Augie once said. "And sometimes we got soft drinks, which made us the envy of the rest of the school."

Born to an Italian mother and residing in Paris, the Tomasso boys and their five other siblings—Fred, Audrey, Joan, Marie, and Denise—suffered in immense poverty during their time in the French city. After inhaling poison gas while fighting for France in Algeria, their father, Ernesto, had died only a few months after Augie was born in 1920. Augie's birth had followed the birth of another boy, also named August, who had lived a mere eight months. With her family (plus the family of her older daughter) living in a rented, one-room flat in the red-light Pigalle district of Paris, Josephine Oliva Tomasso struggled to provide for her children. "Starvation was there," Augie recalled simply—a memory he would retain the rest of his life. When Augie reached the age of seven in 1927, his mother decided she had done all she could do.

Seeking to build his army of the future to the greatest possible strength, Mussolini issued a decree that Italian-born children of expatriates could return to the old country and receive a free education as well as room and board. Believing it was in their best interests, Josephine sent Augie, nine-year-old Louie, and their eleven-year-old sister Denise—the three youngest children, all of whom had been born in Torino—to Italy with the idea of providing a better future for them. Her sons spent the next decade in the cruelest of circumstances, while her daughter fared no better in the girls' camp, where heads were shaved in the name of "order."

When relatives or foreign diplomats visited the schools, fine linens, good food, and bright smiles were put on display—but quickly disappeared on the guests' departure. Outgoing and incoming mail was censored, as the children were completely severed from not only the rest of Italian society but their families as well. After arriving in Italy, Denise, Augie, and Louie were permitted only one momentary in-person visit over the next decade with their mother, who in the interim moved to the United States, uncertain whether she would ever see her children again.

As a break from their perpetual isolation, the Tomasso boys relished the visit from the French soccer team. It was a rare opportunity for interaction—albeit indirect—with the outside world, and the two especially enjoyed hearing their home language once again, having studied only Italian since landing in the camp. That day on the soccer field in 1937, as the ball was kicked off from the center circle, the cunning Louie came up with an idea. Over the next hour and a half, he crafted his plan to perfection while he played.

When the French team got ready to head back home after the game, Louie asked the Italian officials for permission to board the team's train so he could say goodbye to his new friends. Stepping onto the car, he slowly walked down the aisle and shook each team member's hand as he made his way to the back. There, Louie stood in a corner and bent his head toward the window, his heart pounding and his eyes watching out in all directions.

He was still aboard as the train began to inch out of the Milan station. The train soon picked up speed and rolled away into the countryside, with the large city buildings gradually fading from view. Waiting for a moment when the majority of the French boys were occupied in conversations, Louie slipped away into the next car and found an empty seat.

The minutes and scenery continued to creep slowly past. At each stop the train made, the Italian guards eyed Louie with suspicion, but he coolly slipped around them, blending in by uttering a few French phrases. In this manner, he rode to freedom through the rest of northern Italy, across the Alps, and back home into France.

Upon arriving in Paris, Louie's first order of business was to find a pen and paper. He wrote a letter to the priests and nuns who ran the school in Milan, demanding that his sister and brother be released and sent to France as well. The clergy members reached out to representatives of the U.S. Department of State after receiving the letter, and, humiliated by Louie's escape, Mussolini's government offered Louie a deal: if he agreed to return and sign papers pledging to serve in the Italian army until he was twenty-one, he—along with Augie and Denise—would then be permitted to join their mother permanently in the United States.

Deliberating over whether to trust the Italian government, which had already betrayed him and his family once, Louie felt compelled to take the risk because of the opportunity he had to release his siblings from their dire circumstances. "I couldn't believe my eyes the day he returned," Augie said about seeing Louie in Milan once again. "It was like he'd been free and then decided to come back to jail. But I'll always be grateful to my brother for the chance he took."

After Louie put in his time in the Italian army, the government kept its end of the bargain. Twelve years after landing in Mussolini's camp, the three Tomasso children were given permission to go to the United States in 1939— just as Europe, along with the rest of the world, was on the brink of a great catastrophe. Denise reached the shores of liberty first and, after coming through Ellis Island, joined her mother in the upper reaches of New York state. Augie and Louie soon followed, navigating their way in the strange land as best they could with their fluency in French and Italian—but without a single word of English.

The brothers joined Denise and their mother in the city of Rochester, where they had settled into a diverse community of immigrants that included many Italians. The devout Catholic Josephine found a local parish and went to mass nearly every day until her old age—grateful for the unlikely deliverance of her children into a free land. As a tribute to America, she changed the family surname to "Thomas" after remarrying.

The advent of World War II provided employment for Augie as he was drafted into the U.S. Army. Given the assignment to work in ordnance, he also learned how to repair jeeps and other military vehicles and served in the Battle of the Bulge in 1944 in Belgium. Augie then spent the remainder of the war stationed safely, if a little unusually, at a pickle factory in Ireland.

After the war ended and he came home to his mother in the United States for a second time, Augie turned aside offers to play professional soccer in the Midwest and even a chance to try out for the Olympics. Not wishing to be separated from his mother again, he simply sought to stay put in Rochester. Even so, the sport Augie loved so dearly remained a large—and transformative—part of his life.

He began playing with the Rochester Thistles, a semi-pro team composed primarily of Scottish and Irish immigrants. Augie quickly put his exceptional skills on display, capping his first season by scoring eight goals in a single game—every one of which was needed for the Thistles to win the Northwestern Cup (the trophy in a state tournament) by a score of 8–7. In the wake of the triumph, Augie proceeded to form the "Italian American Soccer Team" (along with fellow neighborhood men Larry Saraceni and the Zoccali brothers, Vincent and Guy), which challenged any team the players could find.

The opportunity to continue playing soccer also gave Augie his first extended chance to practice his English and explore jobs he could do around the city. Using the skills he had learned in the Army, he decided to open Augie's Collision Shop on York Street in Rochester, and, in large part because of the honor and work ethic he displayed on the soccer field, people in the community soon came to trust him to fix their vehicles.

In 1947 he met his future wife, Anne Ciavatta, herself an Italian immigrant. By the time he and Anne were married, Augie had saved enough money to make a down payment on a house in a modest, middle-class suburb of Rochester called East Irondequoit. Augie cherished the good fortune that had embraced him—and that he figured was largely owed to the game he loved. Soccer had saved his life in making possible his escape from fascist Italy, and soccer was helping him build a new life as an American. Athletics would further alter the Thomas family for generations to come.

On August 7, 1952, Anne gave birth to a son, and the couple named him Robert Randall Thomas. Three years later, also on August 7, the family welcomed a younger brother for Bob: Richard, whom everyone called "Rick." With two more mouths to feed, Augie made certain that his body shop continued to thrive. "When his business was struggling a little bit, he had to purchase some things at an auto parts store on credit," Rick recalled. "Because of my dad's integrity, the owner of the store thought nothing of it, knowing that my dad would pay him back. And he did."[1]

While Rick would display a preference for the arts, young Bob was soon running up and down the soccer pitch with Augie. "Most of my friends played catch with their fathers after supper," Bob said. "I kicked a soccer ball with mine." Although no youth leagues existed in East Irondequoit at the time, Bob enjoyed a superior level of instruction from his dad. "Back in that day, there wasn't organized sports or park district teams—we had to go out and make our own games. We went out and played soccer or football or kickball in somebody's yard." On occasional weekends, Bob joined Augie at Rochester's Italian American club, where they would sit with other men from the old country and watch 16-mm black-and-white films of European soccer stars.

There was also room for American football in the Thomas household—a sport that Augie quickly came to enjoy in his desire to embrace the culture of his new land. "My dad was a New York Giants fan," Bob explained, "but my dad's sister [Denise] was married to a man named Tony Cuomo who had sons, my cousins, who were big Cleveland Browns fans. Therefore, to poke at my dad a little bit, I started pulling for the Browns. If we were playing out in the yard, I'd always pretend I was Jim Brown or Bobby Mitchell."

Nevertheless, soccer was a priority, and it was Bob's biggest thrill to cheer from the sidelines as he watched his father play—which Augie would do until 1962, when he was forty-two. That year, when Bob was ten years old, Augie exchanged his cleats for a coaching whistle and launched a local youth team called the Baysiders (Irondequoit Bay, part of Lake Ontario, lay just beyond Morin Park, which bordered the Thomas home). Playing with teenagers who had immigrated to Rochester from Italy, Mexico, Greece, Portugal, and other countries, the precocious Bob distinguished himself while Augie searched out other teams for them to play. The Baysiders soon developed a reputation beyond Rochester as one of the finest amateur soccer teams to be found anywhere. "It was a real United Nations," Bob said of the diverse roster, "and gave me a foundation for working with different cultures in the future." His brother agreed. "We had people in our house from Africa, Ireland, Scotland—you name it," Rick said. "In fact, as a kid, the first social event I ever attended with adults was a Portuguese wedding."[2]

Nonetheless, worthy opponents for the Baysiders were difficult to find. While soccer was generally strong in the eastern United States, the sport had yet to fully develop in most parts of the country. There was only one comparable local team with players the same age—the Rochester Juniors, formed largely of the children of local German immigrants. The Baysiders played the remainder of their games against adult teams and youth clubs as far away as Canada and New York City. By the time Bob was in high school, the Baysiders even participated in practice contests against the professional Rochester Lancers—which provided the city with a major league sport in the American (and later North American) Soccer League. The international experiences served to develop Bob in unexpected ways. "I had other interests in life," he said of his formative years, "but it was my ability to kick and dribble a soccer ball that bolstered my self-esteem and actually served as a foundation for my identity."

Faith was also an important cornerstone in the Thomas house as the family attended mass each week, with Bob periodically serving as an altar boy. Music was heard in the home as well, and while attending St. James Grammar School in Rochester, Bob made his first attempts at a variety of instruments, a pursuit he would resume later in life with greater success. "I tried the saxophone," he revealed about his grade school days. "I remember my dad coming into my room one day while I was practicing. He removed the strap from my neck and put it back in the saxophone case. I said, 'Dad, what are you doing?' He said, "After eight months, you should be able to play more than one note.'" Bob had been receiving his music instruction from a nun at St. James who taught lessons in the basement of the convent. She concurred with Augie's assessment of the boy's progress: "The nun called home and told my parents, 'Well, Robert has the nicest saxophone—but the worst notes come out of it.' So that was that."

Next up for audition was the large standing double bass. "I saw this jazz group, and this guy was just plucking the bass and spinning it around, not even using the bow, and he looked really cool. I was willing, but I couldn't take the bass home, so I had to practice at the school. The nun saw me spinning it one day—so that was the end of that." Next was the electric guitar: "I took guitar in the eighth grade, and I was more interested in the fact that the amplifier was somehow picking up the local police calls. So that was the end of that."

When it came time to leave St. James and begin his secondary education, Bob continued his Catholic instruction at McQuaid Jesuit High School, located on Rochester's near south side. Bob jumped right into the soccer program at McQuaid, leading the junior varsity Knights in scoring as a freshman while being elevated for some varsity games as well. He also continued to play for Augie and the Baysiders but was still a self-described "playmaker" in setting up scoring chances for the older players, a role he had performed since starting with the team at the age of ten.

At McQuaid, Bob found new extracurricular outlets beyond soccer. "I was in a couple of plays," he recalled. "The drama teacher, Father O'Malley, was also an English teacher, and I think he liked having someone who was a so-called jock in the plays. I was also in the chorus; but Father O'Malley said I was there because I would sing loud, not because I was any good."

Even before soccer, however, came schoolwork. It was Bob's mother who drove home the importance of doing well in his classes. "My dad was competitive in a sports sense, but my mom was competitive in an academic sense," he noted. When not looking over her boys' homework, Anne occupied her time with a job at a Rochester bank, where she eventually worked her way up to becoming a trust officer.

Anne's true passion, however—and the way she perhaps most fervently displayed her love—was the art of cooking. Every Sunday, the family would gather for large dinners taking place either at the Thomas home or the house of a relative. "It was a very warm family, a very ethnic family," Bob recalled. "I remember taking one of my roommates home from college over the holidays for one of those dinners, and it was course after course after course—it's the soup, then it's the pasta, then it's the meat from the sauce, and then it's the turkey *and* the roast beef, and on and on and on. I would try to excuse myself and go into a room alone for a half-hour or so and watch a game on TV and go back in later. This roommate of mine started looking for me about twenty minutes after I vanished. Finally, he found me, and he said, 'They're killing me in there—I thought we were done with the meal three different times!'" With a great cook in the house, Bob's friends always wanted to come over. "We played a lot of soccer games on Sunday, and when I would wake up on Sunday mornings, I couldn't decide if I was more excited about my game or that we would be having pasta later!"

Around the table at those family dinners, robust discussions on any number of topics would simmer—and sometimes boil over. Anne and her brother-in-law Louie occasionally got into spirited debates about how Louie had escaped from Mussolini's clutches. On one occasion, an agitated Louie said to Anne, "I'm the one who did it—why are you arguing with me about it?!?" Despite the vigor of the dinner-table conversations, it was evident to all that everything Anne did was with an attitude of caring. "I never saw an expression on her face that had any meanness at all," Rick remembered. "My parents were both people of tremendous warmth—simple, humble people, but very kind and generous."[3]

Even during those hectic, delicious Italian dinners, Bob's parents would not permit anything other than English to be spoken in the home. Despite Augie's fluent French and accent-free Italian (with no regional dialect), and even though Anne could speak Italian as well, speaking the European tongues was not allowed because of the discrimination both parents had faced in establishing themselves in their new country and their desire for the family to fit in. "They would always tell me, 'You're an American—we'll speak English,'" Bob said. "I told them later in life that I wished they had spoken Italian or French around the house, so I would have known another language, but they didn't."

When the Sunday dinner was officially declared over, and the men were settled around the television to watch football, Bob and Augie resumed their friendly Giants-Browns needling. Nonetheless, the idea of *playing* football was still remote for Bob halfway through his days at McQuaid. But things were about to change. "A friend's casual suggestion started a chain of events that would redirect my life in ways I could never have imagined," he said in remembering the summer of 1968, when he was about to begin his junior year of high school.

By the mid-1960s, "soccer-style" kickers were coming into vogue in professional football, challenging the traditional, straight-on "toe-punching" technique exclusively used up to that time. With the kicker approaching the ball from a forty-five-degree angle and striking it with his instep, the soccer-style revolution had been launched by Hungarian immigrant Pete Gogolak. Like Augie, Gogolak had come to the United States from Europe as a teenager: in the late 1950s, the Gogolak family had fled their homeland in the wake of Soviet oppression and had settled in the small community of Ogdensburg, New York, a few hours northeast of Rochester on the Saint Lawrence Seaway.

After kicking for Cornell University, in 1964 Gogolak signed with the Buffalo Bills of the American Football League (AFL) and, by 1966, with the Giants of the National Football League (NFL)—teams that Bob and Augie could watch on TV in Rochester. Soon after, other European newcomers to the NFL, such as Jan Stenerud and Garo Yepremian, also mastered the new style and began to influence high-school kickers around the country. Among them was Rolf Benirschke, a teenager growing up in San Diego whose father, a German immigrant, had been an Ivy League medical school professor before moving his family to the West Coast. "In the late 1960s, our heroes were the soccer-style kickers," Benirschke noted. "I actually saw Pete Gogolak kick against Dartmouth when I lived there as a kid. I particularly looked up to Jan Stenerud, because he was a ski racer like me. Back then, we were all soccer players first and learned to kick footballs second."[4]

With Bob's skills on the soccer field having become well known by the spring of his sophomore year at McQuaid, he became a target for his football potential. The high-school team's quarterback, Gary Gianforti, finally caught up with Bob in June. "I was a Giants fan, and they had just signed Gogolak," Gianforti recalled. "Soccer-style kicking was starting to become popular, so I thought it might be worthwhile to reach out to Bobby. I said to him, 'Why don't you give it a try?' We went out to the practice field, and I held the ball for him—and it just exploded out of my hand when he kicked it. As I watched the ball sail through the uprights, I said to myself, 'This is a no-brainer.'"[5]

At first, Thomas was hesitant to commit to the football team at McQuaid if it meant leaving soccer behind. "I'm not giving up ninety minutes a game [of soccer] for five minutes a season [placekicking in football]," he reasoned. Yet, he was intrigued by what football had to offer—and decided he could play both sports. Soon, he was seen practicing with the oblong-shaped ball just as often as the round one. "I enjoyed this strange new endeavor," he admitted, "especially the sudden added prestige I experienced in school as a varsity football player."

Although opposing soccer teams objected, the principal and athletic director from McQuaid, along with soccer coach Vito Marcello and head football coach Tom Seymour, received permission from the state athletic association offices in Albany for Bob to play both sports, provided he put in the requisite amount of practice time for each one. "I think back, and either one of those men could have made an issue of it and forced me to choose between the two," Bob said. "Instead, they went out of their way to make it work."[6]

His parents supported the decision, with Augie providing Bob his first tips for kicking a football. And not surprisingly, both father and son found that football came naturally. "I had a soccer background that was close to European," Bob once said. "Americans have better hands, but as far as feet go, Europeans have much better control. In Europe, it's not a ball in your hand when you're three [years old] but a ball on your foot."[7]

Despite the double-duty workload and the complicated schedule it entailed, Bob was willing to make the necessary commitments. As his new routine began, he sometimes had to scramble between the different practice fields at McQuaid on the same afternoon, joining the football team for the special-teams period and then sprinting back to the soccer field for the rest of their workout.

On the Friday when McQuaid was to open its 1968 football season, Bob was playing in a soccer game late into the afternoon. When the final whistle blew, he hurried to the football stadium with his kicking leg warmed up but his stomach empty. "I hadn't eaten anything," he said, "so Coach Seymour got me a hot dog and a Coke." Scrambling to get into his football gear, which was still relatively new and strange, Bob was finally able to squeeze his helmet onto his head. He found his way to the sidelines, where the makeshift dinner from his coach was waiting for him.

In full view of the crowd, Bob lifted first the hot dog, then the Coke, and then the hot dog again toward his helmeted face, stopping short of his mouth—and then put them back down again. The opening kickoff was to take place in mere moments. Having not yet mastered the intricacies of football equipment, Bob was unable to remove his helmet, even after he set the food and drink down on the bench and furiously attacked the helmet with both hands. When the referee signaled for the game to start and ordered Thomas onto the field, panic set in. Seeing no other alternative, Bob stuffed the hot dog *through his face mask* and then drizzled the Coke onto his face in the same manner—hoping some of the beverage would reach his mouth.

In an era when kickers did not specialize in their craft (especially at the high-school level), Bob's addition to the McQuaid football roster was a novelty in the Rochester area. Bob himself was initially unsure of what his role might be. Most coaches of the day, including McQuaid's Seymour ("old-school and traditional in the Woody Hayes style," as Gianforti put it),[8] preferred players to run or pass for the extra point attempt after touchdowns and rarely if ever to attempt field goals. Seymour thus hesitated to use Bob in the first four games on the schedule. "I think I was viewed by teammates and fans alike as McQuaid's secret weapon," Bob said with a smile about his delayed debut.

Five games into the season, on October 19, McQuaid's big test appeared on the schedule: a road contest against the team's crosstown rival, powerful Aquinas High. Seymour sent Bob in for a pair of extra points, both of which Bob made and which, along with a couple of safeties, contributed to an 18–0 shutout for the Knights. Over the course of his first season on the gridiron, as McQuaid charged to the conference title, Bob did not attempt a single field goal. Seymour, however, was drafting further plans for his "secret weapon" come 1969.

In constructing his game plan against Aquinas that season, Seymour correctly predicted a low-scoring, defensive struggle with opportunities for points at a premium. Late in a scoreless first quarter, a drive by the Knights stalled inside the Aquinas twenty-eight-yard line. Wanting to jump ahead by any means necessary, Seymour decided it was time.

In a move unprecedented in local high school football history, the coach sent Bob into the game to try a forty-five-yard field goal—among the longest ever attempted in New York state history at that time. The distance was so great, in fact, that Aquinas coach Bob Rosmarino could not believe that Seymour would even make the attempt. "Rosmarino was quoted in the local paper as thinking, 'It was nuts,'" Bob said of the reaction to Seymour's decision.

With Gianforti having graduated the past spring, Bob lined up in position with his new holder on a knee. Rosmarino warned his players to be ready for the probable fake. But as the ball came back, after receiving it the holder stayed down. Bob started his steps and fired away: "I made good, solid contact with my kick. I remember watching the football sail up and over the line of scrimmage and on toward the goalposts, which seemed miles away. I lost sight of the ball against the dark night sky, so I never did see whether it went through the uprights. And I was still so new to the sport that I didn't know where to look for the referee's signal."

Behind the goalposts off in the distance, an unconcerned mounted policeman was sitting on his horse. Thinking the kicker was too far away, the policeman had not even bothered to move. However, he quickly had to rein in his spooked animal when the ball unexpectedly landed near them. The first evidence that the kick was good came from the Aquinas sideline, where Rosmarino and his players stood with mouths gaping in stunned silence. The next reaction came from the visitor's side of the stadium: "Suddenly, my own teammates and the McQuaid stands went crazy." The kick was not only the longest field goal anyone around Rochester could remember, but it was also the first field goal *ever* in McQuaid history.

Thereafter, Bob had to remind himself to tone his kicks down when necessary. "When I play football I think football and when I play soccer I think soccer," he told the *Rochester Democrat and Chronicle* that October. "Sometimes when a soccer kick of mine goes over the goal, my friends say I must be thinking of football, but I'm not."[9] He had also gotten off to a hot start on the pitch, netting twelve goals in the first ten games—including five in a single contest against Aquinas.

When Bob graduated from McQuaid in the spring of 1970 a few months later, it was time for him to consider what path his life would take from there. At first, it was his intent to stay close to home, for academic and financial reasons. "I really didn't pursue scholarship offers for soccer," he recalled. "I was thinking about the University of Rochester because they had a good pre-med program and they were offering me a scholarship for football." Lafayette College wanted his services for football as well. But soon another alternative presented itself, which Bob suspected had developed from the publicity generated from his long field goal against Aquinas: "I got a postcard from the University of Notre Dame, from head coach Ara Parseghian, which said, 'You're on file for a possible football scholarship.'"

However, with no further word arriving from Parseghian in the succeeding weeks, Bob decided to accept the offer from Rochester to assist his parents with costs. As he was sitting at his bedroom desk completing the final application form (and having already sent in a fifty-dollar deposit to the admissions office), Augie and Anne appeared in the doorway. "We know you really want to go to Notre Dame," Augie said, sporting a grin that matched his wife's. They knew sending Bob to Notre Dame would be expensive— but making sacrifices for one another was a tradition in the Thomas family.

Paying his way as a non-scholarship player, Bob headed for South Bend, Indiana, that August and arrived at Notre Dame as a walk-on in football, as nondescript as any other student enrolling in fall classes on campus. Once again, sports were about to change a life in the Thomas family.

Chapter 2

SOUTH BEND

The first time I knew something was different was the sound
of how he hit the ball.

—BRIAN DOHERTY, THOMAS'S HOLDER FOR FIELD GOALS
AT NOTRE DAME

When Thomas appeared for his first day of football workouts, he was greeted with the cold dismissal typically given to walk-ons. After waiting in line for the secondhand equipment issued to non-scholarship players, he was given the ignominious jersey number 98—"a tent-sized job," as Bob described it, "last worn by someone at least a hundred pounds heavier than my one-hundred-sixty-or-so pounds."

Gathering the tattered gear into his arms, Bob lugged the bundle down the hallway underneath Notre Dame Stadium, pausing only to glance for a moment at the portal leading to the locker room for the scholarship athletes—which was adorned with new blue carpeting, fresh paint, and large stalls for each player with ample space for the player's equipment and then some.

Ten steps further down, Bob found a door to another locker room—a cramped, unkempt area to which he had been assigned along with seven or eight other walk-ons.

After getting dressed and lacing on his cleats, Thomas stepped outside and fully realized he was in for a tremendous challenge. "Just walking out onto the Notre Dame practice fields for the first time was a pretty intimidating experience. There were a hundred guys out there who were bigger and better football players than anyone I had ever played with or against in high school."

With first-year students ineligible for the varsity at that time, Bob spent his initial year at Notre Dame suiting up for the limited number of freshman football games while also playing in a few contests for the university's club soccer team. Otherwise, he acclimated himself to the milieu of college as he took up residence on the North Quad. "There were no athletic dorms back then. We were in dorms with the other students, and I think that was by design so that you got that flavor of academics instead of being thought of as only being football players."

Brian Doherty, a teammate and close friend of Thomas, agreed. "With Father Hesburgh [president of the University from 1952 to 1987], there was no question that the emphasis at Notre Dame would be on the 'student' part of student-athlete. We had a tutorial department, but if you weren't at the eight a.m. class, someone was pounding on your dorm room door by eight-ten. You were going to make your classes even if it meant skipping football practice, as some had to do. If we missed classes due to away games, they had teachers making those classes up at night. There was no physical education major. You managed it, or you were on the train home the next semester. Bob and I saw that happen with a number of players."[1]

Nonetheless, the players did take time out to have some fun—and one of the ringleaders was Dave Casper, a lineman destined for another position and a fellow member of the 1970 freshman football class. "Of course, those were the days of the 'section parties,'" Casper said of dorm living. "It was where hallmates could come together in a semiprivate atmosphere and loosen up from the previous week's pressures. The 'section' took the place of what other universities call 'fraternities.' There was a bond within the section, and at the center of that bond were the old section parties."[2]

Later in his career at Notre Dame, however, a disappointed Casper would shake his head over a change in campus policy. "Parties must now be expertly planned and the rector must be the guest of honor," he mourned four years later when interviewed by a student paper during his senior year. "Parties that are self-contained within one room are all right as long as you accurately predict attendance and noise levels and do not venture into the hall with a loaded glass of alcohol."[3]

After completing one semester of a pre-med curriculum, Bob realized it would be difficult to continue that concentration while playing football. He took some business courses and ultimately ended up majoring in government studies. Despite doing well in his first round of postsecondary schoolwork, frustration quickly arrived on the football field. "There were three [freshman] games, but I didn't kick in any of them. I was thinking about transferring, because among the freshman guys, I felt I was the best kicker. But in talking to my parents, I just decided to stick it out."

To make "sticking it out" worthwhile, however, Thomas decided he needed to take further initiative at practice and go head-to-head with the 1970 varsity kicker, Scott Hempel. "Coach Parseghian would be out there watching us practice, and I started thinking, 'I have to get someone to notice me.' So, if Hempel would kick from thirty [yards], I'd kick from thirty-five; if he kicked from thirty-five, I'd kick from forty. And I started to notice that Ara was noticing *me*."

It was not just Thomas's unique soccer style that caught the coach's attention (with Hempel being a traditional straight-on kicker), but also the sheer power in Thomas's leg. Other players were seeing it as well—such as Doherty, the starting punter whom Parseghian eventually anointed the holder for extra points and field goals in 1971.

After Doherty received the snap from center and placed the ball down, he recoiled as it fired off the tip of his finger when Bob struck it—just as Gianforti had done back at McQuaid High. "The first time I knew something was different was the sound of how he hit the ball," Doherty said in observing Thomas's kicks from the closest possible vantage point. "He just *thumped* it—and you could hear the difference all over the field as compared to the 'toe' kickers. Thus, we nicknamed him 'Thumper'—kind of like the eighth dwarf."[4]

Thomas was unlike any kicker Doherty and the other players had ever seen. Nearly all kickers and punters of the era usually played other positions (such as Doherty himself, who arrived at Notre Dame as a quarterback and wide receiver, and Hempel, who was a tackle). Thomas, however, was an extreme rarity in that he was *only* a kicker. "Many of us never played against a soccer kicker," Doherty revealed. "All the high school kickers in the 1960s played another position where I came from. There were no punter or kicker specialists."[5]

With Hempel graduating after the 1970 season, Thomas's exhibitions in practice set the stage for an opportunity for him to claim the starting kicker's role in his sophomore year in the fall of 1971. Still a walk-on and listed third on the depth chart as practices got under way, he battled for the top spot with another sophomore, a junior, and a senior who was Thomas's roommate during two-a-day practices. Bob remembered the advice he received: "The senior kicker I was rooming with said he had to wait until he was a senior [to play], and that maybe I would move up the depth chart by then, too. I remember thinking to myself, 'I don't think so—I think I have a chance *right now*.'"

Thomas's confidence was augmented when the junior candidate asked Thomas how he felt on the field with all eyes upon him. "I remember him coming up to me and asking, 'Aren't you nervous when you're out there?' I said, 'No, not really'—but I could tell by the question that *he* was. So, I figured I had a good chance of winning the job."

Unconcerned about the senior and the junior, Thomas was prepared to receive his stiffest challenge from fellow sophomore Cliff Brown, yet another individual who played a regular position and was seeking to become the team's starting quarterback. "Cliff had one of the strongest legs I've ever seen," Bob said. "Accuracy was another issue, however; when he kicked it, you didn't know if it was going right down the middle or would be shanked."

The Fighting Irish opened their 1971 schedule in South Bend on Saturday, September 18, against Northwestern University, the school from which Parseghian was lured in 1964 after his Wildcats had beaten Notre Dame four consecutive times from 1959 to 1962. Less than forty-eight hours from kickoff, at the end of the team's last full workout on Thursday, Thomas was heading onto the field with the number-one field goal unit when it was time for special teams during practice. However, an unpleasant surprise was in store for him the following evening on Friday.

"All of the practices leading up to the Northwestern game had me as the kicker, and I was doing well. The Friday before the Saturday game, they called the field goal team out during the 'walk-through' practice, and I went in. I had been listed everywhere as the number-one kicker. When I went to line up with the field goal team, Parseghian said, '*Cliff Brown—get in there*.'"

Thomas noticed that when Parseghian had made the announcement, the coach was hanging his head and looked as if he was almost embarrassed to do so—suggesting something else was up. To some, the insertion of Brown was seen as a "consolation prize" for the player, as he had failed to win the starting quarterback position.

Having been replaced at the very last moment, a dejected Thomas showered after practice and returned to his residence to call his parents, who were preparing to make the long drive from Rochester to see their son's first college game. He told them not to come. "'I don't know what happened," Bob said over the phone, 'but they put Cliff Brown ahead of me.'"

Unbeknownst to Thomas, however, assistant coach Tom Pagna had also called Bob's father—and told the family to keep their plans to come to South Bend. "I didn't know they had talked," Bob said, "so I didn't even know that my parents were at the game." Augie and Anne left Rochester at 8 p.m. Friday and reached the parking lot outside Notre Dame Stadium early on Saturday morning—where they managed a few hours of sleep inside their car before the gates opened.

As play got under way, the Irish scored early for a 6–0 lead after Walt Patulski blocked a Northwestern punt and Ed Gulyas plunged over from three yards out. As Bob looked on from the sidelines, Brown was sent in to kick the extra point—which scraped just over the crossbar as Parseghian grimaced at the marginal result.

"Ara saw that the kick wasn't very good," Thomas recalled. "So, we score a second time, and again, Cliff's ball just makes it over the crossbar. And again, Ara makes an unpleasant gesture."

Another Notre Dame touchdown followed—and a third consecutive extra point attempt by Brown that barely squeaked between the goalposts, giving the Irish a 21–7 advantage.

Late in the second quarter, a Notre Dame drive stalled at the Northwestern nineteen-yard line. Disappointed with the unpredictable kicks from Brown, Parseghian abruptly summoned a surprised Thomas—who thought he had been permanently banished to the bench—onto the field for a thirty-six-yard field goal try. Bob described the intense moment: "I ran into the game with my heart pounding so loud it drowned out the sounds of the seventy thousand people in the stands."

With the chinstrap to his helmet unbuckled (as it would often be throughout his collegiate career), Thomas lined up in position. Keeping his head down, he concentrated on the striking point of the ball. As he began his steps, however, Bob looked up and noticed something was wrong. "The ball bounced back to Doherty," he said of the snap that dribbled toward the holder. "This is my first kick in a game at Notre Dame after not even knowing that I was going to play."

But the calm Doherty gathered the football and managed to get it down—albeit in a less-than-ideal manner. Bob booted the pigskin as it lay almost sideways. "I basically kicked the ball out of Doherty's hands. And it still went through."

The successful three points started a routine between the two men that continued through their careers at Notre Dame—Doherty would give Thomas a little extra boost when the field goal unit trotted onto the field. "Bob did require a little encouragement now and then—like before every kick," Doherty revealed with a snicker. "I started saying to him before every one, 'Piece of cake, this is a chip shot.'"

The Irish scored another touchdown shortly before halftime, as Brown was sent in once again for the extra point—which he missed. When Notre Dame scored again early in the second half for a 36–7 lead, Brown missed the conversion once more. "I was basically the kicker after that," Thomas said.

After another Irish touchdown moments later, Bob got his first chance at an extra point, which according to Joe Doyle of the *South Bend Tribune* traveled "about fifty rows up into the south stands."[6]

Despite relinquishing the kicking duties to Thomas, Brown had left a significant mark on the afternoon. He became the first African American quarterback in Notre Dame history, as later in the game he relieved starter Pat Steenberge and second-stringer Bill Etter under center, with Parseghian still searching for a permanent replacement for the recently graduated Joe Theismann.

Thomas and the Irish rolled on. In mid-October the team moved to 5–0 with a 16–0 shutout of North Carolina. In this game, Bob nailed three field goals to tie the school record of Gus Dorais set more than a half-century earlier (Dorais, a Notre Dame legend, was also alleged to have thrown the first forward pass in school history—with Knute Rockne on the receiving end). It took Dorais seven tries to get his three field goals in one contest; Bob went a perfect three-for-three. "I think there will be a time when I'll have to kick four or five field goals in a game," Thomas, in the middle of his hot streak, told Steve Klein of the *South Bend Tribune*. "Then a record would really mean something. I don't want to kick four field goals just because it's something I've never done before. Coach Parseghian has a reason for everything."[7]

In solidifying the team's kicking, Thomas had earned the respect of his peers—who approached him with an idea after the North Carolina victory.

"Are you on scholarship?" the players wanted to know.

"No," Thomas responded.

"You should ask Ara for a one," a teammate offered.

"Wouldn't that be opportunistic?"

"*Opportunistic?*" the player responded incredulously. "Ara is opportunistic. He would understand that this is the time you would ask."

The more he listened to them, the more Thomas thought the idea made sense. He phoned Parseghian the following afternoon.

"Coach," his brief proposal began, "I don't want to be opportunistic, but I was wondering if I might be able to get some sort of scholarship. . . ."

Parseghian responded in a sympathetic yet noncommittal tone.

"I don't know, Bob. Scholarships are kind of tight. I might be able to get you some sort of one-eighth scholarship. I have to look into it."

A week after their telephone conversation, Thomas had a late-afternoon exam on the opposite end of campus from the football stadium. Before leaving his room, he called Parseghian again—this time to ask for permission to be a little late to practice that day, a request the coach granted. Before getting off the phone, Parseghian had something to add: "Oh, Bob, by the way, one more thing—you're on full scholarship."

The elated Thomas immediately called home to share the good news. "I was happy the most for my parents, who believed in me and were willing to sacrifice to let me go to Notre Dame in the first place."

Augie began making his attendance at Notre Dame contests part of his weekly schedule. He would leave Rochester right after he closed the body shop on Fridays—usually at 6 p.m.—and drove straight to South Bend, a trip of eight hours. As he and Anne did before the Northwestern game, he would then sleep in his car in the parking lot outside the stadium until he noticed people starting to head for the gates in the early afternoon.

Bob's relationship with Parseghian continued to strengthen. As the rest of the players and coaches left the practice field, the coach often challenged Thomas in a playful manner. "Ara fashioned himself a kicker," Bob mentioned with a smile. "He liked to show how he could drop-kick. He used to enjoy coming out there and competing with me. We started out betting milkshakes. And once he got a promotional deal with Ford [Motor Company], the wager went into Pintos. I would kid him over the years that he owes me thousands of milkshakes and a number of Fords."

The late Parseghian remembered those days well. "I'd challenge him at practice, and we would bet on who could kick the farthest," Ara recalled in early 2017. "I never won anything."[8]

With the athletic Tom Clements taking over as quarterback in 1972, the Irish stormed out of the gate with four straight wins to open the season, which included shutouts of Northwestern and Michigan State. Thomas was perfect on all his kicks through the 4–0 start, making all ten of his extra points and all six of his field goals. Making those field goals enabled him to twice tie his existing school record, of three field goals in one game, against each of the two Big Ten schools with a forty-seven-yarder in both games—the second-longest in school history to that date, while his thirteen points against Northwestern also established a single-game Notre Dame mark for kick scoring. The forty-seven-yarder versus the Wildcats was into a seven-mile-an-hour wind, while the performance against Michigan State prompted Doyle in his *South Bend Tribune* article the following Sunday to proclaim that Thomas was "fast becoming the greatest of all Irish field goal kickers."[9] Bob's conversion attempts were without blemish throughout the remainder of the season, as he made all thirty-four by the end of the year—yet another school record. "Thomas's kicking provided the margin," *The Sporting News* praised about the 16–0 win on the road in East Lansing. "The soccer-styler climaxed three drives."[10]

After a disappointing finish to the season in a 40–6 loss to Nebraska in the Orange Bowl, Parseghian decided to inject some levity into another tension-filled autumn in 1973 by having the offense, defense, and kickers each develop humorous poems about the upcoming opponent every week. The poems would be performed aloud after the Thursday or Friday afternoon practices, and led by Thomas and Doherty, the special teamers raised the bar significantly. They were assisted by Bob's brother, Rick, who was a freshman at Notre Dame and active in the theater community (including as one of the founders of the popular *Keenan Revue* show on campus). To the coach, the recitals were no contest. "Bob's were always the best," Parseghian concluded.[11]

Thomas proudly concurred with the assessment. "They weren't just rhymes about a particular team, but full-fledged songs. We'd do jingles. Some of them we wrote ourselves—but the best ones were probably written by my brother. We'd sneak into the locker room, call Rick, and say, 'Hey—you have any ideas?'"

Defensive lineman Nick Fedorenko remembered the ground-shaking laughter the performances produced at the end of a long, tough week—as well as the camaraderie. "Bobby contributed so much to our team with the spirit he engendered. In addition to his obvious kicking talents, he was a bright, enthusiastic guy who added a lot of fun to our practice sessions."[12]

Nonetheless, Thomas's senior campaign of 1973 did not begin as planned—whether in kicking footballs or performing the end-of-the-week skits at practice. "The week of the [season-opening] Northwestern game, I made up a cheer in which I was supposed to pat Ara on the back at the end. Instead, I got carried away and slapped him on the face. That's the first time since my sophomore year that I'd checked the bulletin board to see if I was dressing for the game."[13]

When the dress roster was announced, Parseghian was forgiving as Thomas participated in a third-straight trouncing of Northwestern to the tune of 44–0. But after making two field goals in a 20–7 defeat of Purdue in week two, Thomas proceeded to miss eight straight—despite the team marching on to another 5–0 start after a 62–3 mauling of Army at West Point in Bob's home state of New York. In that game, Bob's consecutive extra point string was also snapped at 62, which was the second-best in National Collegiate Athletic Association (NCAA) history to that time and a Notre Dame record that stood until sophomore Craig Hentrich surpassed it in 1990.

With the Irish hardly challenged during the first half of the season (save for a narrow 14–10 win against Michigan State), the services of Thomas had not been fully required; therefore, most of his errant kicks received little attention. But in week six, a daunting matchup loomed at Notre Dame Stadium with Coach John McKay's sixth-ranked Trojans of the University of Southern California.

USC came into the contest unbeaten in its previous twenty-three games—including a 45–23 destruction of the Irish the previous season that was still fresh in many minds. Moreover, a national television audience would be watching. These things occupied Bob's mind as his confidence admittedly began to waver.

"I said a prayer at the beginning of the season, and I told God that I didn't want any recognition all season if I could just have it for the Southern Cal game," he went on to say to a campus reporter. "After breaking my PAT [points after touchdown, or extra points] streak at Army and missing a couple of field goals, one of which I thought was good, I walked back to my sixth-floor room. I opened the curtains and looked toward heaven and said, 'I know I told you I didn't want any big games until USC, but this is getting ridiculous."[14]

As usual, Parseghian knew the correct approach to get his kicker back in a positive groove. At the end of the week's final practice on Friday afternoon, with the USC game slated for the following day (and with threatening, dark skies foreboding a rain-soaked battle), Thomas and Parseghian had another of their friendly kicking competitions. The coach proceeded to drop-kick the ball through the uprights from thirty-two yards away. "He turned to me and asked if I had seen that," Thomas continued. "I nodded. He then reminded me that I had missed a few from just that far."[15]

Parseghian then finished the quick lesson: "We haven't needed your kicks so far this season, but let me tell you something, Bob—you're going to win the game for us tomorrow." For Thomas, the much-needed boost was further confirmation that Parseghian—named that month as the new chair of the National Multiple Sclerosis Society, a disease that had stricken the coach's younger sister—had an instinct for reaching his players. "We called Ara 'The Man' for a reason. He had his hands on every aspect of the program. He was a great psychologist."

Having observed Parseghian and Thomas talking that day, Doherty described the scene as a vintage Ara moment. "He knew when to chew you up and, most importantly, when and how to build you up. Bob was pretty down on himself.

"Coach was a renaissance man. He was a scratch golfer and played the piano. I think he knew forty or fifty college fight songs. You could spend a weekend with him and be fascinated, as he could talk of world affairs without ever speaking a word about football. You could not say that about many coaches, then or now. He taught us about honesty with yourself and your team, the responsibility of never letting your teammates down, being accountable for your actions on and off the field, and putting it all out every down, every practice. Seeing Coach live that way, and clearly expect no less from you each and every day, it wore on you—the right way. He truly made men out of boys."[16]

Excitement for the impending game grew to a fever pitch that Friday evening, as Parseghian spoke to a pep rally assembled near the library as the USC Marching Band set up its own impromptu gathering on another part of campus—the first time the Southern Cal band had accompanied the Tro-jan team to South Bend since 1927.

When the battle finally got under way, the tension of the afternoon was felt at the outset. On USC's first play from scrimmage, Irish defensive back Luther Bradley separated star Trojan receiver Lynn Swann from his helmet with a vicious hit. After an exchange of punts, the second Notre Dame drive ended deep in USC territory with seven minutes and eight seconds left in the first quarter as the struggling Thomas entered the game for a thirty-two-yard field goal attempt—the exact distance of Parseghian's dropkick after practice the previous day.

As was their custom, Bob's holder once again reassured him that it was a chip shot. Doherty settled himself upon the left hash mark as the kicker got ready with his patented flexing of the lower leg, like a bull preparing to charge. After Doherty grabbed a high snap, he swiftly put it down as Thomas fired the ball authoritatively through the posts for a 3–0 Notre Dame lead. Relieved that he had liberated himself from his slump, a jubilant Thomas pumped his fists while sprinting back to the sideline as the "Victory March" blared from the stands.

With just over five minutes to play in the first half and Notre Dame trail-ing 7–3, the Irish offense stalled a second time in USC territory as Thomas was again summoned. Again he responded, blasting another solid kick from thirty-three yards, which brought his team to within a point. At the end of the third quarter, with the rainfall starting to intensify, Thomas matched his own school record with his third field goal of the day from thirty-two yards, giving Notre Dame a 23–14 advantage that proved to be the final score.

Bob's performance earned him the Offensive Player of the Game Award from both Chevrolet and the Notre Dame Quarterback Club in the Irish's first victory over the Trojans since 1966. "Boy, those holds were beautiful to watch, too," Doherty was sure to add about the day's events.[17]

The Notre Dame stampede went unabated from there. Four straight de-cisive victories followed, capped by a 44–0 thrashing of Miami on Decem-ber 1, after which the team sported a perfect 10–0 record. Notre Dame was thus invited to the fortieth Sugar Bowl in New Orleans on New Year's Eve to play Coach Bear Bryant's Alabama Crimson Tide for the national title.

The 1973 Sugar Bowl was the first meeting ever in football between Notre Dame and Alabama, with the historic powers having gotten together only once for basketball in 1955. The record crowd of 85,161 at Tulane Stadium was not deterred by the tornado warnings that had been issued around New Orleans earlier in the day, in spite of talk of the game being postponed. Although the threat of funnel clouds would subside, a cold rain persisted throughout the first quarter as strong winds shifted directions frequently—impacting the strategies of the coaches and the concentration of the kickers. The players and the football itself skidded across the damp, smooth fibers of the artificial turf all evening long—suggesting that one kick might make the difference in the game.

The Irish jumped ahead late in the first quarter, as junior fullback Wayne Bullock charged over the goal line from a yard out to cap a six-play, sixty-four-yard drive in just over two minutes. Thomas, however, would not get a chance at the extra point, as Doherty was unable to corral the snap, which rattled in his hands and fell to the ground, leaving the Notre Dame lead at 6–0.

Parseghian's defense dominated much of the first half, holding the powerful Alabama offense—third in the nation in scoring with 41.3 points per game coming into the Sugar Bowl—to zero net yards midway through the second period. But after turnovers by both teams, Crimson Tide running back Randy Billingsley crossed the goal line, after which a Bill Davis conversion provided 'Bama with a 7–6 lead.

As suddenly as the lightning flashing outside the stadium, Notre Dame answered. Al Hunter grabbed the ensuing kickoff and scampered around the Alabama coverage for a ninety-three-yard touchdown, breaking a Sugar Bowl record that had stood for thirty-eight years. As Hunter excitedly circled through the end zone, the entire Irish team rushed there to greet him—behavior that was then still permissible under NCAA rules.

They all returned to the sidelines—including Thomas, as Parseghian left his offense on the field and decided to go for the two-point conversion. It was successful, giving the Irish a 14–7 lead with Thomas having yet to attempt a placement kick.

To get the Crimson Tide offense going, Bryant decided to insert quarterback Richard Todd into the game late in the second quarter in place of starter Gary Rutledge. Despite being listed as Rutledge's backup, Todd—a sophomore from Mobile—came into the Sugar Bowl as Alabama's second leading rusher on the season with 560 yards. He had also thrown for four touchdowns as well; as testimony to the team's tremendous depth, which Bryant was notorious for stockpiling, Todd was one of sixty players Bryant used in the first half of the game *alone.*

Calling Todd "one of the most gifted athletes he has ever coached, with even a quicker release on his passes than Joe Namath,"[18] Bryant turned him loose. Todd drove the Tide down the field and put Davis in position for a thirty-nine-yard field goal attempt, which he sent through successfully to pull Alabama to within 14–10, as the winds from the passing storms continued to howl.

With one second left to play in the first half, Thomas finally got his first chance, as Clements had taken the Irish to the Alabama thirty-one-yard line when Parseghian decided to give his strong-legged senior an opportunity. Slamming the ball into the teeth of a bayou monsoon, Thomas left the forty-nine-yard effort just short as the teams ducked for cover from the elements by speeding to the locker rooms.

Even though the rains had stopped as the teams emerged for the second half, the conditions remained perilous. Boys were bringing out towels and newly wiped footballs to the officials on nearly every play. And despite great care taken by ballcarriers on both sides, a flurry of turnovers on the wet turf emerged in the opening minutes of the third quarter.

Thomas posted his first point with a conversion after another Notre Dame score to put the Irish ahead 21–17. The lead, however, was once again short-lived. The Tide's Mike Stock—a native of Elkhart, Indiana, a small city in the shadow of South Bend—next found the end zone. The extra point, however, was wide, keeping the game at 23–21.

Coolly, Clements navigated the Irish offense down the field yet again to the four-yard line, setting up first-and-goal. Two running plays netted only a single yard, placing the ball at the two. When Clements missed on a pass to the corner of the end zone, it was fourth down. Four and a half minutes were left on the clock.

Parseghian sent Thomas in for a nineteen-yard field goal try—the result of which would likely determine the national championship.

"Bob was one of the most confident kids I had ever met," Parseghian said. "But that kick in the Sugar Bowl was the only time I had ever seen him overly excited or nervous. Before he went in, I told him, 'It's just another extra point or field goal.'"[19]

The only problem was that Doherty, on this one occasion, had failed to utter his usual reminder: "Piece of cake, Bob—this is a chip shot."

The holder had his mind on other things—particularly, on making amends for what had happened earlier in the game: "On the first extra point I dropped the snap. So, when it came to the winning field goal, I was making sure I caught that sucker and got it down.

"As I am about to call for the snap, I hear from behind me: 'Say it!'

"'Say *what*?' I asked Bob.

"'Say, *'Piece of cake, it's a chip shot!'*'"

Doherty complied and uttered the magic words. "We kid each other about that often over the years. I won't get started on his superstitions."[20]

Thomas fixed his eyes on the spot where Doherty would place the ball and again flexed his lower right leg a few times—a gyration that would become his trademark in the years to come. He closed his ears to the raucous Irish cheers and Tide jeers thundering through the Louisiana night. "It was as if I were struck deaf," he would reveal decades later about his strategy for concentrating during a kick. "You knew the crowd was making noise, but you had to be so focused that you shut off the world."[21]

Doherty grabbed the snap and expertly settled it on the tee sunk into the soggy turf. A second later, he gazed upward.

"He kicked it through the uprights, and the rest is history."[22]

In the sixth lead change of the game, the football sneaked just inside the goal-post. The kick not only gave Notre Dame a 24–23 advantage but also gave Thomas a new single-season Irish field goal mark with ten—surpassing yet another of his own records, set earlier in the season.

The colorful Dave Casper, meanwhile, minced no words decades later with his own assessment about the narrow margin of the boot. "Bob scared the heck out of us. Here it is, a nineteen-yard kick, and he just barely squeezes it through the right upright. He came off the field and I said, 'It's nineteen yards—why don't you just kick it down the middle?' When I watch replays of it, I still get nervous and think it's going to sail wide."[23]

As for himself, Thomas could not understand all the fuss. "If it was right down the middle, no one would be talking about it," he reasoned.

"Just like a kicker, he always had an excuse," Casper snipped back. "We all knew he'd become a lawyer. Doherty's the same way—and he's a lawyer too."[24]

Whenever the 1973 Notre Dame team gets back together, in fact, Casper keeps all the special-teamers on a short leash. "We had a close-knit team, and as captain, I get to delegate duties whenever we have a reunion," he proudly said. "And one rule I always have is that kickers aren't allowed to speak. He and Doherty would talk the whole time if we let them."[25]

After a last stand by the Irish defense, Clements and the offense sealed the victory and the national title for Notre Dame. The 24–23 score stood as the final, in a contest that would later be called "the game of the century."

Afterward in the locker room, the media asked Thomas about the field goal. "When their guy missed the extra point on their last score and it was 23–21, I knew I might be kicking for it," he said. "I didn't want to hit it too hard. When you punch it, you know the ball will curve on you, but I felt we were in so close it wouldn't matter."[26] A newspaperman photographed Bob's famous foot the next morning in his New Orleans hotel room, propped atop a golden helmet.

Thomas finished his Notre Dame career second on the kick-scoring charts with 161 points, just behind his predecessor Hempel's total of 164. Thomas also received the campus-wide John W. McMullan Award as the player who "best exemplifies the spirit of the scholar-athlete."

To Parseghian, none was more deserving. "He had a God-given talent to get along with the entire team," the coach said of Thomas in early 2017. "He was a great kicker, but I knew he'd also be a success in whatever he did off the field. He has a personality that melts neatly anywhere he wants to go."[27]

Chapter 3

Claimed on Waivers

"Welcome to the Chicago Bears."
—Chicago Bears Personnel Director Carl Marasco
in a phone call to Thomas, January 1975

After a few days back home in Rochester basking in success, it was time for Bob to return to South Bend for the start of classes in January 1974. As the month of snowy northern Indiana winter crept along, Thomas's thoughts turned to what would be occurring at the Americana Hotel in New York City beginning on January 29—the National Football League draft.

When draft day arrived, Bob went about his usual business on campus as the selection process got under way in New York. These days, elaborate "draft parties" are held at the homes of every worthy and unworthy prospect, and dramatic announcements are televised live from their parents' living rooms; but those drafted in the 1970s—including those selected in the early rounds— were typically notified by a simple telephone call from the personnel office of the NFL team.

Bob thought he might be a first-day selection, but no such call came for him on January 29. With no classes to attend on the second and final day of the draft on January 30, Bob realized he was doing himself no good sitting around anxiously by the phone. To release some stress, he decided to head over to the athletic complex and work out.

Upon arriving at the facility, he ran into Notre Dame Sports Information Director Roger Valdeserri, who told Bob that he had been looking for him, and that he had good news. Thomas shrugged nonchalantly, trying to hide his excitement as he waited for Valdeserri to say which NFL team had chosen him.

"You've just been named a unanimous first-team Academic All-American!"

Stunned, Bob showed his displeasure. "I don't know if anyone's ever been disappointed in getting the call to be named Academic All-American," he later said, "but I was kind of deflated." While being named was a nice honor, Bob viewed it as a consolation prize, a cheap memento that merely punctuated the end of his football career. He felt as if he was receiving a virtual telegram from the twenty-six NFL teams saying, "Thanks, but no thanks."

His thoughts went back to the hours that immediately followed the Sugar Bowl. During the celebration on Bourbon Street, Bob had run into a bigtime Notre Dame booster. "I greeted the man by name, expecting the kind of congratulatory response I'd been getting from Irish fans all evening long. Instead he said, 'Why should I talk to you? You're old news. You're graduating.'

"While he said it in a teasing, tongue-in-cheek tone, I recognized the underlying truth to his words. I may have been the toast of Notre Dame football fans all over the world that night because I was the Irish kicker who scored the winning field goal, but come morning, I would be just another graduating senior. There would be another kicker for the team next year. I would have to find a new identity."

The call came from the Los Angeles Rams, informing Bob he had been their fifteenth-round selection in the draft. His close friend Doherty—working to recover from a lingering knee injury—had been taken in the ninth round by the Buffalo Bills. Twelve picks prior to Thomas, the Green Bay Packers—while also considering a kicker—instead selected University of Pittsburgh tackle Dave Wannstedt.

Bob felt anxious, despite the good news. He knew the Rams already had a veteran kicker in David Ray, Bryant's former player at Alabama, who had led the league in scoring in 1973. Thomas began getting his law school application materials ready as a backup plan. Then suddenly, a different opportunity arrived in the form of a new competitor with the NFL.

Founded a year earlier and preparing for its first season in the summer of 1974, the World Football League (WFL) was dangling large sums to money to lure all sorts of players onto its rosters—including active NFL rookies and veterans. Each move made by the maverick league stood in brash defiance of the pro football establishment; the WFL planned a longer twenty-game schedule that would start in midsummer and then run parallel to the NFL slate through November (with most games on Wednesday nights in addition to a featured game on Sundays), television contracts of its own (some of which conflicted with existing NFL deals), and even its own draft—making certain it took place a week before the NFL version on January 22.

While Thomas went unselected in the WFL draft, he received a call in March from Fran Monaco, the owner of the Jacksonville Sharks. After a try-out, the Sharks were prepared to give Bob a guaranteed salary of $60,000 in addition to a flashy new Datsun 280-Z, while the Rams were offering him only $25,000. "Being an impressionable kid, I took the Sharks' deal," he said. But Thomas quickly discovered—as did the rest of the WFL players, sooner or later—that the league was built on sand. Furthermore, he also found that much of the day-to-day operations displayed a lack of professionalism.

At one of his first practices with the Sharks (practices that sometimes were delayed because of a shortage of clean socks for the team), Bob was directed to take part in a tackling drill, as the coaching staff claimed he needed to be prepared to make stops on kickoffs. The exercise was known as the "Oklahoma" drill; the defender had to shed a blocker and bring down a ball carrier before he passed by. Obediently, Bob readied himself as he stared across at the much larger players facing him. Using his quick feet, he evaded the blocker and bore down on one of the team's larger running backs. After successfully (but painfully) taking the runner down to the turf, Thomas received some inside information from his adversary as they helped each other up. "Hey, I don't know you from Adam," the running back said to Thomas while pointing toward one of the assistant coaches standing on the sideline. "But that guy over there told me to try to hurt you."

Bob rolled with the punches, and was in uniform for the Sharks' first exhibition game against the Birmingham Americans. Even so, he still felt as if something was not on the level. "I was kicking the ball better than the other guy. I had two blocked, and in looking at the film it was pretty obvious they weren't trying to block anybody as the defense came right up the middle."

Thomas was cut from the team the following week. He maintained a friendly relationship with owner Monaco, who offered Thomas a front office job that he turned down. "So, I was out of there, but I had the guaranteed contract which means I was paid until the Sharks went belly-up—which was about eight weeks later."

Hearing of his release, Thomas's college coach contacted Bob. Parseghian had phoned Don Klosterman, the general manager of the Rams. "He can kick under pressure," the Notre Dame grid boss told him. "If you keep using him, he will come through for you."[1] After packing his things in Jacksonville, Bob headed for the opposite coast and arrived in Orange County in time to join the Rams at the start of their training camp in Fullerton on July 16.

Encouraged by the first-class surroundings, facilities, and treatment that the Rams and the NFL had offered, Thomas immediately opened eyes in southern California. Battling six other kickers in camp, Bob nailed four straight field goals in a late July scrimmage against the Denver Broncos and then a fifty-seven-yarder in practice two days later—despite it being his first extended experience in kicking directly off the ground (in collegiate play at that time, the kicker could opt to use a block tee for placement kicks). "A lot of the kickers in college used the two-inch tee, but I used the one-inch variety," Thomas pointed out about his time at Notre Dame. "So, I was used to kicking lower to the ground. There was some adjustment time for me, too, but it came relatively easily." In contrast to the Sharks, Rams staff carefully charted each kick in practice, and the data clearly showed that Bob was outperforming the competition. Moreover, the goalposts were in a familiar position to him—in 1974, the NFL decided to follow the college practice and moved the posts off the goal line and ten yards deeper to the back line of the end zone.

Before long, Thomas was the only kicker remaining on the active Los Angeles roster, as yet to report was Ray, one of many veterans around the league on strike during a labor dispute between the NFL and its players' union. The conflict was giving rookies and free agents extra looks as the preseason moved along.

To the local media, Bob was a refreshing change from the typical player at his position. An impressed Jim Murray of the *Los Angeles Times* claimed that Thomas was "clearly an impostor" and could not be a real kicker—for "he could (1) speak English, (2) was nearly five-foot-ten, and (3) had entered the country in a hospital delivery room and not through a customs office," Murray penned. "Everyone knows race horses come from Kentucky, comedians come from the Lower East Side, swimmers come from Santa Clara, and place kickers come from Armenia, Romania, Vienna, the West German Republic, or Norway. . . . What the Jacksonville Sharks didn't know was that Bob Thomas had played as much soccer as a kid in Rochester as a boy growing up in Leeds or in the shadow of the Moscow Dynamo."[2]

After making his mark in training camp, Bob's next objective was a strong showing in his first NFL competition with the opening of the Rams' 1974 exhibition schedule on August 2. Murray gave a qualifying advisory to his readers: "He will get his chance under real combat conditions in the game against the Cleveland Browns at the [Los Angeles] Coliseum Friday night."[3]

Using a roster full of youngsters making their NFL debuts—including the 1973 Heisman Trophy–winning running back John Cappelletti out of Penn State—the Rams defeated Bob's boyhood-favorite Browns, 24–21, as Thomas made the difference by drilling a nineteen-yard field goal with two seconds remaining. "Thank heavens for Bob Thomas," wrote a grateful Joe Hendrickson in the *Pasadena Star-News* after the rookie kicker ended the game in regulation. "A 15-minute overtime tie-breaking session wasn't needed by the newspapermen who never have an easy time making late night deadlines."[4] But despite the boot giving Los Angeles the victory, Thomas noticed that the reaction he received from his teammates and coaches was stoic in comparison with the response to the last field goal he had kicked for Notre Dame in New Orleans: "Both were easy nineteen-yarders. But where the Sugar Bowl kick had triggered a night-long celebration and worldwide recognition the following day, I don't remember anything more than a simple pat on the back from [Rams' Head] Coach [Chuck] Knox. That may have been the first time I realized kicking was now my job. Success was expected."

He shared the positive update with the folks back home in Rochester. "I've really enjoyed it here," he said when Michael Lewis interviewed Thomas by telephone for the *Democrat and Chronicle*. "I'm in a state of limbo. Inevitably, it will come down to a showdown between Ray and me. Right now though, I'm the number-one kicker. I'm in camp, Ray's not. When they [the Rams] drafted me, they wanted a pressure kicker. Last year Ray missed several field goals in tight situations. I have a decent shot at the job. I haven't seen him kick and I have faith in my kicking."[5] With Ray still absent the

following week, Bob excelled in the second preseason contest as well, kicking a pair of twenty-two-yard field goals for the only Rams points in a 13–6
loss to the Dallas Cowboys at the Coliseum on August 9.

Viewing his progress from a distance were the Sharks and their followers—
with one local newspaperman suggesting the deck had been stacked against
Bob in Jacksonville from the start. "There are those close to the Sharks who
say it was politics which prompted Thomas's demise," wrote John Smith in
Brevard County's *Florida Today* on August 4. "Jacksonville's kicking coach,
Bugsy Engelberg, formerly held similar positions with Florida State University and the NFL Buffalo Bills. And the man who Engelberg decided was
superior to Thomas, Grant Guthrie, just happened to be Engelberg's field
goal kicker at FSU and with the Bills."[6]

Perhaps sensing an impending loss of his job, Ray came back for the Rams'
third preseason game against the Kansas City Chiefs on August 17. Immediately inserted as the starting kicker by Knox, Ray was given the initial kicking opportunities. Bob was subsequently sent in during the second half, where
he was successful on four of five extra points in the Rams' 58–16 drubbing of
Hank Stram's team in the Coliseum. Knox employed a similar pattern the
next week against the defending champion Miami Dolphins as well, with
Ray handling the first-half chores while Thomas went three-for-three in the
second half on extra points as the Rams won again in Los Angeles, 31–13.

A strange feeling was starting to overcome the first-year player. The
momentum that Thomas had established appeared to be eroding after Ray
arrived from nowhere to take over. As the Rams closed out their exhibition
schedule with games in San Diego and San Francisco, Bob was not sent in
for any placement kicks. With the preseason games in the books, the statistics showed Thomas being three-for-three in field goals and ten-for-eleven
on extra points, while Ray was six-for-nine and nine-for-nine, respectively.

On Thursday, September 12—just seventy-two hours before the Rams
were scheduled to open the regular season in Denver against the Broncos—
Knox called the rookie into his office. Thomas recalled the brief meeting:
"He said, 'Bob, you've really won the kicking job, but we think we're going
to the Super Bowl this year. David had a good year last year, so we have to
go with the veteran.'"

Denied employment on both coasts, Thomas departed California bitter about
football. He had outperformed his competition on two different teams in two

different leagues in a matter of a months, but at the end of the day, he was left on the outside looking in. "If I had failed miserably, it would bother me," he concluded. "But I kicked well." While being cut late in the preseason might have hurt his chances of being picked up by another team, it was also evidence to Thomas that he had given a quality performance. "If I had been cut early, it would have meant I was no good."[7]

Sitting at home in in East Irondequoit and following the news from Los Angeles was Augie Thomas, who was also disappointed—but not in Bob. "Maybe I'm partial because he is my son," he told a writer from St. Petersburg, Florida, who had phoned the Thomas household. "But I don't miss a game on television, and when I see things that I see on television, I know that my son is better than a good 35 percent of the kickers. It hurts me to see him not playing. Maybe it hurts me more than it hurts my own son. He takes it better than I do."[8]

Bob did *not* take it well enough, however, to give up. With his personal belongings moved out of the Rams' facility, Thomas was committed to making one last go of it. He began poring over the rosters of other NFL teams, looking for one in need of a kicker. One such team appeared to be the Cowboys. Bob was disappointed to learn, however, that Dallas had just signed the longtime Chicago Bears kicker Mac Percival, who had kicked in only four games for the Bears in 1973 before being replaced by rookie Mirro Roder.

After Percival was successful on only two out of eight field goals in the first three games, he was released. Staying in touch with the club in Texas, coach Tom Landry summoned Thomas to Dallas in early October to vie for the job. Competing with him was Efren Herrera, a Detroit Lions castoff from the University of California, Los Angeles (UCLA), who had been selected before Thomas in the seventh round of the 1974 draft and was cut from the Lions the same day Bob was let go in Los Angeles.

Taking advantage of the opportunity, Thomas put on a tremendous display. He boomed kicks from every part of the Cowboys' practice field as everything clicked. "I didn't miss in Dallas," he said. But on Wednesday, October 3—in advance of the Cowboys' fourth game of the season three days later—Herrera was signed. Thomas, once again, was sent away empty-handed: "Very disappointed, I went back to Rochester, worked a few different jobs, and thought about law school."

After some time at home, Bob returned to Notre Dame. There he reunited with his old friend Doherty, who was able to empathize, having been cut by the Bills in the final week of the preseason. The two got an apartment to-gether and continued working out in the hope of getting *just one more shot.* "But also to relive some of the glory days," Bob admitted with a smile. "Soon, we got the idea of starting a bar, forgetting about football, and just living in South Bend." They approached an influential Notre Dame fan with their idea and asked for his financial backing. The man was willing, on the con-dition that they work in a bar for six months, cleaning up spills and hauling kegs up from the basement—and then tell him if they *really* wanted to open a bar. "Well, he was very wise—because obviously we didn't want any of that. We just wanted to be bar owners and tell football stories to kids who were twenty-one years old. So, we never did it. And it worked out fine."

The pair also were seeing football slowly recede in the rearview mirror but continued hitting the gym and the practice fields every day to kick. "I've got a conflict because I'd love to play, and I want to play," Thomas proclaimed as he and Doherty continued to work out. "But if I go and make it to the last cut again, I won't be able to get into law school until 1976. That's a long time."[9]

As the two sat in their apartment in the fall of 1974 and watched the NFL season unfold, the Rams marched to a 10–4 record and their second-straight Western Division title. Ray struggled throughout the regular season, and Bob received another call from Klosterman, this one informing Thomas there was a chance he could be activated for the playoffs. Ray had suffered an in-jury, and his availability was in question. No such activation would occur. Ray stayed in the game, and the Rams beat the Washington Redskins in the opening round, only to be defeated in the conference championship game by the Minnesota Vikings the following week.

In February 1975, a third phone call came from Los Angeles. "The Rams contacted me again, and said they wanted to re-sign me. I said I didn't want to do it; what could I do more than I did last year? They admitted that Ray didn't have a good season and told me that this was still the best situation for me and that they knew what I could do. So, I signed with them."

A few days later, the tables turned once again as Bob's phone rang yet an-other time. Now it was Carl Marasco, the personnel director from a differ-ent NFL team. "Welcome to the Chicago Bears!" Marasco told him. "Well, that's very flattering," Bob responded after hesitating, "but I just signed with the Rams."

"They didn't tell you?"

"Tell me what?"

"You've been claimed on waivers."

Marasco explained that Bob's name had to pass through "procedural waivers"—a formality whereby a player who is signed, released, and then signed again by the same team must be made temporarily available through the waiver wire to all the other teams (to forbid a team from stockpiling players). Chicago and Washington were the two teams that had expressed an interest in Thomas; and as the Bears (4–10) finished with a worse record than the Redskins (10 4) in 1974, Thomas was awarded to the Chicago team.

A new coach had just arrived in the Windy City: Jack Pardee, a hard-nosed linebacker during his playing days with the Rams and Redskins who had also received overtures to replace the coaches in Atlanta and Cleveland. He finished his NFL playing career only two years earlier, retiring after the 1972 season to tutor George Allen's linebackers in Washington and, in 1974, leading the Florida Blazers to the WFL championship game as the head coach and general manager. Much like the Jacksonville Sharks and other WFL clubs, the cash-strapped Blazers, despite their success, were not able to meet their payroll in the second half of the season, and Pardee himself was not paid during his final four months of work.

As a collegian at Texas A&M University in 1954, Pardee had been a survivor of Bear Bryant's infamous preseason training camp at Junction, Texas, in Bryant's first year at that school. As Pardee spent his first few hours in Chicago working at his new job on New Year's Day, Bryant and Parseghian were preparing for their rematch that night in the 1975 Orange Bowl. One of Pardee's first tasks was to collaborate with new general manager Jim Finks in preparation for the upcoming college draft, taking place at the end of January.

The Bears opened and closed their selections with a pair of running backs from smaller schools in the South, taking Jackson State's Walter Payton with the fourth overall pick in the first round and Louisiana Tech's Roland Harper in the seventeenth round at pick number 420. After what was considered a solid pick with defensive end Mike Hartenstine of Penn State in the second round, Chicago went after relatively obscure players in cornerback Virgil Livers of Western Kentucky, guard Revie Sorey and linebacker Tom Hicks of Illinois, quarterback Bob Avellini of Maryland, and defensive tackle Roger Stillwell of Stanford, among others—all considered quality college talent but questionable prospects for the NFL. "The first two or three rounds of the draft, it's not difficult to choose players," Marasco said of the new crop of potential Bears when the second day of the draft was finished. "After that it gets tough. You go for a kid who shows you something—attitude, desire, etc."[10]

By the eleventh round, Finks felt it was time to address the kicking game. The third-year placekicker Roder, a Czechoslovakian immigrant and soccer player who had been a bricklayer in the old country to support himself, made only half his attempts in his rookie season before improving his field goal accuracy to 69 percent in 1974. To challenge him, Finks selected Mike Dean from the University of Texas. Dean had shown a strong leg in the Southwest Conference by nailing a fifty-six-yard field goal the previous November against Texas Christian, as well as a fifty-yarder against Rice two seasons earlier. Dean had punted the past two years for the Longhorns and was also seen as potentially taking over that position on the Bears by unseating Bob Parsons, a tight end for the prior three seasons and, in 1974, doing the punting as well.

Following Dean for the Bears in the twelfth round was Ohio State defensive back Doug Plank. Plank had gone unnoticed by most NFL teams, having seen the field only sparingly for the Buckeyes in starting just five games in three varsity seasons. Nonetheless, Plank was one of the peripheral players who had grabbed Marasco's attention because of his toughness and tenacity.

Three weeks had passed since the draft when Thomas received the call from Marasco on February 21, letting him know he had been added to the Bears' growing list of young talent. Three weeks later on March 13, the team signed Doherty as well.

"I went home to Portland and blew out my knee for the second time in December, right before getting the letter from Chicago about trying out," Doherty recalled of late 1974. "Bob got his invitation too, and we decided I would come out to Rochester and let his mom heal me with a huge Italian dinner every night for two months. It worked. I got my left leg strengthened enough to punt, and away we went to the Bears training camp in early summer.[11]

Appropriate for a team with so many new faces, the Bears opened their 1975 training camp on July 12 in a new location. After spending the previous 31 years in Rensselaer, Indiana, the team's new preseason home became Lake Forest College, north of Chicago. As had been the case when arriving at Notre Dame from Rochester, Thomas showed up at the Bears training camp in relative anonymity, receiving the nominal $200 a week allotted to rookies and free agents until they either made the permanent roster or were cut. But perhaps as an earned measure of respect, he was issued jersey number 16 with the Bears—in contrast to his college days when he received that oversized jersey number 98. Thomas's fellow rookie Avellini was one of the first people Bob met. "I had just driven in from New York, and I saw him in the parking lot," the quarterback remembered about the kicker. "We introduced ourselves, and we sort of gravitated toward each other because we had things in common."[12]

It was immediately clear that all jobs were up for grabs—a stark contrast to the environment Thomas had experienced when vying to join the powerful, established Rams the previous year. "There was no allegiance to the players who were there before," Bob said of the attitude Pardee and his staff held toward the few remaining holdovers from the 1974 Chicago roster. "It's not like the Bears were winning; it's not like the coaches had memories of Mirro Roder kicking game-winning field goals. It was a completely different situation than when I competed in Los Angeles."

Doherty was the first player sent packing. His bad knee resurfaced and prevented him from passing the required physical exam. "I was disappointed," Bob recalled, "mostly for Brian of course, but also for me as he could have been my holder once again."

The Bears' 1975 preseason opener on August 9 took Thomas back to the West Coast in a game against the Chargers in San Diego. As Roder nursed a cracked bone in his left foot, Thomas took advantage of the extra opportunities. He kicked three field goals from distances of 18, 26, and 42 yards in a 22–0 Bears win, making a strong first impression on Pardee in the duel for the placekicking job. "Most pressure, at least for a kicker, is self-imposed," Thomas noted the following week when asked of the inherent anxiety associated with the position. "It depends on what the kick means, what the distance is, on the game situation. But to say to yourself, 'If I miss this kick I might be cut,' that can't help but create an unnecessary burden."[13]

Roder—"a very pleasant guy, a big burly guy, who seemed a lot older than me," as Thomas recalled his first impressions—was absent for the second exhibition game as well, a rain-soaked, windswept contest on a muddy field in Milwaukee County Stadium against the Packers on August 16, which ended in a 13–9 Chicago loss. Thrust into the starting role once again, Thomas initially struggled, missing two of three field goal attempts and an extra point, but the coaching staff was encouraged to see that he composed himself to succeed on his third try, a forty-five-yarder under adverse conditions.

Perhaps feeling the same type of pressure from Thomas that David Ray had experienced a year earlier, Roder returned a week later in the third exhibition against the Cardinals on August 23, a game played at Memorial Stadium in Champaign, Illinois. A sweat-soaked total of nineteen thousand fans sat through a sizzling 91-degree Saturday afternoon on the prairie as temperatures on the new Astroturf reached as high as 150 degrees. With Thomas watching from the bench, Roder trudged onto the field, after a Bears touchdown tied the game at 13–13 with 30 seconds to go, and booted his second extra point of the day for the victory.

Bob was once again getting the notion that a football career was perhaps not meant to be. After the Bears were shut out 13–0 by the Broncos in the first home preseason game of the year at Soldier Field in the fourth week, Thomas witnessed Roder's automatic reinsertion by Pardee as the starting kicker—as had been the case with Ray and the Rams.

On the following Monday morning, he set aside his frustration and went out early on the cool, dew-laden Lake Forest field before the start of practice. Something was strange. "I'm the only one there," he recalled. "There was nobody else—not the holders or the other kickers, including Roder, so I'm out there working by myself." Bob boomed kick after kick through the uprights, some of which went through the open windows of a gymnasium which sat well beyond the practice field.

The first person he saw that morning was Pardee, who was impressed that Bob was the only player coming out early to put in extra work. It was the final confirmation the coach needed to solidify one of the many positions he had to fill on the young team. "He sees me, and walks up to me and says, 'You're my kicker.'—and that was it," Thomas said.

"He fit right in," *Chicago Tribune* writer Don Pierson remembered in 2018 of Thomas joining the team. "Kickers always seem to be separate from the team, but he wasn't just a soccer player from nowhere; he was from Notre Dame and had won a national championship, so he was accepted by the other players very quickly."[14]

Having won the kicking job free and clear, Bob next worked to get better acquainted with veteran quarterback Bobby Douglass, the man slotted to be his holder. By the time of the fifth preseason game the following week against the Miami Dolphins at Soldier Field (in which Payton finally made his Bears debut after a lingering elbow injury), the two were not yet in sync. "Douglass is holding for me, and he kneels down after I mark the spot. But just before the snap, Douglass jumps up a yard; so, I quickly try to adjust and move up a yard myself. But then, he jumps up again, and moves *back* a yard-and-a-half—so *I* try to back up. The ball comes back during one of these transitions. I'm so messed up, I miss the kick.

"We come back to the sidelines. Pardee saw the whole thing, so he grabs Douglass and asks, 'Bobby, what the heck were you doing out there, jumping back and forth?' Douglass said, 'I just didn't feel like we were at seven yards.' So I said, 'Bobby, you see those little hash marks out there? Every one of them is a yard.'"

Avellini and another quarterback, Gary Huff, then took over the duty. "Bobby was a good athlete," Avellini said of his fellow quarterback, "but wasn't a perfectionist about putting the ball in the right spot. Bob didn't feel comfortable with him, so I held for him a little my rookie season."[15]

Like Thomas, Plank was another rookie who had survived; their resilience ultimately brought the two together as roommates. "As players started to get cut from the team, those who remained were consolidated into the same rooms," Plank recalled about the waning days of the training camp at Lake Forest. "Bob and I wound up together because the guys with whom we were rooming kept getting cut."[16]

They also roomed together in hotels, on the road as well as in the North Shore Hilton outside Chicago on Saturday nights before home games. "If I have one complaint about Bob, it's the following," Plank said in 2017. "Some television station in Chicago would play highlights from the previous day's Notre Dame game at six o'clock on Sunday morning. Bob was always up early watching it while I was trying to get some sleep."[17]

Plank, Thomas, and Payton were among thirteen new starters on the roster as Pardee and his young Bears kicked off the 1975 season on September 21 at home against the Baltimore Colts. With Chicago baseball followers seeing the Cubs obliterated by the Pittsburgh Pirates, 22–0 in the past week at Wrigley Field, local sports fans were looking for hope. Not enough of them made their way to Chicago's ancient lakefront stadium, however, to keep the game from being blacked out on area televisions.

In an ominous sign, in arriving at Soldier Field, the Bears players found their locker room flooded with six inches of backed-up sewage. "And then we went out and stunk up the place," Pardee said in reviewing the day.[18]

The newly outfitted Bears defense could not contain the Colts' scrambling third-year quarterback Bert Jones, who led Baltimore to a crushing 35–7 win. Douglass, soon to be released after struggling through an eight-for-twenty day of passing, snuck over from a yard out in the fourth quarter to give Chicago its only touchdown as Thomas notched his first NFL point on the conversion. Observers mocked the familiar product. "The Bears looked as remodeled as their Soldier Field home," Pierson wrote. "New paint and new names on the outside, same old problems on the inside."[19]

Payton, who ran for a net total of zero yards on eight carries that afternoon, left many wondering if whether his small-college competition had made him capable of playing in the NFL. When coming through Mississippi on a recruiting trip in 1970, Florida State University assistant coach Bill Parcells judged the high-schooler Payton too small and not good enough. "We've got six backs better than him at Florida State," Parcells told Payton's coach.[20]

Following intense pressure from the media and fans, Pardee inserted Huff as the starting quarterback the following week at home against the Philadelphia Eagles. With eleven seconds to go and Huff kneeling on the turf to hold, Thomas sent through a twenty-four-yard field goal—his third of the day—for a 15–13 win. The performance earned him the Golden Toe Award from the publication *Pro Football Weekly* for the most impressive performance in the preceding week by a kicker. "Thomas was suddenly in the driver's seat," the paper marveled. "Last week he proved he can handle the NFL roads as smooth as anyone."[21]

Huff remembered that day. "Bob was a real class guy, with a great sense of humor," the quarterback reflected in 2017. "He wasn't like a normal kicker. Often, kickers aren't part of the team—but Bob was. He had a lot of confidence and competitiveness. As the holder, when I looked up at him, I could see the determined look on his face."[22]

Fans in Los Angeles were now looking on with envy, as the struggling David Ray had been released from the Rams before the season started. "Bob Thomas, who won a 15–13 game last week for Chicago with his third field goal, has one thing in common with St. Louis kicker Jim Bakken," mourned Bob Oates from the *Los Angeles Times*, comparing Thomas with the All-Pro in St. Louis. "Both were originally drafted and cut by the Rams."[23]

Signed by Finks to take Douglass's spot on the roster was first-year wide receiver Steve Schubert, recently released by the New England Patriots and yet another youngster eager for an opportunity. "There were a lot of hungry individuals who came to the Bears as rookies or free agents," Schubert spoke of those days, "and who wanted to prove that they were capable of playing in the NFL—and playing at a high level. Bob, I, and several others were like that."[24]

But as young teams do, the Bears struggled through their growing pains. Had it not been for Thomas's heroics against Philadelphia, Chicago would have lost its first seven games in 1975. A particularly agonizing stretch included defeats to three league powerhouses in Minnesota, Pittsburgh, and Miami by a composite 108–19 score as Thomas was the lone reliable offensive weapon in nailing five straight field goals—including the Bears' only points in a 34–3 trouncing at the hands of the champion Steelers. "It proved a difficult adjustment," Thomas said of the pounding he and his new teammates were taking, "having come from a national championship team at Notre Dame where we were favored to win every week."

Still, he maintained his sense of humor. "Bob always had a good story or a good joke that would keep everyone loose—even when we were losing early on," said Plank. "He was, indeed, a true leader—and not just toward the end of his career. He was a leader on the Bears in both good times and in bad."[25] The recognition Thomas and Plank were gaining around Chicago afforded them opportunities for public service, as defensive back Terry Schmidt recalled. "Bob and Doug would often visit schools to speak in the off-season. Bob typically spoke first and talked about how academics were highly stressed at Notre Dame—that it was important to go to class, get your degree, and so forth. When Plank got up next, he would say to the students, 'At Ohio State, we didn't have to go to class—playing football was all that mattered.' The kids would cheer loudly at that." When they got back to the car in the school parking lot, Thomas shook his head in disbelief: "Doug, what were you thinking?!?"

"I thought that's what they'd want to hear," Plank reasoned.[26]

The losses continued with a 31–3 pummeling at San Francisco on November 16. On the subsequent Sunday, the battered team had to make another long journey back to the West Coast, to face Knox's mighty Rams in the Coliseum in Los Angeles as the brutal schedule wore on.

Bob's pregame regimen had been carefully monitored by John Hilton, the Bears' first-year special-teams coach who had finished his playing days for Pardee with the Blazers the previous year. "I was a rookie, and I listened to what *everyone* was saying," Bob recalled about the early stages of his career.

"He [Hilton] insisted that I kicked better when I warmed up for an inordinate amount of time. Even though it was late November, it was a hot day in Los Angeles. I had kicked so much in pregame that I got dehydrated and had to come back in the locker room."

With twenty-seven seconds left in the first quarter and the Bears already down 14–0, a promising Chicago drive stalled at the Rams' thirty-eight-yard-line. Taking a stab at some precious points in whatever manner he could, Pardee sent in Thomas to attempt a mammoth fifty-five-yard field goal.

Trotting onto the same field where he had competed for the Rams' kicking job a year earlier, Bob ignored the gulf between him and the goalposts in the cavernous old stadium. He marked his spot for Huff on the historic grass and began counting off his steps. Suddenly, he heard a familiar voice call out to him. It was Rams defensive Fred Dryer, whom Thomas had gotten to know during his time in Los Angeles and who was getting ready to rush the attempt.

"Hey Bob!" Dryer hollered. "Man, this a pretty long kick. It's a little out of your range, isn't it?'"

"I don't know, Fred," Thomas responded without looking up. "But I'm going to have to try it."

"Well, I'm going to have to try and *block* it," Dryer countered in getting into his three-point stance. Bob let it fly: "So, I kick it, and because it's a long one, it takes a little while to get there. Fred and I stood next to each other, watching it." The ball soared far through the southern California sky in slow, beautiful, end-over-end fashion, finally landing perfectly in between the uprights for three points.

"Fred turns to me and says, 'Man, good kick!'—and he runs off the field."

Thomas jogged off the field with a little smile. "Take that, Knox," he thought to himself, glancing back over his shoulder at the other sideline. It was the fourth-longest field goal in NFL history, the longest since 1972, and it remained the league's longest for another four years. It was also the longest in the Bears' annals (breaking the thirty-five-year-old team record by three yards) and was a record for a professional game in the Coliseum, second only to a fifty-nine-yarder by collegian Rod Garcia of Stanford against USC two years previously. Later in the game, Thomas nearly nailed another long one, hitting the crossbar in falling just short from fifty yards.

Taking pride in Bob's blast was the special-teams coach, who attributed the success to the pregame workload he had placed on the kicker. "After

I made the long field goal, Hilton said, 'See, I told you!'—so we had to continue to have long pregame kicking sessions."

Despite the overall struggles and a repeat of their 4–10 record from 1974, Pardee was pleased with the development of his young Bears in his first season in 1975—and believed they had set the table for greater things to come in 1976. "Jack was the type of coach that got the most out of teams," Bob concluded in thinking back to his rookie year. "That's how he struck me as a linebacker—he was a very hard worker. And as that type of guy, who must work very hard, sometimes you don't have the natural abilities as others, and you're aware of your own weaknesses. And I think that's how he looked at that 1975 Bears team—that we can accomplish things, but we have to be aware of our limitations."

One of the team strengths on which Pardee could build was his rookie kicker, as Thomas netted a team-leading 57 points on thirteen field goals and 18 extra points—far outdistancing the second-place finisher, Payton, with his 42 points on seven touchdowns. The Bears would not draft another kicker for ten more years.

Chapter 4

The Meadowlands

Mr. Finks tried to bring in individuals who were both good athletes
and good people. Bob was one of those people.

—Brian Baschnagel, 2017

Heightened expectations greeted Thomas and his teammates when they
arrived for training camp at Lake Forest during the nation's bicentennial
month of July 1976. A second harvest of draft picks and free agents joined
Pardee's evolving ranks. After University of Wisconsin offensive tackle Dennis Lick, a Chicago native, was claimed in the first round, the Bears next
chose wide receiver Brian Baschnagel from Ohio State. A teammate of
Plank's in Columbus, Baschnagel hailed from the same football-rich region
outside of Pittsburgh. He had been the first running back in Western Penn-
sylvania Interscholastic Athletic League history to rush for more than four
hundred yards in a high school game and, like Thomas, also an Academic
All-American in college.

When Thomas hung around after practice to get in some extra kicking
work, the eager Baschnagel badgered Bob about letting the receiver hold for
field goals. Thomas preferred to stick exclusively with Huff. "Bob was very
particular about his holder," Baschnagel recalled of his first few days with

the Bears. "One day I said, 'Bob—why don't you just let me *try* it?' So, I started holding for him when Huff was busy with his quarterback duties."[1]

Among the qualities that captured Pardee's eye was Baschnagel's work ethic, which comported with what the coach felt was the high honor bestowed in being chosen to play in the NFL. The players quickly got a sense of Pardee's approach in this respect, exemplified in the training camp misfortune of Carl Gersbach, a backup linebacker who had joined the Bears for ten games in 1975. "Jack thought it was a real privilege to play pro football, and of course it was," Thomas said. "One day, we were having a particularly bad practice, and it was ninety degrees and humid. Ordinarily we did ten hundred-yard sprints at the end, but Jack was ticked off—so we did twenty.

"When we were finished running, I just happened to be walking by as Jack came up to Gersbach. Jack said, 'By the way, Carl—I put you on waivers before practice.' And I thought, 'Are you kidding me? You made this guy run sprints *after* you cut him?' But that was Jack—he thought it was a privilege."

Nor would Pardee let Thomas rest on *his* laurels, despite Bob's strong showing in his rookie season. Brought into camp to compete with him was free agent kicker Rick Danmeier from the University of Sioux Falls, who had received a tryout with Minnesota as a rookie the previous year. In the 1976 preseason opener in Denver on July 31, two field goals by Thomas and one by Danmeier were enough to push the Bears past the Broncos 15–14—a victory saved in the last minute when a bone-jarring hit by Plank caused a Denver fumble.

Another win out west followed in the second exhibition game, as the Bears beat the expansion Seattle Seahawks, the members of whose no-name roster nonetheless had, on average, a full year more of professional experience than the youthful Bears. Danmeier kept pace with Thomas as each man booted one field goal.

Danmeier was somewhat known, having been in the Vikings camp the prior summer. In a culture full of rich personalities, however, few in the kicking community could match the stories—real and imagined—of the well-traveled Ed Strickland, who looked to be a second challenger for Thomas when he arrived at the Bears facility.

Prior to kicking for two different colleges, two WFL teams, and two semi-pro teams, Strickland had earned a Purple Heart with the Marines in Vietnam—from a casualty that occurred while "peeling potatoes," he said.[2]

He had since supported himself and his wife by selling used cars while keeping his kicking leg in shape in hopes of a shot in the NFL. Strickland had wired Jim Finks the following succinct message before leaving his home in Alabama to drive to the Chicago area: "Don't care who you sign—I'm the best kicker."

Unfortunately, Strickland's automobile caused trouble along the way. "Delayed by bad valves in Indianapolis, he was the last man into camp, last to get his physical, last to get his picture taken," as Pierson chronicled the journey.[3] When Strickland's car finally sputtered to a stop in Lake Forest, he sought to corner any reporters he could find. "I know what you're going to ask," he announced with a smile and a wave of his hand. "Can I break the NFL field goal record of sixty-three yards? I say if it's a hot day and I'm hot and the wind is blowing right, that's when I've got it. I want to be known as the greatest long-distance kicker in history. . . . When the pressure comes from the defense, it'll tell right there. When they start rushing, that's when I start smoking." (Strickland's claims of hitting a record fifty-three-yard field goal in the WFL and a sixty-seven-yarder in an amateur game were never verified.)[4]

Hungry for a meal as well as a roster spot, Strickland was not shy about piling on the food while moving through the lunch line in the Bears' residence hall cafeteria. Following close behind him one day was Finks, clandestinely removing one item after another from Strickland's tray without the player realizing that the roast beef, mashed potatoes, gravy, and dessert were being returned to the serving pans.

Watching with amusement was Thomas, who later pulled the general manager aside. "Mr. Finks, I couldn't help but notice you were removing all the food from Ed's tray."

Finks rolled his eyes in frustration. "If we keep feeding him," he responded, "we'll never get rid of him."

As training camp wore on, Bob fended off Danmeier and Strickland with an exceptional preseason performance. After hitting two field goals in a 25–14 win over the Colts on August 14 (including a fifty-yarder, the longest in a pro game in Soldier Field's history to that time), Thomas kicked a forty-four-yarder—his sixth of the summer—with one minute and forty-four seconds left as the Bears squeaked past the Tampa Bay Buccaneers in Florida by a 10–7 score two weeks later. "John McKay can't escape Notre Dame, even in professional football," Jim Selman of the *Tampa Tribune* wrote of the latest encounter with Thomas for the new Bucs coach, who had left USC to take on the challenge of leading the NFL's other expansion franchise in 1976.[5]

The game-winner was supposed to be Danmeier's, as he was slated to take the second-half kicks while Thomas had the first half. But with the game on the line, Pardee went with his regular man. "Great kick!" the coach told Bob as the two headed for the locker room. "Great coaching decision!" Bob replied with a wink.

By the time of the last exhibition game of the season on September 3 in Washington, Thomas had put an indelible stamp on the kicking job. He rescued yet another win for the Bears with three more field goals (for a preseason total of nine), hitting the final one with four minutes and forty-one seconds remaining to beat the Redskins 9–7 in RFK Stadium. Danmeier had already been released the previous Wednesday, and Strickland a couple of weeks earlier.

Danmeier refused to quit. The following season, he again signed with Minnesota and, in 1978, became the team's starting kicker by replacing veteran Fred Cox. When the toe-kicking Danmeier departed from the Vikings in 1983, Mark Moseley of the Redskins became the lone straight-on kicker remaining in the NFL, with all others utilizing the soccer style Thomas had helped popularize.

The young Bears were ready to conquer new territory and got off to a strong start in 1976. After a 10–3 win over the Lions on opening day, the team took two of the next three as well, a stretch that culminated with a 33–7 devastation of the Redskins at Soldier Field on October 3. Thomas hit four field goals, navigating a stiff breeze all afternoon, and netted another Golden Toe Award from *Pro Football Weekly*. After a year and a half of playing in Chicago, Bob believed he had decoded most of the wind patterns in the Bears' lakefront home. "One end zone I have figured out," he stated about his examination of Soldier Field. "That's the [south] end where the stadium is enclosed, and the wind always blows from right to left."

It was the north end that harbored the unpredictable winds—in part because of portable stands that had been installed directly behind the end zone to bring fans closer to field than had the permanent, original enclosure a hundred feet farther beyond. "The other end I don't even think about," he admitted. "Just hit it down the middle, relax with the wind, and let form do the rest."

That wind had a role in what followed over the next few weeks as the Bears went into a downward spiral and the kicker's faith in himself was suddenly shaken.

In week five at Minnesota, Bob ran headlong into the Vikings' six-foot-five linebacker Matt Blair on an extra point attempt. Blair, a specialist at blocking kicks, knocked the ball out of the air to keep a Minnesota lead at 17–13. Later, Thomas was unsuccessful with yet another extra point try in skimming it wide, leaving the Vikings with a 20–19 advantage, which proved to be the final score. Bob had a chance to redeem himself with three minutes and sixteen seconds left, but a gust of wind blew a fifty-two-yard field goal attempt astray of the goalposts. "I have never been on a team which has lost by the margin of one of my kicks before," he said afterward. "I don't like that feeling."[6] The entire kicking game struggled, as Parsons shanked punts of 10, 18, and 19 yards in the first half. "I can't speak for Parsons, but I came into the game aware of the successes the Vikings have had against their opponents' kicking games this year," Bob added. "There is no such thing as a routine kick against the Vikings."[7]

After dealing with reporters, Bob did not want to face his teammates. He lingered in various parts of the visitor's locker room and made certain he was the last one to shower as he slipped inconspicuously out of Metropolitan Stadium. "I trudged out the door with my head hung low."

On the way to the team bus, there was a person waiting for him.

A ten-year-old boy was sitting in a wheelchair in the hallway, holding a game program, a Bears' pennant, and a wide smile—all of which he directed at Thomas, who stopped to autograph the items. "You'd have thought I'd have given the boy the world," Bob remembered. "He got so excited just to have me stop and talk to him, I wondered if he might fall out of his chair."

The two became instant friends. "After a few moments, I bid my young fan a reluctant goodbye and walked out of that stadium, forever changed by the brief encounter. The experience both humiliated and humbled me. I was humiliated by the contrast I saw between the joy of that handicapped kid and the total dejection I felt in the face of a lost football game. He was an example to me—not the other way around."

The inspiration was well-timed. Looming ahead for the Bears was the hottest team in football: the 7–1 Oakland Raiders who arrived at Soldier Field on November 7, a day that would become among Bob's toughest as a professional.

The up-and-coming Bears refused to be intimidated as they traded blows with the Raiders all afternoon. Chicago surged ahead near the end of the third quarter, 27–21 after a two-yard Payton touchdown run, which was parlayed on the ensuing play with the recovery of an onside kick off the foot of Thomas. What made the onside kick even sweeter for Bob was that it allowed him to take a jab at his kicker-hating college teammate, Dave Casper, who was quickly becoming a star tight end for Oakland. "We noticed on film that Casper left early to go back and get his block rather than wait to see if there was an onside kick," Bob recalled gleefully.

After the Raiders slipped back ahead 28–27 in the fourth quarter, the Bears advanced the ball to the Oakland fourteen-yard line. Letting the clock run down to twenty seconds remaining, Pardee called a time-out. Bob gazed across the field and looked up toward the east side of the venerable stadium, watching the flags that lined the columns. Zephyrs had been blowing out of the west all day long at a consistent 17 to 20 miles per hour, occasionally spiking to 30.

As he trotted out for the thirty-one-yard field goal attempt, Thomas was also checking out the flags on top of the goalposts at the north end, but any indications he could decipher were inconclusive. "One flag was blowing left to right, and another was blowing right to left," he would later say.[8]

Huff knelt at the placement spot and waited for the snap from center Dan Neal. Bob sprang into action and swung his leg mightily. "I was confident when I hit it. It rotated well."[9]

In the short distance the football traveled, it seemed to be yanked in different directions every few feet by the blasts of wind shooting toward Lake Michigan. "I thought it was good and I started to walk away," Bob told Kevin Lamb of the *Chicago Daily News*. "I don't know what happened."[10]

Suddenly, the ball's path was impeded, like a bird flying into a building. It hit high on the right goalpost, bouncing directly back into the field of play. Bob's hands, raised in triumph over his head a second earlier, descended slowly to his hips as a couple of Oakland players began taunting him.

If the wind in that millisecond had provided an inch the other way, the ball would have scraped through for a Bears win. Instead, victory belonged to Oakland with a 28–27 final.

It was the first time Bob had ever missed a last-second, game-deciding kick. Just before halftime, his attempt from thirty-three yards had blown just left of the goalposts at the other end of the field. "The life seemed to drain out of that Soldier Field crowd at that moment," Thomas noticed, "and with it, any real hope for mounting a late-season charge to a berth in the playoffs was dashed."

In the Bears' locker room, reporters looked to pin responsibility somewhere for the loss. In answering them, Pardee was just as supportive of his kicker as anyone else on the roster. "There is not a 'gimme' field goal any time, especially when you're playing in a gusty wind." The coach added that Thomas had been eager to get on the field to do the job—even from a longer distance a moment earlier. "He wanted to kick from the 40, but I said to wait."[11]

In front of Bob's locker, Revie Sorey came over, sat down, and put his arm around him. "A couple of the guys are going out later for a beer," Sorey said. "Why don't you come along? We'd love to have you."

"Thanks, but no thanks," Thomas responded as he gritted his teeth and turned toward his stall.

Thomas thought of the Oakland loss together with the critical Minnesota game as a missed chance to beat both powerhouse teams, which would eventually meet in the Super Bowl after the 1976 season. He mumbled a final comment: "I've had two of the saddest days a kicker could have."[12]

Decades later, Pierson not only viewed Thomas as blameless in the defeat but even saw the game as a positive, watershed moment for the growth of the Bears as a whole. "I never remember a time when he wasn't willing to talk to the media—whether he made or missed a big kick," the longtime beat writer reflected in 2018. "He was very respectful to the press and was never reluctant to take responsibility. That Raiders game, however, win or lose, was such a big step forward for the Bears in showing they could compete with the best in the NFL at that point. I don't think anyone blamed Bob for that loss."[13]

As he faced the media again on Monday, Bob tried to put a positive spin on his difficulties over the past few weeks by labeling them as "character-building." "What I have to prevent from happening is letting it affect the next one. I can't dwell on this or I'll really be in trouble."[14] He had now missed seven times in his last eight field goal attempts, reminiscent of his senior-year struggles at Notre Dame. "I'm really looking forward to the next kick," he assured the fans about the home game against the rival Packers to take place the following Sunday. "I'm sure before I take the field there are going to be boos. This is pro football; I'm a pro, and everybody has been booed at times. But confidence comes from within."[15]

And in what would prove to be a prescient statement leading up to the following week's game, he added, "I think we have one of the strongest kick coverage teams in football."[16]

Along with the support of Pardee, Thomas had the complete backing of the general manager. "I got a paycheck after that game," Bob recalled of the week following the Raiders debacle, "and Jim Finks wrote on the stub of the check, 'Cox, Bakken, or Stenerud? I'll take Thomas.'" It felt good knowing Bob had the general manager's trust. Nonetheless, Bob arrived at the Soldier Field locker room for the Green Bay game and noticed some disturbing news written on the chalkboard.

Pardee had decided that the kickoff coverage unit would be the one introduced to the home crowd before the game instead of the usual offense or defense. "I had just missed the kick against Oakland, and Bears fans are the most rabid in the world," Thomas remembered. "I thought, 'Are you kidding me?' I went up to him and I said, 'Jack, I know you're a new head coach, but before the game, you don't introduce the *kickoff coverage team*—especially when *I'm on it*!'"

The kickoff team was nevertheless introduced. And as Bob expected, the crowd in Soldier Field unleashed its anger at him, the derision cascading down in waves from the top row to the bottom. Two people sat silently and heard the jeers with painful sympathy—Augie and Anne Thomas.

The anger of the faithful was still audible once the game got under way. "When he was kicking into the net and warming up on the sidelines, you should have heard some of the things the fans were saying to him," Plank said in disgust when thinking back to the scene. "He can't make it up to them by suddenly going out there and kicking a fifty-five-yard field goal. He can't even go out and tackle someone like I can when I'm frustrated."[17]

But that afternoon, whether trying to make amends or not, Bob *did* seek a chance to tackle someone.

He had been regularly asking Plank for advice on what to do when blockers went after him on kickoff returns. "Bobby," Plank told him. "Don't worry about it. If a guy is coming toward you, just stand still. He'll get one look at that little jersey number 16, that little single-bar face mask, and the little guy wearing them, and he'll go right around you."[18]

Thomas had largely followed the instructions, adding further protection for himself by hanging back as a "deep safety" (as kickers typically do) to guard against a long return. But on one of his kickoffs against the Packers, he was finally called into the melee.

"I made a quick move around a big guy who was charging down toward me. As the return man was going down the sidelines, I turned around to get an angle on him. Meanwhile, the guy I faked out is peeling back around and looking for me. And as I turned around, I got hit harder than I ever had been before—or since."

It was a situation which football players refer to as getting "ear-holed"— whereby the player takes a vicious hit from the side that he never sees coming, usually occurring on kickoff and punt returns because of the zigzagging paths taken by the blockers.

"When I hit the ground, I looked like the crash dummy on one of those TV commercials for cars," Bob continued with a nervous chuckle about the incident. "It was almost like a whiplash thing. My head went back, and I hit the turf. I got up, and then I hit the ground again. Then, I was helped from the field."

Or, as Terry Schmidt described the scene, "It looked like one of those Bugs Bunny cartoons where a character is knocked head over heels."

Bob convalesced from the attack and proceeded on his mission to win the fans back over. With the Bears leading 21–13 in the fourth quarter, he drove a forty-six-yard field goal through the oncoming wind for the final points in a 24–13 Chicago victory. While the field goal wound up being insignificant in the outcome of the game, his teammates nevertheless mobbed him in supportive jubilation—as Bob could hear the crowd cheering once again from underneath the congratulatory pile. "That's why I think this club is headed for big things," Thomas would say in the following off-season. "The camaraderie between the front office, the coaching staff, and the players is tremendous. There's the feeling that we're all in this thing together. There's a spirit that's hard to define . . . at Notre Dame we had that same kind of feeling."[19]

When the Bears assembled for their film session the following day, the hit Thomas sustained on the kickoff return was the talk of the meeting room.

"On Mondays, Pardee would give out awards from the previous game," Bob said. "I think a television was the top award, but Jack always seemed to be most thrilled about potentially giving away a cooler—just a little Igloo cooler.

"We're in the meeting room, and I received a bottle of wine for the 'Coming of Age Award' for 'coming of age as a football player,' as Jack put it, as he re-wound the tape and showed the 'highlight' of me getting hit about ten times."

While most of the other Bears were falling off their chairs, one teammate did not find it humorous—a player who had been through the rough-and-tumble wars of the NFL countless times.

"Everyone was laughing—except Doug Buffone, who was sitting next to me. I said, 'Doug, I noticed you weren't laughing during the film.' He said, 'Bob, the guy was pretty much standing still when he hit you. If he had been running full speed, you'd be dead.'"

The special-teams coach Hilton, a nine-year veteran as a player himself, was equally unamused. Like Buffone, he was shaking his head in horror while watching and claimed it was the hardest he had ever seen anyone be hit.

The insight from the two men gave Thomas pause. He was ready to move on from one of the toughest stretches of his career.

"After that kickoff, I brought new meaning to the term 'deep safety'—for I was never seen in the television camera angle on kickoffs ever again."

Both Thomas and the Bears had fought back from the midseason adversity. Despite falling short of the playoffs, the team won three of its last five games to finish with an even 7–7 record, while Bob nailed five of his next six field goals after the Oakland miss.

To stay on the cutting edge, however, Thomas decided that an overhaul of his style was necessary for the following campaign. Determined to right himself, he prepped for training camp by kicking 150 to 200 balls with his father in Rochester nearly every day from April to June 1977. While doing so, Bob discovered that striking the football with his entire instep instead of using some of his toe, as he had always done, was producing more power. "The kicks were not only long, but they were high—higher even than my extra points," Thomas told a reporter that summer.[20]

Despite his confidence being restored, abuse continued to be delivered toward Bob from the segment of fans who chose to focus on the memory of the Oakland game.

At the team's first public workout in late July (annually dubbed the "Welcome Home Scrimmage"), Thomas was booed by a majority of the fifteen thousand fans in attendance. Once again, Plank had been amazed at the lack of forgiveness: "I couldn't believe the bitterness toward him whenever I went to a banquet in the off-season."[21]

The boos were still coming when the Bears concluded their preseason schedule at Soldier Field on September 10 against the Cincinnati Bengals. Once again, Pardee chose an odd and ill-timed way to thrust his kicker into the public eye, naming Thomas one of the captains to supervise the pregame coin toss as the veteran Buffone headed to midfield for the ritual as well. "Stay away from me," he said to Thomas jokingly as they strutted out along the fifty-yard line. "They might be throwing grenades."[22]

Thomas generally managed to ignore the mistreatment, as he looked forward to a long NFL tenure yet to come. It did not prevent him, however, from making plans for second career.

The past spring, Bob's brother, Rick, had graduated from Notre Dame and started attending law school at Loyola University in Chicago. The dean of Loyola Law was Charles "Bud" Murdock, who had previously been a professor in South Bend. He read in the newspaper of Bob's interest in attending law school and invited the player to breakfast one morning where the two discussed the idea.

"When are you going to start?" Murdock asked.

"Maybe next off-season," Thomas responded.

"How about *this* season?"

Murdock assured Bob that his schedule of classes could be arranged around his football duties, with him technically being classified as a "day student" (the full-time designation) yet being permitted to take the four-year duration normally followed by "night students" to complete his degree.

"OK, maybe I will."

Next, Bob had to approach Finks with the idea. "He said that if I had played any other position, it would not work. But, considering the fact I was kicker, he actually thought it was a good thing that I would have something else to occupy my time."

Thomas sent in his application, was accepted, and enrolled at Loyola for five hours of classes for the fall semester of 1977 with plans to take ten more hours in the spring and summer. "I'd like to practice law someday, but it's more than just the drive to be a lawyer," he told the *Rochester Times-Union* as the Bears' season was about to get under way. "It's just good to get your mind working again. Once you're out of college, you don't have to worry about current events. The only thing you read is the sports page. I'm ready to go back to school."[23]

Bob's decision surprised few of his peers—especially those who valued higher education themselves. "Jim Finks brought in atypical players," said Schmidt, who became a dentist after his NFL career, serving at Veterans Administration facilities and on mission trips abroad. "We had people who went on to earn graduate degrees. Bob was someone who always had 'other plans' for life after football. We often sat together at team meetings and meals, and just sort of gravitated together. I loved his sense of humor and quick wit."[24] Baschnagel agreed that the roster was being stocked with well-rounded men. "Mr. Finks tried to bring in individuals who were both good athletes and good people. Bob was one of those people."[25]

The new off-field objective gave Thomas a revived sense of vigor as he further honed his kicking craft. But again in 1977, a season that began with high hopes for him and his teammates quickly fell into disarray.

After an opening day win over the Lions at home for the second year in a row, the Bears dropped five of their next seven, culminating with a 47–0 blowout at the hands of the Houston Oilers in the Astrodome. Only a last-second extra point by Thomas the following week for a 28–27 squeaker over the Kansas City Chiefs at Soldier Field kept the team's playoff hopes alive. Each subsequent week, however, became increasingly important, with the team still teetering on edge of elimination.

The Bears pushed through a dreary, overcast, rain-soaked day at Soldier Field the following Sunday, November 20, as Payton broke the NFL single-game rushing record with 275 yards while a field goal by Thomas once again made the difference. But the 10–7 victory over the Vikings also came at an immediate, tangible cost—a cost that affected Bob directly. On a play in the fourth quarter, Baschnagel tore the deltoid ligament in his left ankle and was lost for the remainder of the season.

The team kept the momentum going. Wins on the road against the Lions (four days later, on Thanksgiving) and the Bucs followed, making four victories in a row.

The Packers were the fifth straight opponent to fall by a 21–10 count on December 11 in front of the third-smallest crowd in the Bears' seven years at Soldier Field (33,557). Despite the Bears' push for the playoffs, a temperature of 10 degrees and a wind chill factor of –3 at kickoff, plummeting to –10 at times, had kept many away from the final home game. But even with the reduced showing, the Bears' Soldier Field attendance in 1977 of 401,513 for seven games was their highest since moving into the Park District stadium.

The five straight triumphs moved the Bears' record to 8–5, evening them with the first-place Vikings and leaving only a victory in the season's final week over the Giants in New York standing between the Bears and their first playoff appearance since 1963.

During the winning steak, the effect of Baschnagel's absence on Bob's kicking had been palpable. In the first ten games with Baschnagel holding for field goals, Thomas had been ten-for-sixteen; but over the next three games with reserve quarterback Vince Evans performing the duty, Bob had gone two-for-seven. "He was missing spots and was putting too much pressure on the ball," Bob said sympathetically about Evans having no experience at the job. "He was kind of unsure of himself. After we kicked one, he would ask me if he had made a good hold or not."

Thomas was surprised that Avellini—who had held in college at Maryland while Evans had *not* done so for McKay at USC—was not given the role. Pardee, however, was adamant.

"'I've got to get him on the field,' Jack told me. 'He's a good athlete.'

"'Well, just make him a punt returner!' I said. 'Don't make him a *holder!*'"

Pardee entertained Bob's opinion, but nothing changed.

In the Tuesday and Wednesday practices leading up to the season finale, Evans was still sent out with the field goal unit. With the all-important contest looming, Thomas took his case to a higher court.

"So, we get to the Giants game, and I have to talk to *somebody*—so I go see Jim Finks. Lo and behold, Bob Avellini becomes the holder."

After winning his case against Pardee, Bob drove from Lake Forest into the city later that week to complete his final exams for his first semester of law school. Upon heading back home to gather his things, he prepared to join his teammates on the fateful journey out east.

With temperature readings at nearby Newark Airport showing thirty degrees at the 1 p.m. kickoff on December 18, the blanket that covered Giants Stadium at the Meadowlands appeared on CBS to be beautiful, delicate, soft snow. Closer examination revealed a sheet of ice. When the two teams conducted their pregame warmups an hour earlier, the field was in perfect condition; but at game time, the yard lines were nowhere to be found as a result of the sudden blast of arctic precipitation. The temperature was expected to drop to twenty by the end of the afternoon, with the ice entombing the As-troturf deeper as each hour passed. Packers' legend Paul Hornung, serving as one of the television broadcasters for the game, said it was the worst field he had ever seen—despite his many years toiling in Green Bay. Considering the circumstances, no one gave Payton a chance for the 199 yards he needed to break O. J. Simpson's single-season record of 2,003. To make matters more challenging for the Bears, several players were battling the flu. One was Ro-land Harper, who on Saturday had stayed in his bed at the team's Sheraton Hotel in Hasbrouck Heights, New Jersey, all day while Payton, his room mate and benefactor of Harper's blocking, brought him soup.

As hearty souls began filling the seats in the frosted rows of Giants Sta-dium, among them were Augie and Anne, who had made a seven-and-half hour drive across the state from Rochester, staying just ahead of the foul weather.

When Thomas's counterpart Joe Danelo got set to conduct the opening kickoff for New York, CBS cameras showed the tiny icicles hanging from the crossbars of the goalposts while pellets of hail smacked against the play-ers' helmets.

Joe McConnell, the Bears' play-by-play announcer on WBBM Radio, told his listeners, "Bob Thomas, the Bears' placekicker, may be the big man of the day as he loosens up behind the Bears' bench on the near side." McCon-nell's sidekick, Brad Palmer, was quick to point out that Thomas "had missed eight of his last eleven field goals."

At the 10:50 mark of the first quarter, the Chicago kicker lined up behind Avellini on a cleared strip on the right hash mark and drilled a thirty-two-yarder through the uprights, giving the Bears the first lead of the day at 3–0. Danelo soon after hit from thirty-eight yards away at the opposite end for a 3–3 tie.

The rest of the first half remained an offensive stalemate, with neither team able to gain traction and the kickers exchanging misses. Thomas went wide on a twenty-four-yard attempt as he pulled the ball and banged it off the left goalpost, while Danelo pushed a try too far to the right to leave the score knotted at the break.

With six minutes and two seconds remaining in the game and shortly after Danelo kicked another field goal, fullback Robin Earl spurred his cleats into the ice and barged over the goal line from four yards out for a 9–6 Chi-cago lead. Thomas's extra point was deflected out of the air, however, permitting Danelo to tie the game at 9–9 with another three-pointer before regulation ended to send the game into sudden-death overtime.

It was the second overtime game in Bears' history, the first having occurred just two months earlier in Minnesota when the team lost to the Vikings on a touchdown scored on a fake field goal, giving the Vikes a 22–16 win. In that game, Blair had blocked yet another of Thomas's extra points.

If neither team was able to score and the game ended in a tie, the Bears season would be over and the Redskins would get into the playoffs in Chicago's place. Pardee's troops had to find a way, amid the storm, to put points on the board—and do so before the Giants did.

Things looked favorable for Chicago early in the extra period. After the Bears kicked off, Plank intercepted a pass and returned it to the New York twenty-seven-yard line. Three plays later, the Bears were left with a fourth-and-one; but Thomas missed a field goal try from thirty-six yards away, hooking his kick wide of the left post. "The snap was a bit low," a disappointed McConnell said over WBBM, "and Avellini did a heck of a job to get it down."

The Chicago defense held once again on the Giants' second possession in overtime, getting Avellini the ball back with just five minutes and six seconds to go. The offense navigated its way down to the New York ten, as the field goal unit entered again with three minutes and four seconds left. For the second straight possession, the offense failed to get a first down on third-and-inches. "Let's don't mishandle this one, guys," McConnell advised the special-teams group.

But once again, Neal's snap hit the ground on its way back to Avellini. Thomas skidded to a stop without getting a chance to kick, as the quarterback scooped up the ball and flung a desperation pass to the man on the end of the line, Buffone, who had the ball jarred loose from his grasp by a New York defender. "As the holder, when you put the ball down, there's a little clock that goes off in your head," Avellini said. "When I realized Bob wasn't going to kick, I picked the ball up and rolled out and tossed it to Buffone. He got broken in two." Buffone was interested only in giving out shots on defense—not *taking* them on offense. "When we came back to the bench, Doug said, 'Don't ever throw me the ball again.'"[26]

With a second chance having gone by the wayside, Thomas—and everyone else—imagined that getting a third was impossible. The field was now a virtual hockey rink, with the temperature continuing to plummet. It was destined to be another heartbreaking end to a Chicago sports season.

Despondent on the sideline, Bob received some much-needed words of encouragement from one of the team's few veterans. "Mike Phipps came up to me," Thomas said of the quarterback, "and told me a story about when he was in Cleveland. Don Cockroft [the Browns' kicker] had missed three in one game, but he came back to get the last one to win. Mike said that Cockroft just mentioned, 'No matter what happens, life goes on. One missed kick doesn't mutually exclude another.' Mike really picked my spirits up."[27]

Having taken away both Bears' scoring chances, the Giants looked to run out the clock. But on third down, the team committed a costly clipping penalty, which forced a punt, giving Chicago one last shot. The unheralded Bears defense—which had permitted only two touchdowns in the previous five games since the Kansas City win—had halted the opposition yet again.

After completing a pass to tight end Greg Latta over the middle, Avellini quickly called the Bears' final time-out. He next found Payton in the flat for fourteen yards and a first down, which advanced the ball to the Giants' eleven-yard line. On the play, Payton chose to veer back into the field for extra yardage instead of getting out of bounds—a decision that kept the clock running. "I thought they would take away the outside stuff, since the only way we could stop the clock was to get out of bounds," Avellini said later in analyzing the New York defense. "But I saw they *didn't* take away the outside. I threw to Payton quick, hoping he'd get out of bounds. Why he cut back, I really don't know."[28]

Twenty seconds were left, and the clock was moving. With time—and the season—ticking away, Avellini got ready to take another snap and fire the ball into the stands to stop the clock. "But I saw the field goal team running onto the field," he continued, "and you can't send them back. I figured we had time to kick, but I didn't want to rush anything."[29]

This *was* the last chance. There would be no more opportunities. Bob sprinted out onto the frozen field one more time and took his spot. "We had no time-outs left, and people were running in all directions," Thomas remembered. "I saw so many out there that I thought we were going to be penalized for too many men on the field. People were yelling at me from both the offense and the field goal unit, and I couldn't understand a word they were saying. All I saw was a bunch of white shirts all around me."[30]

Amid the chaos, Bob Parsons found Thomas. The six-foot-three, 240-pound punter grabbed the five-foot-ten, 175-pound kicker by the collar of his jersey and lifted him up three inches off the ground. "You'd better make *this* kick," Parsons said, "or I'm going to break your f——ing neck." After his feet landed back on the icy turf, Thomas looked up at Parsons. "You obviously weren't a psychology major at Penn State, were you?" To this day, Thomas never lets him forget the exchange. "Bob reminds me of it all the time," Parsons affirmed.[31] If he missed again, Bob figured that having to face Parsons afterward would be only the beginning: "He was my teammate and friend. I didn't even want to think about the potential fan reaction back in Chicago."

Over on the sidelines, Pardee, who had been wearing an old-fashioned naval watch cap pulled down tight over his head all day against the bitter wind, was vigorously scrubbing his scalp. "Jack would always take off his cap and rub his head—out of nervousness, thinking, or whatever," Thomas said.

Bob's teammates were doing everything they could to assist. The original clearing of the hash marks by the grounds crew—which had contributed to Bob's first field goal on the afternoon—had long faded, giving way to another wave of ice. "Payton and Harper were lying on turf making snow angels in a desperate attempt to clear a small spot where I could get better footing," the kicker appreciatively remembered.

But it was the snapper, Neal, who recognized that something had been amiss on the earlier field goal tries—and this time, it was corrected. "We noticed that, on the first two attempts in overtime, my snaps had been coming up short," Neal said in 2017. "My snaps were actually fine; but if you look at the film, you can see that Avellini was setting up at eight yards—not seven, probably due to the field being covered in ice. Now, for our last chance, the whole team was clearing out a spot for Bob at exactly seven yards."[32]

With the game meaning nothing to the Giants in terms of their own postseason possibilities, much of the home crowd had departed by the time Avellini went down to a knee. But the next play carried all the hopes of Chicago with it, including those of the Bears fans who could not bear to watch—in particular, the kicker's mother.

A combination of the bitter weather and the kick's importance had driven Anne Thomas out of the stands and into the ladies' room at Giants' Stadium, where she performed her usual ritual when Bob attempted a field goal: saying a prayer to St. Jude. "Mom—that's the patron saint of lost causes," Bob once said crossly when Anne revealed the practice to him. "Yes, I know," was her matter-of-fact reply.

This time, Avellini grabbed a perfect snap from Neal. He took a split-second to spot a reasonable piece of turf and set the ball down as Bob gingerly began his steps, trying not to slip. Seconds after Bob struck the football, another lady ran into the bathroom where Anne was sitting. Anne could not see the lady, who began shouting hysterically, "We won!!! We won!!!"

Believing the woman had to be a Giants fan, Anne's eyes began to tear up at the thought of Bob being ridiculed. But the woman was Jack Pardee's wife.

Once Anne realized this, she barged out of the stall, hugged Mrs. Pardee, and hurried back into the stadium to celebrate the Bears' victory with her husband. "She found Mr. Thomas jumping up and down in an aisle, chanting *'Bobby did it! Bobby did it!'*" wrote John Schulian of the *Chicago Daily News*.[33]

Thus ended the longest contest in Bears' history to that time after 74 minutes and 51 seconds had gone off the game clock. In 2019, Pierson and fellow Bears' beat writer Dan Pompei cited the field goal as the second-greatest kick in team history.[34]

As Bob was hoisted into the air by a mob of teammates, the field goal set off a wave of celebrations that stretched from the Bears' sideline to taverns and living rooms across the Chicago area. Parsons and Neal rolled around the slick turf together in a laughing embrace. Eight seconds from a tie that would have precluded them from a playoff spot, the Bears were headed to the postseason while also owning the NFL's longest current winning streak at six.

Years later, *Chicago Sun-Times* writer Dan Bickley recounted what that moment meant to the team's owner as he watched the game from a television in his office. "After the kick, Bears founder George Halas looked out the window and saw no traffic on Sheridan Road. That sight, he later confided to a friend, proved that the Bears finally had recaptured the soul of the city."[35]

After some quick handshakes with the Giants players, the Bears quickly exited the frigid field. They lingered happily in the warmth of the visitors' locker room, basking in the hot water of the shower and in the glory of their triumph. Peeling off their white road jerseys with the navy-blue numbers still glistening from the sleet, players shared congratulations all around—but particularly for Thomas and Avellini. The latter blamed none of the missed chances on the kicker nor on Neal. "People just took turns screwing up for him," the quarterback shrugged apologetically toward Bob. "One time I set the ball up wrong. Another time there was too much penetration. Another time I set up too far back."[36]

Had Thomas's future with the Bears hinged on that last kick? Some, including Pierson, suggested so—even in memorializing the happy moment. "Don't say the Bears belong in the playoffs," he wrote. "They belong in the Bible. Right under miracles. With the clock running out in overtime and in a season and perhaps in a career, warmth returned to Dan Neal's hands and Bob Avellini's fingers and Bob Thomas's toe, bringing tears to the eyes of coaches and players and thousands of Chicagoans who have waited 14 years for something good to cry about after a football game."[37]

As for Bob, what would he have done if he missed the final chance? "I saw an exit sign to the left," he remarked about the end of the facility where the kick took place. "I would have had them forward my mail to Asia." All was forgiven. "They can send it to Dallas instead," Pierson wrote in conclusion.[38]

A trip to Texas Stadium was the team's prize for victory, where the powerful Cowboys awaited as the Bears' assignment. The Cowboys' own field goal specialist was suffering through a slump. Herrera failed on three field goals on the season's final day—in *good* weather conditions—in the Cowboys' 14–6 home win over the Broncos. The misses prevented the Dallas kicker from taking the National Football Conference (NFC) scoring title away from Payton, as the Chicago running back finished three points ahead, ninety-six to ninety-three—netting Payton a $5,000 bonus per his contract.

As the Bears got into their street clothes and made their way out of Giants Stadium, Avellini, a native of Queens, suggested that Bob skip the team flight back home and, with Augie and Anne, join Avellini and his parents for dinner—tamer plans than the bachelors' usual pursuits, as Avellini remembered. "In 1977, I moved out to Northbrook (Illinois) in the Mission Hills area. A few months later, Bob bought a place in the same building. So, we hung around a lot.

"Bob always had this little sports car—he was really into cars. He was also really into line dancing—and remember, this was the disco era. Bob would practice his line dancing in front of the mirror at home, so that when we went out to the clubs, he would be good at it. He really worked at it, because I can't say he's a gifted athlete. Sometimes, when you're a kicker, you're not looked at as a 'real' football player—and Bob tried to make up for it in other ways. But he was good on the dance floor. He could do all the moves."[39]

Fatigued after the epic game, Avellini and Thomas decided that dinner with the parents would suffice. "My dad was following the Avellinis' car to the restaurant, but they accidentally lost us along the way," Bob recalled. "We're in New York City with no idea of where to go. This is before cell phones, and I figured Avellini and I have already missed the team flight back home. So, I say to my parents, 'Would you mind if we go to the airport to get a flight to Chicago?' They said it was no problem, so I got a ticket for a commercial flight back to O'Hare." After settling into a coach seat, Bob saw a familiar face walking down the aisle from first class. It was CBS television broadcaster Brent Musburger, who relinquished his premium spot to sit next to Thomas for the trip to Chicago, where Musburger had launched his career ten years earlier. "We get to O'Hare," Bob continued, "and my plane lands before the Bears' charter—which isn't unusual, because they had to pack up all the gear, wait for the interviews to be finished, and so forth."

Getting off their plane, Thomas and Musburger immediately noticed a swarm of about five thousand Bears fans clustered around a security-staffed gate that had been constructed near where the team's charter flight would roll in. "Because all those fans were there, they were not letting anyone through," Thomas went on. "I'm trying to make my way past the crowd to the gate. I finally get to the front and I said to the cops, 'I'd like to get in there, because my teammates are coming back, and it would be fun to be there and greet them.'

"They said, '*Your* teammates? You think we were born yesterday?!?'

"I said, 'It's a long story . . . I took a different flight. . . .'"

"Get out of here!" one of the officers yelled back in Bob's face.

"So, they're not letting me in. And then someone in the crowd says, 'Hey, that's Bob Thomas!' And the cop said, 'Oh yeah—you are!'—And they grabbed me and lifted me over the gate so I could get to the team plane."

Unbeknownst to Thomas at the time, his lengthy appearance on national television after the Giants' game had also garnered him some corporate interest. On Monday, he received a visit from the Chicago-area marketing representative for Wilson Sporting Goods. When Musburger in the "NFL Today" studios sent CBS broadcaster Johnny Morris outside the Bears' locker room for interviews, Bob had already removed his jersey and thus had his shoulder pads showing. Happily for Wilson, the company logo was clearly displayed on the pads while the camera was rolling.

"Do you know how much free advertising time you gave us yesterday?" the rep said happily when greeting Bob. "We want to do something for you."

An avid golfer, Thomas quickly offered an idea: "How about a set of Staff irons?"

The rep tapped on his chin. He then countered the proposal: "How about a racquetball racquet instead?"

"I'll take it."

Bob's heroics in New York had inspired other people in profound ways around Chicago. "A woman called Wally Phillips," Pierson wrote of the legendary WGN Radio personality, "to report she had watched the Giants game from her hospital labor room and decided to name her son Robert Thomas Smith."[40]

The day after Christmas in Dallas, Thomas and the Bears were overrun by the ferocious Cowboys by a 37–7 score. Nonetheless, a promising foundation for the team's future success had been laid.

Chapter 5

MAGGIE

Every point counted. And Bob came through.

—ROBIN EARL, RECALLING THE BEARS'
CHARGE TO THE 1979 PLAYOFFS

In January 1978 as Bob was packing up his football gear and starting his second semester of law school, a bombshell hit the Bears' offices. On Thursday, January 19, it was announced that Pardee was out as head coach, as the former Washington player and assistant coach had landed the top job with the Redskins. In taking nearly a month to land a replacement, Finks got the man he wanted—a trusted colleague from his days in Minnesota. On February 16, Neill Armstrong was introduced to the Chicago media.

Armstrong had been a head coach in the Canadian Football League for six years before becoming the defensive coordinator for Vikings head coach Bud Grant in 1970. He had not applied for the Bears' position; rather, Finks made it a point to pursue the coach. "I'm just up here doing my job," Armstrong said of sitting in his home outside the Twin Cities, "and someone calls me at midnight to ask if I'm a candidate. I figured if Jim didn't call me three years ago when the job was open, why should he call this time?"[1]

The choice surprised many of the Bears, many of whom were unfamiliar with Armstrong—and even confused him with the famous astronaut Neil

Armstrong. In the days preceding the announcement, rumors had circulated that Stanford head coach Bill Walsh would be given the job. "I was shocked—I thought it would be Walsh," said Plank.[2]

As he and his teammates adapted to the coaching staff change, Bob settled into a new set of classes at Loyola while also making another round of speaking engagements and autograph signings at banquets, charity events, and shopping malls, along with the usual school appearances. One school he visited was Robina Lyle Elementary School in the southwest Chicago suburb of Bridgeview, a community near where his good friends Ron and Mary Lynn Colosimo lived. Mary Lynn was a counselor at the school, and in early March asked Bob to take part in a career day the staff was offering students.

After completing a workout in Lake Forest and heading out to his car on the morning of the event, Bob was disgruntled to find that the weather was much the same as it had been at the Meadowlands a couple months earlier. "It was a terrible, icy, windy day," he recalled in dreading the long trip he was facing from one end of the Chicago area to the other. "I'm thinking, 'What the heck am I doing this for?'" As he inched along the treacherous roads, he fought an inclination to turn around several times. Something inside told him to keep going.

Arriving late at the school, Bob expected to get a negative reception—considering his tardiness as well as the animosity he had been experiencing from his missed kicks in the past year despite the game-winner against the Giants. "I was a little surprised when I heard cheers as I walked into the gymnasium. I then knew it was a grammar school and not a high school—because high-school kids probably would have been booing."

After making some opening comments, Bob put a Bears highlight film on the projector for the students to watch: "As the reel started playing, I saw this cute kindergarten teacher out of the corner of my eye."

Her name was Margaret Mary Murphy, sitting near the front of the stands with an empty seat next to her. Bob coolly sauntered over. She offered him the chair, but Bob politely refused. He preferred to stand, he responded. Because it was a highlight reel of the Bears' *offense*, Bob figured he did not have a lot of time to act. He got right to work. "I asked if she was married. For some reason she thought *I* was married—I don't know why. She said no, she was not married. I said, 'That's a plus!'—for which, to this day, she makes fun of me."

The highlight film quickly spun to its end, and Bob returned to the front of the gym to answer the students' questions. "After my presentation was over, Mary Lynn came up to me and said the teachers wanted to know if I'd like to join them at a nearby restaurant. I said, 'Only if the kindergarten teacher is going.'" As it was the end of the school day, Margaret had gone back to her classroom to help her students put on their coats for the bus trip home. Mary Lynn came skipping in. "He said he'll go if the kindergarten teacher goes!" she proclaimed. "He's in love! He's in love!"

The sudden outburst of enthusiasm tipped off Margaret that something was up. "I respected Mary Lynn highly," she said in 2017. "She was an excellent guidance counselor and the utmost professional. That's what made it funny to see her so giddy about the whole thing."[3] Margaret agreed to go. But because of some schoolwork she needed to finish, she was the last one to arrive at the restaurant. When she walked in, several of the teachers were already gathered around a large table. Once again, there was one empty chair—but this time, the roles were reversed as the lone available space was next to Bob. "Bob says I planned it that way," Margaret asserted with a smile. "But it's not true."[4]

After chatting and sharing several laughs, the two said goodbye as Bob returned to his apartment in Northbrook to prepare for an out-of-town trip. "The next day, I had to fly to Conway, Arkansas, as a friend of mine from Notre Dame was getting married. On the way back home, I had to get on this little puddle-jumper and fly through a lightning storm."

He called Margaret before boarding and told her what a great time he had in meeting her. "When we ascended up into the storm, I started thinking to myself, 'I just met the girl I am going to marry—but I'm going to die in this flight!'" Nonetheless, he made it back to Chicago safely and started exclusively seeing Margaret, whom he would call "Maggie."

Bob picked her up for their first date in his 1957 Thunderbird, which Augie had restored for him. When the couple drove through downtown Chicago, she noticed that a lot of people were staring at them. "She was thinking, 'Is this guy really that famous?'" Bob remembered. "They weren't recognizing *me*. They were looking at the *car*."

With the grind of the season behind him, Bob continued the rigor of the first year of law school as new friendships were forged at Loyola with study groups among the students. Certain classes and instructors stood out to him as favorites—such as Professor Richard A. Michael. "He was an icon,"

Thomas remembered fondly. "He wrote a textbook on civil procedure, but he was more known for his teaching style. He had an unusual way of speaking and we affectionately called him 'The RAM' because of his initials. We always looked forward to his classes—in part because he was such a character."

Michael employed the Socratic method with his pedagogy—and like any good teacher, kept all the students on their toes. "You never knew when the spotlight was going to fall on you and he was going to ask you a particular holding of a case," Bob recalled. "You would have to stand up in front of the class and give it."

One day in the civil procedure course, Michael was gazing up toward the top rows of the auditorium during his lecture. His eyes landed on Thomas. The professor required a response.

"I stood up and gave the answer to his question," Bob remembered.

Pausing for a moment, Michael offered his assessment—which he voiced in a language Bob could understand from his other profession. "Misterrr Thommmas . . ." Michael drew out the name in his urbane murmur.

"Yes, Professor Michael?" Bob responded, eagerly awaiting the evaluation of his answer.

"Wiiide rrright."

In Michael's estimation, this attempt by Thomas did not split the up-rights. And while perhaps not the equivalent of missing a game-winning field goal, the moment lives on in humorous posterity among Bob's family, friends, and colleagues. "Even the president of the senate here in Illinois, John Cullerton—who does a great Professor Michael impression—will tell this story," Thomas admitted. "He's told it at judicial conferences and many other places."

Despite the one "shank," Thomas performed consistently well in his classes and cited his holdings correctly more often than not. Due to the diligence he displayed in his studies, Bob was selected to take part in an advanced trial practice course in the summer of 1978 at Loyola, an honor granted by invitation only. "Bob was a bright student," his old friend Doherty affirmed, who was in the process of finishing his own law training as well. "He would often argue his point of view when we lived together, so Casper was right—a lawyer was in the making from the start. We both had our reasons for going the law route, but he did it while managing a day job as an NFL kicker. All I can say is that my training at Notre Dame in spending at least fifty hours a week with football while attending a very competitive university made law school easier. I knew I could just outwork everyone else—which was required in my case."[5]

With the Bears training camp of 1978 ready to start in July, Armstrong had his coaching staff in place. Handpicked as his new defensive coordinator was James "Buddy" Ryan, who as the defensive line coach in Minnesota had, along with Armstrong, tried to corral Payton for the past couple of seasons. Irascible from the outset, Ryan displayed a lack of fondness for kickers—and his feelings surfaced in the very first defensive platoon meeting he led before workouts began. "Thomas was in the back of the room when Ryan was explaining secrets to blocking the kicks of 'those squirrely guys,'" Pierson recounted.

Bob was not fazed. "Thomas loved the attention. He made a friendly bet with Ryan that none of his kicks would be blocked in the first practice. Thomas won."[6]

In having coached Blair and the rest of the Vikings' kick-swatting machine, Armstrong made it a point to provide solid blocking for Thomas along the offensive line on the Bears' field goal unit. "I'm really excited about it," Bob told Pierson as he competed with rookie kickers Bruce Carlson and Tony DiRienzo trying to unseat him. "When have you seen coaches take that much pride in field goal protection this early in camp?"[7]

Armstrong was also searching for someone on the roster to assume the role of Blair on the Bears' field goal block team—and believed he had found him in the six-foot-three tight end Latta. "He's got good height and good timing and can jump," the coach pointed out. "He'll get first crack at it."[8] Armstrong soon unleashed Latta and the rest of the kick-blocking unit against Thomas in training camp, as the drill was done at full speed— something not seen under Pardee. "Neill told me that when I get through practicing," Bob said, "kicking in games will be easy because no one will come harder than we do in practice."[9]

As easygoing as Thomas was, the team noticed he would tense up a bit when it was time for the field goal team to take the practice field. "Bob had a quick quip—he would always zing somebody and had a great sense of humor," recalled John Skibinski, a rookie running back in camp in 1978. "But he was very serious when it came time for field goals in practice. So of course, that was our turn to mess with *him*. Gary Campbell, a linebacker, would sometimes drop his pants just as Bob was about to kick. Or sometimes, as the blockers, we would all turn around and rush him after the ball was snapped."[10] On other occasions, Payton would throw a football in trying to intercept Thomas's kicks as they left his foot.

By the time the preseason schedule started, Armstrong's attention to special teams was apparent from the very beginning.

In the opener against the Raiders on August 5 at Soldier Field, Art Best—Thomas's teammate on the 1973 Notre Dame national championship squad—blocked a punt against Oakland's Ray Guy as lineman Jerry Meyers, a Chicago native out of Northern Illinois University, scooped up the ball and ran it in for a touchdown. In his five years in the league to that time, the incomparable Guy (perhaps the greatest punter who ever lived) had only one other punt blocked—which occurred in the Super Bowl against Armstrong and the Vikings in January 1977.

Another young Bears team took the field in 1978, with seventeen of the twenty-two starters having been in the NFL for three years or fewer. Despite their inexperience, they sprinted out to a 3–0 record; but the hot start merely preluded another midseason swoon—a free fall virtually unparalleled in team history that included eight straight defeats. Ironically, for Thomas, the team's drought occurred during one of the greatest individual runs of his career.

By October 1 Bob had hit nine straight field goals to start the season, and ten dating back to the game-winning Giants' kick. The feat tied Percival's team record, with Thomas's eyes now set on the NFL mark of sixteen shared by Stenerud and Cockroft. A factor in Bob's hot streak had been the return of Baschnagel as the holder, who was happy to be back in action after missing out on the historic victory in New York and subsequent playoff appearance in Dallas. "This year, I can think of several times the snap from center came back on a bounce or came back high, but each time Brian made a great hold to keep my streak going," Bob told a writer during the 1978 season.[11] Armstrong, who had watched Paul Krause do the job for many years in Minnesota, concurred. "Brian Baschnagel is a magician," the coach stated. "I've seen a lot of good holders, but he's the best."[12] In one of his *Tribune* columns, Pierson even suggested that the rest of the Bears should take an example from how Thomas and Baschnagel coordinated their efforts on placement kicks. "If such teamwork was more widespread," he offered, "there wouldn't be a losing streak."[13]

After tying Percival's team record of ten in a row, Bob's run ended when he missed a forty-five-yarder into the wind at Green Bay. But he proceeded to hit another six field goals in a row, leaving him fifteen-for-sixteen by mid-November for a percentage of .938—well above the pace of the league record of .885 set by Lou Groza of Cleveland in 1953. "It really does mean something," he told the *Sun-Times* about shooting for the all-time mark. "It has stood such a long time, and when you think of placekicking, Lou Groza's the one you think of, the Hall of Famer. Even if it is a disappointing season, you have to have personal goals. I don't think that's a conflict of interest."[14] But on November 12, Thomas's second streak ended in an eerie repeat of history at Minnesota.

As Bob was attempting a game-tying field goal late in a rematch against the Vikings in Bloomington, Blair's virtual twin—fellow linebacker Fred McNeill—slipped through a missed assignment in offensive line and blocked it, sealing a 17–14 win at Metropolitan Stadium to post the Bears' eighth loss in a row. When asked afterward about his decisive play, McNeill said that he "got in so quickly on Thomas that he almost overran the ball."[15]

NFL statistics had Thomas at 17-for-22 in field goals when 1978 ended (a Bears record .773 percentage), but he was actually 18-for-23 that year—as a marriage proposal to Maggie was successful as well, corresponding with a more relaxed approach to his job. "Bob is concerned about a lot less now," Plank noticed during the season. "Getting engaged had to help. That's security. Whatever it is, he's had more self-confidence this year."[16] Thomas agreed: "Each year I get better physically and mentally, but the mental aspect is more important. A lot of guys can kick when there's no rush and no pressure, but the successful kickers are the ones who can handle the mental part."[17]

The happy day for Bob and Maggie arrived on June 23, 1979, as they were wed at Holy Name Cathedral near the Magnificent Mile in downtown Chicago. A reception followed at Sweetwater on Rush Street (of which Buffone was a part owner), which sits on the current location of Gibson's Steakhouse. "It was an unusually cool day for June," Bob remembered. "It was a short, chilly walk to Sweetwater. The food was great, but there was limited space with seating for only about ninety people. Maggie had a big family, and I had many family members and close friends there as well. So, along with Neill [Armstrong], there were only so many players who could be invited."

As the crowd swelled inside the restaurant, the couple became concerned about where to put them all. "Jim Finks originally indicated he couldn't make the wedding—but then he and his wife showed up. We got to the restaurant, and I had to tell Dennis Lick and his wife that they had to eat at the bar—because Mr. Finks and his wife were definitely going to get a seat!"

A honeymoon to Hawaii followed, with four days on Kauai and several more on Oahu. While in Honolulu, Bob made sure to keep his leg in shape with the start of training camp looming only a few weeks later. "I had called the University of Hawaii to make arrangements to kick while I was out there," he said of planning the itinerary. In making the university's football field one of their tourist destinations, the new Mrs. Thomas therefore had to assist with the workouts. "We didn't have those little gadgets to hold the ball back then, so Maggie had to hold for me. I always say that she was certainly my *best-looking* holder, but not my *best* holder—she kept wanting to pull her hand away too quickly, like Lucy in the Charlie Brown cartoons."

When the couple returned to the mainland in July, Bob found that much had changed at the Bears' facilities. Not only was the team getting ready to move into new office headquarters at Halas Hall in Lake Forest, but Soldier Field had been renovated as well—with new lights, new artificial turf, improved seating, and rebuilt dressing rooms for the 1979 season. "At least sewage was no longer flowing by our lockers," Thomas scoffed.

Halfway through the schedule, the Bears stood with a 3–5 mark—the same figure at which hopes for the 1977 been shelved two years earlier. With some deeming another season already over, the mettle of Armstrong and his plan was tested. Thomas and the rest of the team stood by the coach as he demonstrated a willingness to take players' input into account on a variety of issues—unusual for an NFL head coach in that era. "Doug Buffone always said that Neill really ran a democracy," Bob recalled the veteran linebacker saying, "and probably the best example of that is a story we all tell and laugh about a lot.

"The grass fields in Lake Forest were so bad by the middle of fall that we had to go down to Dyche Stadium at Northwestern and practice on the Astroturf. A lot of us, including myself, lived in downtown Chicago. Obviously, Evanston is closer to downtown than Lake Forest. We asked Neill if we could drive to Dyche Stadium and, after practice, just go home with our gear and come back the next day instead of going back to Lake Forest—and he said yes."

Unfamiliar with the area, however, was rookie wide receiver and Texas native Rickey Watts. Watts drove up and down the lakefront in Evanston looking for the Northwestern campus. "Somehow, he got lost—and he ends up coming to practice with only fifteen minutes left. So, the next day we're in the meeting room in Lake Forest. Neill got up in front of the team and, because of what happened with Watts, issued an order in his Oklahoman drawl: "'Gentlemen, today, we're all gettin' on the bus, going down to Dyche Stadium, practicin' at Dyche Stadium, gettin' back on the bus, and then comin' back to Lake Forest. You can shower here—then, you can get into your cars and go downtown. You understan' me? Everybody on the bus . . . Dyche Stadium . . . back on the bus . . . Lake Forest . . . and you leave from here. Ev'body understan'?'

"Gary Fencik was slouched in a chair in the back of the room. He raises his hand.

"'Neill says, 'Yeah, Gary?'

"Fencik says, 'Neill—that's *ridiculous*.'

"And Neill says, 'Good point—you can all drive.'"

To everyone's surprise in the room, the coach had changed his tune as the result of a single complaint. "But we all thought, 'Hey, there aren't many coaches like this, who will take the players' wishes into account,'" as Bob summarized the team's sentiment toward Armstrong. "We had to go to bat for him."

The mutual confidence ultimately paid off. And as in 1977, a single, miraculous comeback win propelled the Bears forward from their 3–5 record. Avellini was given one more chance and went five-of-thirteen with three interceptions in the loss at Minnesota in week eight (two weeks after Finks reportedly turned down a trade offer from the Raiders for Ken Stabler—"We told the Raiders that we weren't interested," the general manager explained; "we felt like our quarterback situation was okay"[18]). Then Phipps took over. The veteran pulled out a 28–27 squeaker over Walsh and the 49ers, positioning Chicago in a scenario that was now eerily similar to 1977 when the Bears beat the Chiefs by the same score at the same time in the season.

The victory set in motion a run of six wins in seven weeks, as by December 9 the Bears had improved all the way to 9–6. Thomas undid the Packers in Green Bay, as his three field goals secured a razor-thin 15–14 decision on the cold-crisped grass of Lambeau Field. But even if the Bears could defeat St. Louis in the regular season finale at Soldier Field on December 16, a 10–6 mark would not get them in the playoffs—unless either Tampa Bay lost or the Bears were able to beat the Cardinals by at least thirty-three points, with Pardee's Redskins also needing to lose in Dallas.

With the team preparing for the game that would decide its postseason fate, Bob was also scrambling to finish up his law classes at the end of the semester. "Loyola has been very good about it," he said of the school's continued accommodation of his day job while the Bears were prepping for the Cardinals. "I had one exam scheduled this Friday during the day. I had to have it rescheduled later in the day because of practice, and then they let me postpone it until after the game."[19]

In yet another ironic parallel to the 1977 finale in New York, the Bears would once again be forced to overcome inclement weather as well as the opponent. While not as treacherous as the famous day at the Meadowlands, the snow from a recent Chicago blizzard had been plowed to the edge of the Soldier Field stands, while temperatures hovered in the upper twenties by kickoff with wind chills nearing the single digits. As he did before every game, Bob conferred with Armstrong after pregame warmups on the maximum distance at which he felt confident attempting field goals from both ends of the field. Thomas knew that each kick would be critical. "Every point counted," Robin Earl remembered about the afternoon. "And Bob came through."[20]

Playing with an urgency that met the occasion, Bob and the rest of the Bears were on pace for the necessary tallies by halftime. Two touchdown runs by Payton and a scoring toss from Phipps to Dave Williams were all followed by Thomas conversions, sending the team into the tunnel with a 21–0 lead—but there was still work to be done.

Warming themselves for a few minutes in the locker room, the players were upset to learn that McKay's surprising and defense-oriented Buccaneers had beaten the Chiefs in Tampa by a 3–0 score on a fourth-quarter field goal, in a game that had started an hour earlier than the Bears-Cardinals contest in Chicago. With their only possible route to the playoffs now being a complete demolition of the Cardinals by thirty-three points or more, the pressure was ramped up on the Bears as they strapped their helmets back on.

"I didn't want them to know," Armstrong said of learning the Tampa score as his team exited the clubhouse. "I didn't want anything negative." But unbeknownst to the coach, the players were one step ahead of him. "There was a TV set in the back of the room," Fencik revealed. Armstrong ultimately saw the television before heading out the door. He realized there was only one thing left to do: "Word got out. So, yes, we did go out [in the second half] thinking we had to score points."[21]

The Cardinals struck first in the third quarter with a touchdown, but Steve Little—the first Cardinals kicker since 1962 not named Jim Bakken, who had retired after the previous season—missed the extra point to keep the score at 21–6. From that moment, the rookie Watts and the determined Payton put the game on their shoulders. Grabbing the ensuing kickoff from Little, the first-year receiver bolted eighty-three yards down the east sideline for a touchdown, and later hauled in a thirty-five-yard score from Phipps by spinning away from defenders and outrunning them down the west sideline. In doing so, Watts made all twenty-four of his 1979 catches in the final six weeks of the season and appeared to be an emerging star.

Payton added his third score of the day; Thomas remained perfect in nailing every extra point; and even Buffone, in his last appearance in Chicago, joined the fun in catching a twenty-two-yard pass from Parsons off a fake punt while also making a touchdown-saving tackle.

When the final gun went off, the Chicago Park District scoreboard at the south end of Soldier Field read 42–6—the necessary spread having been topped with three points to spare in a consummate team effort. But the excitement was tempered by what still needed to take place later that afternoon in Dallas, beginning with a 3:00 kickoff between the Cowboys and the Redskins.

Long after the media had asked all of their questions, Armstrong returned to his office and privately tuned into the Cowboys-Redskins game on a small transistor radio. Meanwhile, several of the players—including Thomas— gathered around Robin Earl's vehicle in the players' parking lot underneath Soldier Field, as Earl cranked up the broadcast on his car stereo to listen to the events from Texas. "Those were the days before regular updates on ESPN," Earl said, "and the only thing we could do was get the game on the radio. Our wives brought us some beers, and it was a lot of fun."[22]

They listened intently as the Cowboys, trailing 34–21 late in the fourth quarter, rode back in a stampede on the arm of Roger Staubach. He tossed two touchdown passes in the final two minutes to give Dallas a 35–34 win, leaving Pardee and the Redskins out of the playoffs and putting the Bears in. "When Dallas finally won, we sprayed beer all over the parking garage," Earl added with a laugh.[23]

Just as in 1977, everything had fallen into place as Thomas and the Bears traveled to Philadelphia for the postseason. But while holding their own on the road against an up-and-coming Eagles team, the Bears were beaten 27–17, bringing down the curtain on Buffone's long career. "We had a running joke about the injury chalkboard that stood outside the locker room," Thomas laughed in thinking respectfully of his teammate who had first come to the Bears in 1966. "Guys were listed as *'Questionable—Ankle,' 'Probable—Shoulder,'* and so forth. And with Buffone, someone would write, *'Doubtful—Old.'*"

Skibinski had his own pregame memories of the venerable linebacker. "You knew it was getting close to game time when Buffone started dry heaving in one of the bathroom stalls—just after he had smoked a bunch of cigarettes. Everyone would hear him because his gagging would echo throughout the entire locker room. When the coaches heard Doug doing that, they told us it was time to take the field—they didn't even need to look at the clock on the wall." The image still haunts Skibinski to this day—but with a hearty laugh. "As a kid, I remember idolizing Buffone and collecting bubble-gum pictures of him. Now, I was listening to him dry heaving in the toilet. That is how I knew I had made the big-time in the NFL."[24]

As for Thomas, one of the things he would miss the most about Buffone was his skill as the end man on the line of scrimmage for field goals and extra points. "That blocker usually has to handle two rushers—one on the inside and one on the outside," Bob pointed out. "No one did it better than Doug. He blocked down on the inside man, and then got just enough of a piece of the outside man to keep him off me—which is exactly how you're supposed to do it. I wanted Doug to teach the next guy to do it the same way."

Indeed, Buffone's lessons in leadership would reverberate on the team for years to come. "In the middle of the losing stretch in 1979," Bob continued, "Buffone was the one who stood up in the middle of a team meeting and said, 'We need to turn this thing around'—and we did." Now, it was up to Bob and the other remaining veterans to lead the Bears into the next decade.

Thomas entered 1980 as the Bears' career percentage leader in field goals, hitting 58 percent (72-for-124), having passed Percival's previous mark (54 percent) midway through the 1979 campaign. The team started 3–5 for the fourth straight year—but this time, there would be no magical run from that point to the playoffs. The record ended disappointingly at 7–9, while by season's end Thomas found himself third on the team's all-time scoring list with 422 points, behind Percival (456) and George Blanda (541). But instead of setting his sights on those figures, Bob in 1981 would face a series of unprecedented challenges in his personal and professional life that deeply tested his faith.

Chapter 6

CUT

If I would have seen anything clear-cut either way, it would have made
the decision a lot easier.

—MIKE DITKA ON CHOOSING HIS KICKER, SEPTEMBER, 1982

After a four-year journey with tiresome nights of classes while balancing
professional football and being a new husband, Bob got set to tackle his
final term at Loyola in the spring semester of 1981. His daily routine required driving to Lake Forest for meetings and practices from his home in
the western suburbs, into Chicago for law school in the evenings, and then
commuting back home. By May, he had plowed through the remainder of
his coursework. Only the bar exam—looming in late July—stood between
him and his goal of becoming a practicing attorney.

He took a break from his studies in early June and returned to Rochester
to continue a summer tradition with his father. For the past several years,
Augie had run a two-week kicking camp with which Bob assisted. It was
one of the few places where youngsters could learn the finer points of the
soccer style. In retrospect, Bob was indeed proud of the results his father had
attained at the camp—but was equally impressed with what an *innovator*
Augie was. "He had a history of being able to train people to kick in the NFL
when very few people knew anything about soccer-style kicking. These kids

he helped get Division One college scholarships were just coming out of a little kicking camp. It's not like the best high-school kickers from across the country were flying into Rochester—these were raw, local kids from a very small population of *potential* kickers."

After working with Augie while getting ready for the 1981 training camp with the Bears, Bob spent several quiet evenings in upstate New York in a final review of his textbooks and class notes. Excused from practice by Armstrong for two days, his bar exam was set for July 28 and 29 in downtown Chicago.

Upon getting into the city, Bob checked into a room at the Drake Hotel, situated near the testing location at the northern edge of Michigan Avenue along the lakefront. The first day of the exam consisted of essay questions on Illinois law, followed by the multistate exam the second day, composed of multiple-choice questions.

When Bob got seated on the first day, he took a moment to gaze around the large hall at the other candidates. Among them was George McCaskey, grandson of George Halas, who had just completed his undergraduate and legal studies at Arizona State University. But while George appeared to be confident, Bob noticed that most of the other examinees were so nervous they could hardly move. "I remember thinking, 'Wow, these people look pretty tense.'"

The proctor began the high-stakes event by taking attendance in alphabetical order, impersonally bellowing out the surnames with his eyes never rising from his clipboard. "When he got to 'Thomas,' there must have been three or four other Thomases taking the test," Bob remembered. "Finally, he gets to me." Figuring *somebody* had to break the ice and put an end to the stifling silence, Bob glanced at his namesakes scattered about the room. "Oh, mother would have been so proud!" he suddenly exclaimed. The stillness in the examination hall remained unbroken. "Not one of them even smiled," Bob recalled about the anxiety-filled atmosphere. "I know it wasn't the greatest joke in the world, but at least *one of them* could have *smiled*."

Bob approached the exam without trepidation—not because he was an NFL kicker and accustomed to pressure, but for the reason that he had relatively little time to prepare for the test *because he was an NFL kicker*. "There were study groups, and some of the other students were studying twelve hours a day. During two-a-days, I only had an hour here and there to study. I'd wake up early and read for a couple of hours. Then, we'd have our two practices, I'd go to dinner and meetings, and then I'd come back and study for as long as I could keep my eyes open. But even while studying when I could find the time, my mind was also somewhere else—because I was also trying to keep my job with the Bears."

Before his trip to Rochester, Bob had managed to fit in a bar review course to his schedule, offered by the Kent Law School in Chicago where Bob commuted each day on the train from his home in Lisle, just outside of Naperville. "They gave us a book," Bob said of the review. "I would read the materials for the day, and then highlight whatever they had talked about—because I knew I wasn't going to have enough time to read it all. They also had sample questions from past exams on which I also focused as I rode the train back and forth. Then, when training camp began, that's all I had time to look over—the portions I had highlighted and the sample questions."

Therefore, when the proctor directed the examinees to open their exam booklets and begin, Bob felt he had an advantage over his highly stressed peers. "I didn't feel a lot of pressure because I didn't have a lot of time to study. If I had the time, I'm sure I would have been spending all those hours like those study groups had done, and probably would have been worried that I missed something."

He did the best he could, and closed his test answer booklet. After returning it to the proctor, he got into his car and headed up to Lake Forest. The results would arrive in early October.

When Thomas returned to the Bears training camp on Thursday, July 30, he found that nothing had changed in his department. As usual, standing idle under the goalposts and watching the offense and defense practice were the other specialists, the same scene Bob saw when departing three days earlier. "Every year, every team brings in extra kickers," Pierson yawned about the foregone conclusion of Thomas and Parsons once again handling the Bears' special-teams chores. The reliable combination had now been together for six seasons, with Parsons' individual tenure on the team dating back to 1972. "Five or six years ago, the Bears did it to provide competition for Bob Thomas. Now, they do it to provide companionship. It gets lonely out there among the tees."[1]

For the summer of 1981, the rookie kicker brought in to provide Bob some company was Denmark native Hans Nielsen. Like Thomas, Nielsen was twenty-nine years old, but he was seeking his first roster spot on an NFL team. Having unsuccessfully competed in tryouts with Atlanta and Philadelphia over the past three years, Nielsen had last kicked in game competition as a twenty-five-year-old senior at Michigan State in 1977. "Bob Thomas is very good," Nielsen granted while watching the veteran wearing jersey number 16 resume rocketing balls through the uprights with authority. "Other teams need a kicker worse."[2]

Between his shifts working at a restaurant back in East Lansing, Nielsen had been practicing with a fellow Dane, Michigan State's current kicker Morten Andersen, when he caught the attention of a Bears scout who happened to be passing through town. "I think the scout saw Morten and not me," Nielsen suggested in self-deprecation.[3]

Offered a chance in the Bears' preseason opener against the Giants on August 8 at Soldier Field, Nielsen missed his only field goal attempt from forty yards away while Thomas converted an extra point in a 23–7 loss. When the team was shut out 13–0 in Kansas City the following week, Nielsen was sent packing after another miss. "The Danish placekicker was cut as expected Tuesday," Larry Casey reported in the *Tribune* on Thursday, August 20.

While Bob's job once again appeared to be safe, it did not stop his teammates from chiding him. "When incumbent Bob Thomas missed his first field goal in practice Wednesday," Casey continued, "his teammates chanted 'Hans . . . Hans . . . Hans!' Yelled Doug Plank, 'He's not out of the country yet!'"[4]

Having thus outlasted yet another challenger for the seventh straight year, Bob ignored the teasing and returned to the practice field on Friday as the team went through a very light "walk-through" workout, in advance of the third exhibition game against the Cincinnati Bengals on Saturday night at Soldier Field. Despite the game just over twenty-four hours away, the players were required to run vigorous wind sprints at the conclusion of the Friday workout.

While charging down the Lake Forest grass with his teammates, Bob suddenly pulled up lame. He hopped along for the last twenty yards to finish the dash, grasping the back of his kicking leg as he crossed the goal line. "I felt something pop." He had torn his hamstring. In looking back upon the moment, Thomas felt it was a situation that could have been easily avoided. "If I was the special teams' coach, I wouldn't have my kickers doing sprints."

The medical staff assisted him onto a cart and into the locker room. But while teammates stopped in to offer support and encouragement, Bob received what sounded like an ominous warning from another visitor—the general manager. "I'm in the training room getting treatment, and Jim Finks comes up to me and says, "One of the reasons you've been around here so long is that you never get hurt.'"

The next morning, Nielsen was awakened by a phone call from Finks at Nielsen's Arlington Heights apartment—informing him that not only was he was going to be re-signed to a new contract, but he was also going be the Bears' kicker that night against the Bengals.

Nielsen was not even supposed to have been in the Chicago area by the time Finks called. The kicker planned to immediately return to Michigan after being released but was stranded in the suburbs without transportation after another rookie free agent hopeful with the Bears, Joe Noonan, wrecked Hans's car. "He was in an accident with my Audi last weekend while I was with the team was in Kansas City," Nielsen explained. "Because my car is being fixed, I was still around to get the call."[5] To make room for Nielsen on the roster, the Bears released backup guard Paul Tabor, while another offensive lineman (who could also snap for field goals) had already made the team—Jay Hilgenberg from the University of Iowa, yet another undrafted rookie free agent.

Over the course of the ensuing several hours, Nielsen's life took a dramatic turn. After the Bears' 24–21 victory over the Bengals, he found himself receiving a game ball in the locker room from his once-again teammates for kicking the winning thirty-seven-yard field goal. He had made all three extra point attempts as well and had another forty-yard field goal wiped off the scoreboard as a Cincinnati penalty allowed a Bears drive to continue.

A friend of Nielsen's from East Lansing, meanwhile, had driven all the way to Chicago with plans to watch the game with him from the Soldier Field seats before towing Nielsen and his belongings back to Michigan. "He's probably out there waiting and upset that I wasn't in the stands with him," Nielsen told the writers after the game in peeking out toward the parking lot.[6]

Armstrong was impressed with the way the rookie had performed. "I wouldn't be too happy about putting him on the street again," the coach said. Then, in a lighthearted poke at the Bears' regular kicker, he added, "I wouldn't feel bad about Thomas taking his time to get well." Bob, however, took the challenge seriously. "I'll be ready to play by the next game," he told the *Tribune* stoutly.[7]

When the hamstring did not respond to treatments as he had hoped, however, Thomas and the medical staff decided it was prudent for him to sit out the Bears' final preseason game against the Cardinals on August 29 in St. Louis. The result was a 31–27 Chicago victory, in which Nielsen made a stronger case for a place somewhere in the league—or at least kept Armstrong in a holding pattern regarding a decision on when to bring the starter back. "Kicking in the place of injured Bob Thomas for the second week, Nielsen hit a 21-yard field goal, barely missed a 43-yarder, hit his kickoffs deep, was perfect on extra points, and generally managed to set up a difficult season for Thomas," Pierson concluded of the exhibition finale.[8]

But less than forty-eight hours later, Nielsen was cut yet again—as Armstrong and Finks held out hope that Bob's leg would heal in time for the regular season opener on September 6 against the Packers at Soldier Field. One the same day Nielsen was once again clearing out his things from the Lake Forest complex, Don Cockroft was released from the Browns after fourteen years in Cleveland while the San Diego Chargers decided at the last moment to keep Rolf Benirschke after a challenge from Mike Wood.

With the hamstring issue still lingering as the game-week preparations for the Packers proceeded, Armstrong worried further about developing a contingency plan in the event Thomas was unable to go. Payton, who had kicked in high school and for Jackson State (and for fun at practice), offered his services, but the coach refused. For the previous five seasons, defensive tackle Ron Rydalch had been an unofficial, yet never-needed, emergency kicker in the event Bob suffered an injury—but like Nielsen, Rydalch had also been released in the past week. The only remaining possibility appeared to be rookie defensive back Jeff Fisher, who informed Armstrong that he had had served as a backup kicker at USC—and that he liked to do so barefooted. But after one poor demonstration in practice in which Fisher (wearing only a sock on his kicking foot) shanked four consecutive field goal attempts, Armstrong sent him to the showers.

Despite the injury not having fully healed, Bob decided to kick in the opener against the Packers and missed an extra point in a 16–9 loss. When one of his field goal tries went wide in a 28–17 defeat in San Francisco in week two, the hamstring was aggravated once again; Kevin Lamb (now writing for the *Sun-Times*) noticed on the flight home that Bob's leg had swollen further since the team had boarded the plane.

On the team's arrival back in Chicago, Finks placed Thomas on injured reserve. According to league rules, Bob had to spend a minimum of four weeks on that list. "It's better for me and for the team that I don't kick," he told Pierson resignedly.[9]

On the following Wednesday, September 16, the phone rang at Nielsen's apartment in Arlington Heights once again. Nielsen had decided to stay permanently in the Chicago area after all. He was attempting to get a sales job with a copier company while continuing to work out on the football field of John Hersey High School in the hopes of catching on with another NFL team—but he was also kicking for the simple enjoyment of it. "Even if someone told me a definite 'no' in the league, I'd still kick," Nielsen said of the pleasure he derived from the activity. "People think that's strange, but a lot of people go out and play golf. I think that's strange."[10]

Assuring Finks he had kept his leg in shape, Nielsen was ordered to the Bears' offices for a third time and re-issued a uniform as Bob watched him practice from the sidelines. "Neill told me, 'You're the new kicking coach,'" Thomas said with a nervous chuckle. "I'll be glad to lend any suggestions."[11]

By Saturday, Nielsen found himself sitting in a room at the North Shore Hilton with the rest of the team, nervously attempting to pass the time in anticipation of his NFL debut the following afternoon against Tampa Bay at Soldier Field. Flipping through the channels on the television, he came across the Michigan State–Ohio State game from Columbus. He watched as his countryman Andersen took advantage of a fifteen-mile-per-hour wind at his back and unloaded a Big Ten record sixty-three-yard field goal, a cannon shot that cleared the crossbar in Ohio Stadium by ten feet in the Spartans' 27–13 loss to the Buckeyes.

The following day, as Nielsen joined the Bears in pregame warm-ups, he gazed toward the other end of Soldier Field and took notice of Garo Yepremian, one of Bob's soccer-style mentors from the late 1960s. In vying for the Bucs' placekicking position, the thirty-seven-year-old Yepremian had recently fought off a challenge from a rookie free agent, John Roveto.

Benefiting from the Bears' forcing three Tampa turnovers and an eighty-eight-yard punt return by Fisher, Nielsen made all four of his extra point attempts (while missing a field goal) in a 28–17 win. In missing a field goal himself, it would be Yepremian's last NFL game as he was replaced the following week by rookie Bill Capece. "They need a new transmission," Yepremian said derisively of McKay's decision to get rid of him. "So they changed a tire."[12]

As Yepremian closed out his career in being released by the Bucs the following day on Monday, September 21, Nielsen joined Thomas at the team meetings in Lake Forest to review the game film. When Bob returned back home to Lisle afterwards, he and Maggie received a phone call that evening that would change their lives forever.

Since their marriage, the couple had yearned to add to their family and have children. Upon prayer and reflection, they ultimately decided to consider adoption. Sometime earlier, Bob happened to run into a fellow law school student from Loyola who was also an obstetric-gynecological doctor at a large clinic in the Chicago area. "He asked if we were interested in adopting," Bob said.

Joining their family on Thursday of that week was son Brendan, who went home with Bob and Maggie four days after he was born on September 21—as the happy husband and wife went on the scramble for baby items that accompanies a sudden adoption. "With a pregnancy, it's nine months—and with Brendan it was four days," Bob laughed in remembering the instant need for supplies. "So, we were scurrying around to get him a crib and all that."

With Bob's leg still recuperating as he simultaneously adjusted to fatherhood, Armstrong refrained from using Nielsen on field goals the following week in a 24–7 loss to the Rams, passing on a pair of attempts from forty-nine and forty-eight yards early in the game (the latter with the wind at the team's back) while the score was still close. "I didn't feel confident we could make it," Armstrong grunted afterward.[13] Instead, Nielsen hoped for a chance the following week in the Bears' perennial house of horrors—Metropolitan Stadium in Bloomington, where the team had not beaten the Minnesota Vikings since 1971.

Battling to within three points at 24–21 near the end of regulation, the Chicago offense put together one last thrust in moving the ball to the Vikings' nine-yard line with one second remaining. As the rookie snapper Hilgenberg took his place, the ball sat squarely in the middle of the field with the goalposts staring back at the rookie kicker. "It was a very simple task, nothing to be confused about," Nielsen said after the game about the chip shot that would send the game into overtime.[14]

But after Baschnagel set his hold and the kicker went into his steps, Nielsen hooked it wildly. The ball skidded along the grass far to the left of the posts, more akin to a double-play grounder on the Minnesota Twins' baseball infield than a field goal try. The shank preserved the Vikings' win, and stuffed the Bears deeper in the standings with a 1–4 record. "An Annual Event: The Bears Swoon in Vikingland," was the headline in the *Tribune* sports section the following day.

As Nielsen was showering in the visitors' dressing room, the reporters had already clustered around his locker in preparation for an inquisition. When he emerged from his bathing wrapped in a towel, the kicker saw the assembly. Discouraged, he stopped after a few steps, wondering what he would say as he made his way back toward his clothes.

Suddenly, the star of the team stood up and stopped Nielsen before he got there, offering a measure of comfort and sensitivity which had become one of his personal trademarks. "Payton gripped him by the shoulder," wrote Steve Daley in the *Tribune*, "and, for no more than a moment or two, made Hans Nielsen listen . . . he managed to invest Nielsen with enough dignity and pride to get him through the moment. In the ensuing hail of questions, someone wanted to know if the kicker's teammates had been supportive. 'They are the best,' Nielsen offered in forcing a smile."[15] The kicker had few other words for the assembled throng: "This was my great opportunity. I guess I didn't come through."[16] It would be his last official act with the team.

On Tuesday, October 6—the same day Bob received word that he had passed the bar exam on his first attempt—Nielsen was released from the Bears for the third time in just under two months. "It's sad," he said in a tone that, despite the important miss in Minnesota, was less understanding than the first couple of times he was let go. "I'm surprised because there is only one game left until Thomas can come back. I'm disappointed obviously because they think I'm so bad I can't be used at least one more game."[17]

Meanwhile, flying into Chicago from Atlanta that same morning—where he had been working at his family's tire store—was John Roveto. While the Bears were battling the Vikings in Minnesota on Sunday, Roveto had been busy with customers and was thus unable to catch any of the NFL scores from the afternoon. Later in the day, his brother popped into the store for a visit. "He told me the Bears missed a field goal with one second left," Roveto said. "I didn't think nothing of it."[18]

Unable to reach Roveto directly on Monday morning, Finks got in touch with his parents—who located him at ten o'clock that night and told their son he had to be in Lake Forest the following afternoon for a tryout with the Bears. Prior to losing out to Yepremian in Tampa, Roveto had also failed to unseat the Cowboys' Rafael Septien a year earlier, whom Roveto had ironically followed as the kicker at the University of Louisiana–Lafayette in 1977.

Impressing the coaches with deep kickoffs at the tryout, Roveto was signed as the Chicago Bears' kicker after about twenty swings of his leg. "His job with the Bears may last only one week," Pierson wrote, "until regular kicker Bob Thomas is able to return."[19] That date, circled on the Thomas calendar at home, was October 19—the end of Bob's requisite four-week period on the injured reserve list, with the Bears scheduled to play the Lions in Detroit on *Monday Night Football* that evening. Thomas insisted that all signs were positive in the leg's continued recovery. "I've been working with weights with no pain," he told the media in one room at Halas Hall just as Roveto was arriving at another part of the facility. "Their feeling [the team physicians] is the hamstring has healed. It's just a question of getting strength back. I should be kicking by the end of this week or Monday [October 12]." He added his sympathies for Nielsen after learning of his release. "I felt bad for Hans in Minnesota. I got to know him, and I liked him."[20]

After signing his contract, Roveto was given a room at the Ramada Inn in Highwood and made no permanent plans to remain in the Chicago area. "They were straight with me," he said of his negotiations with the Bears. "They don't want me to think I'm just going to kick for one week, but at the same time, they don't want me to think it will last the whole season. That's just the way it is."[21]

After striking the opening kickoff, Roveto mostly sat on the sidelines in watching the Bears fall behind 24–0 to the Redskins at Soldier Field the following Sunday. He booted his first NFL point after a late touchdown, which did nothing to alter the outcome as the Bears fell to a 1–5 mark in a 24–7 loss (as the team continued to struggle, Bears officials installed an awning over the north tunnel at Soldier Field, protecting Armstrong and the players from beer cups and other projectiles fired their way from angry fans as the team went to and from the locker room). Thomas watched the game anxiously, eager to return to full throttle in practice and reclaim his position.

Looking to salvage the season, Armstrong and his staff had an extra day's preparation the following week in advance of the Monday night game in Detroit. With the practice schedule thus being moved back a day, the team had an unusual full Friday workout in pads on October 16. At the end of the afternoon, Armstrong summoned Thomas and Roveto to go head-to-head in a field goal competition—much to the delight of the other players.

As the two kickers got ready, Mike Phipps jogged down to the end of the field and stood under the goalposts. Trying to entertain the others as the competition commenced, the quarterback emphatically raised or crossed his arms after each kick to announce the result.

By the time the duel was finished, the official summary had the rookie coming out on top. "It was reported that Roveto converted nine straight attempts from 28 to 43 yards while Thomas was 4-for-8," wrote Howard Balzer in *The Sporting News*. But as a result of Phipps trying to have some fun with his friend Thomas, the tally was inaccurate. A writer for the *Sun-Times*, Brian Hewitt, had been relying on Phipps for the count instead of watching the football—and unfortunately for Thomas, Phipps was messing with Bob in waving off his successful kicks while sarcastically signaling "good" for several that Roveto actually had missed. "After that report was printed in a Chicago paper, Thomas noted that he was 6-for-8 and that Roveto had missed more in the drill," wrote Balzer, revising the story.[22] With his livelihood at stake, the misinformation prompted Bob to contact Hewitt. "Brian, I don't typically do this—but didn't you see what happened?'" Hewitt retracted his claim and amended the results—albeit in the typical, inconspicuous "Corrections" portion of the paper in a subsequent issue.

When the time came for Armstrong and Finks to decide, Roveto remained in place for the Monday night game against the Lions game despite Bob being eligible and healthy.

In front of a national television audience, second-year Lions quarterback Eric Hipple threw for 336 yards and four touchdowns in his first NFL start as Detroit annihilated the Bears 48–17, dropping Chicago to 1–6.

Another sure defeat for the struggling team was in order the following week as the high-powered and Super Bowl–contending Chargers arrived at Soldier Field. Once again, Roveto was announced as the kicker as Thomas—his leg now 100 percent—was left in the dark as to the reasoning.

The Chicago team held tough, heading into overtime tied at 17–17. They had squandered opportunities to put San Diego away in regulation, due in part to Roveto missing two field goals (including an eighteen-yarder). But when Roveto was able to hit from twenty-six yards away to give the Bears an improbable 20–17 win, the scribes were suddenly prompted to ask Armstrong whether there was an impending kicker controversy. The coach seemed unwilling to confront the issue. "Why do I have to answer the question?" he responded curtly.[23]

The writers—and Bob himself—were left with little understanding about where Thomas stood. The only plausible explanation was that the team was permitted to make only a limited number of transactions from the injured reserve list over the course of the season, as running back Dave Williams and linebacker Jerry Muckensturm were among several others recuperating. "Thomas, whose leg is healthy enough to play again, appears to be in limbo as long as Roveto doesn't dip into the Hans Nielsen playbook and miss a costly field goal," penned Mike Kiley in the *Tribune* on the Tuesday following the win over the Chargers. "The Bears can bring three players off injured reserve and, if Roveto is doing well, they don't want to use up a move on Thomas."[24]

Thus, Bob remained idle as the controversy heated up two weeks later. Roveto made three field goals—including another game-winner in overtime—to beat Kansas City on the road, 16–13. But on Thanksgiving Day, Roveto's missed extra point and two missed field goals denied the Bears a chance to beat the Cowboys in Dallas, with the team falling 10–9. For the remainder of the season, Roveto was successful on only one of his last four field goal tries—with Thomas still watching from afar and with further frustration settling in as Armstrong continued to assert there were no plans to bring Bob off the injured reserve list. His patience at an end, Bob felt he deserved a straight answer from the head coach.

"I had a pretty close relationship with Neill," he remembered. "I went up to him said, 'Neill, I'm healthy—and I've been healthy for several weeks.' He basically told me, 'You're on injured reserve; you're getting paid, and as long as I don't cut John, *he's* getting paid.'"

"I said, 'Neill—you're going to keep a guy on the roster who's missing kicks for you because you want to keep giving him a salary?' I was just mystified. I could understand if a guy was doing gangbusters, and you were injured—of course he wouldn't get pulled in that situation. But this wasn't the case."

Even so, it was clear to Thomas that God had placed the right people in Bob's life at the right time, which included Roveto and Armstrong. Being able to come home to Maggie—and now Brendan—not only gave him perspective, but it also galvanized his faith. "You realize that there is something greater in your life than football," he said in recollection of those trying moments of fall 1981, when he feared losing his grip on one career while also trying to start another in law. "It made it easier. While it was frustrating not to play, I still had the beauty of family and a child."

When the Bears' dismal 1981 season finally ended with a 6–10 record and Christmas approached, Armstrong took Bob aside and assured him that everything would be all right: "Neill told me, 'You know you're my kicker next year.'"

Unfortunately, there was no next season for Armstrong. As had been the case four years earlier, the team chose the holiday season to inform the press of a change in leadership on January 4, 1982. "Neill Armstrong, a nice guy who finished last, was fired as head coach of the Bears by owner George Halas," reported Pierson.[25] It was also revealed that Halas planned another press conference at the end of the week—causing some to wonder whether Finks was on the chopping block as well, as the general manager had publicly displayed his anger at not being consulted by the owner on the selection of the next head coach.

Candidates for the position were viewed coming and going from the Bears' offices. John Robinson, who had followed McKay as the USC head coach, rescheduled a meeting with the New England Patriots for their head coaching position so that he could interview in Lake Forest, while Hugh Campbell, who had won five straight Grey Cups in the Canadian Football League with the Edmonton Eskimos, had been seen on the premises as well.

But on January 20, Halas decided on his rugged tight end from the 1960s to bring his team back to prominence. Despite Mike Ditka's strong historical ties to the Bears (and the fact that he reportedly had expressed an interest in the job to Halas several years earlier), the choice was a surprise to most observers. While Ditka had been an assistant for Tom Landry in Dallas for the past nine seasons since retiring as a player from the Cowboys in 1972, Ditka's responsibilities had been limited to overseeing Landry's special teams, and he had never been an offensive or defensive coordinator.

Nonetheless, Halas was convinced it was the right move. And once the Cowboys were eliminated in the NFC Championship Game against the 49ers on January 10, he got on the phone with Ditka, and an agreement was quickly reached.

For Ditka to get the job, however, the owner had attached some strings, as Thomas remembered: "Before the season ended in 1981, the entire Bears' defense sent a letter to Halas—saying that if Armstrong was fired, they wanted Buddy Ryan retained as defensive coordinator." The idea had reportedly come from the rookie linebacker Mike Singletary. "Alan Page wrote the letter," Jim Osborne recalled. "We knew if they let Buddy go the defense would be set back another three or four years. We all signed the letter and sent it off, hoping for the best." While Page was willing to do it, he knew it could be risky. "When you write something like that, you never know how it will be perceived. We could have been looking for work."[26]

Halas granted the request and instructed Ditka to keep Ryan on staff. Inherent difficulties immediately arose as Ryan openly wanted—and felt he deserved—the head job himself. "I remember Buddy making the statement that 'No one has done more for Neill Armstrong than Buddy Ryan,'" Bob continued. "I'm fairly confident that Buddy knew about the letter. As an older guy on the team, I was pretty vocal in saying that the letter was wrong—that you don't do that to a guy *before* he gets fired."

Shortly thereafter, Thomas got the feeling that Roveto was favored over him within certain facets of the organization: "My relationship with Buddy completely changed from that point on." With a new head coach in place, an open battle for the Bears' kicking job was thus on the horizon for training camp 1982. And while preparing for a fight to keep his job in one profession, Bob was also looking to establish himself in another. While picking up a few things at a grocery store near his home, a man approached him in the cereal aisle.

"Aren't you Bob Thomas of the Bears?" asked the man, as people often did in seeing Bob around town. The man was Ted Kuzniar, a partner in the law firm of Bochte and Kuzniar in Elburn, Illinois, a small community in a rural area to the northwest of Naperville. "Kuzniar is quite a sports enthusiast, so we began talking about football," Bob said in a 1982 interview with the *Aurora Beacon-News*. "I signed an autograph for his son and mailed him an autographed picture. Later, I received a letter back thanking me and saying he appreciated the fact I was down to earth with him."[27] Kuzniar also mentioned in the letter that he was aware Bob was in law school—and to let him know if he had any questions about the profession.

With Bob looking for work as a lawyer in the off-season from football, he had garnered interest from a few firms in Chicago. Yet, in conversations with Maggie, he did not feel fully comfortable with any of them. "Probably because I played professional football, an entertainment firm contacted me when I got out of law school, likely because they thought I'd have an 'in' for bringing in some athlete clients. But that was really something that never interested me." With his extensive experience in public speaking, Bob instead sought a position where he could immediately jump into the courtroom. "I figured litigation would be an area of strength for me."

One day in early January 1982, while cleaning out a desk drawer at home, he came upon Kuzniar's letter once again. "I decided to call him." A couple of days later, he met Kuzniar and Bill Bochte for dinner. The trio hit it off. The partners offered Bob a position at the firm, and he walked into his first day at work on Tuesday, January 26. "I feel I am being accepted here as a full-time lawyer rather than a football player who practices law in the off-season," he said once he was settled in. "Ted and Bill are offering the type of law I want to practice. I'll have a chance here to do different types of cases much quicker than I would with a larger firm. I think I'll have a varied exposure to law here."[28]

Commuting westward from Lisle to Elburn and other parts of Kane County, Bob ultimately found his way to the Kane County Courthouse and began making his arguments. Steep challenges quickly arrived at his desk, as the firm performed a lot of divorce services. One of the first cases to which Bob was assigned involved a client's volatile husband. "I knew divorce wasn't the kind of work I wanted to do long term, but the position was getting me some litigation experience."

With three attorneys in a small, busy office, the firm was a constant beehive of activity. Often, its occupants did not even a break for a meal. "Soon after I started, I noticed there was always a pot of coffee going in the office—but also that Ted and Bill never broke for lunch," Bob recalled. "So, as the new guy, I didn't dare take a lunch break either. It reminded me of football players back in those days who avoided drinking water at a hot practice—it was a badge of honor not to need it. So, in a similar way, we followed the proud thinking of 'You don't need to eat!'" The pace, however, eventually caught up to him. "One day, while driving back home, my hands started shaking and I almost went off the road. I realized I had eaten no food, but probably drank twelve cups of coffee—and not the decaffeinated kind. At that point I said to Ted and Bill, 'I don't care what you guys say—there's a hot dog stand down the block, and I'm taking five minutes to go get something at lunch!'"

Thomas took the heavy workload in stride, and soon discovered that a law office did not present anything much more difficult than his typical months away from the Bears. "There was always something different for me to do in the off-season anyway. I had been going to law school full-time in the spring and summer, and now that simply turned into *practicing* law full-time in the off-season—which was more enjoyable than just *studying* it."

Shortly after his arrival, the firm moved eastward to the larger community of St. Charles, placing Bob slightly closer to his home in Lisle. Before long, he demonstrated enough capability to earn a seat at the second chair for some of the firm's trials, after which the partners placed his name on the company letterhead alongside their own.

One football responsibility for which Thomas needed to make time during the off-season of 1982 was "mini-camp"—a three-day period in the spring when teams evaluate newly signed rookies and free agents while veterans have a chance to work off some rust. Because Ditka was a new head coach, the NFL granted him an extra mini-camp in 1982 to take place in Arizona in April in addition to the traditional one at the end of May in Lake Forest. "It was really successful," Thomas said at the conclusion of the Arizona experience, where he got to know the new leader for the first time. "He [Ditka] stressed loyalty, discipline, and conditioning, and the team generally came away with the feeling that we got something accomplished and that he feels we have a chance to win the Central Division."

Reflecting upon his first interactions with Ditka, Thomas in 2017 spoke of the "reversal of atmosphere" the team encountered with the brash new coach on the scene. "Guys [on the Bears] who knew players in Dallas were shocked because he was a special-teams coach. They were letting us know how fiery this guy was. He came in, and he was totally different from Armstrong in terms of personality. He established himself as a disciplinarian from the get-go, and that he wasn't going to take anything."

Looking to get a jump on things—and especially on Roveto—Bob had arrived in Arizona a week early "because the weather was so bad around here," he said of the surprise snowstorm that hit Chicago in early April. Thomas also put to rest any concerns about his hamstring injury. "The leg feels fine. It felt smooth and I was hitting the ball well."[29]

Through the rest of the spring, Bob continued to confront his battles in the courtroom—and then returned to Lake Forest in July to find himself in a battle on the field as well. "I'm not going to worry about how John does," Thomas said of Roveto. "I have no control over that. But I do have control over what I do, and that's why I'm going to try to get the best out of my ability." Bob added that the injury may have actually been a blessing in disguise, as it had him arriving to two-a-days with a new hunger. "I think I'll be bringing some rookie enthusiasm to camp. When you sit on the sideline, you realize how much you like to compete."[30]

The new boss was noncommittal in his opening statement about the kickers. "I saw Roveto at Dallas," Ditka said of watching him trying to take Septien's job in 1980, while also coaching against Armstrong's Bears in the 1981 Thanksgiving Day game in which Roveto's missed kicks were the difference in the Bears' one-point loss. "He has to work on his form to get more consistent.

That would improve his accuracy quite a bit. We felt very confident about him in Dallas. Thomas didn't have the distance on kickoffs and longer field goals, but he was very accurate. We hope his injury has healed and he can compete."[31]

Thomas signed his 1982 contract on July 16, with his thirtieth birthday looming in a few weeks on August 7. "Sitting out last year made me realize how much I love the game," he told the media as the team assembled on the practice field for the first time. "Playing football comes before law, because law will be there when my football career ends."[32]

After going toe-to-toe in the July heat, Thomas and Roveto took their showcase to the exhibition schedule with the new staff looking on. The new offense struggled in the Ditka's debut in the preseason opener at San Diego on August 16, with the team falling behind early 28–7 and its only score being an eighty-four-yard punt return by rookie Dennis Gentry after Thomas missed a thirty-three-yard field goal. But in the second half, rookie first-round draft choice Jim McMahon entered the game at quarterback and ignited the attack, bringing the team within a point at 28–27, which proved to be the final score.

The jury was still out on the kicking decision by the preseason finale on September 4 against the Colts in Chicago. Bob kicked the lone Bears' field goal in the game, a thirty-three-yarder, as part of a 26–17 loss (with both kickers successful on an extra point tries). With the exhibition schedule completed, the statistics showed Thomas two-of-three on field goals while Roveto had missed both of his attempts.

Yet, with Thomas standing a mere fifteen field goals shy of the Bears' career record, he was dismissed when the final cuts were announced on Monday, September 6, as Roveto was the one retained.

Everyone was stunned. "This move even surprised Finks," a baffled Pierson wrote, "the man who hired Thomas but had no say in his departure."[33] Ditka said the move to keep Roveto was a "staff decision" that he "almost overruled before deferring to the recommendation of special teams coach Steve Kazor and other assistants," Pierson continued. "Kazor put more emphasis on kickoff distance than Ditka did. Leg strength and potential obviously played a bigger role than past performance."[34] In reflecting on that difficult moment years later, Bob believed the presence of a new coaching staff may have played a role in the choice. "My guess is perhaps that Kazor, as a young special-teams coach, was more comfortable with a younger kicker— and I think Ditka just went with it."

For the first time in seven years, the most accurate kicker in Bears' history was jobless in the NFL; and when questioned by Pierson and other newspaper writers, Thomas pulled no punches in his dissent from the verdict. "I have no idea what criteria he used," he said of Ditka's move. "It was tough for him to tell me. He said he thought I was a good kicker under pressure. After talking to him, I had less indication about 'why' than I had before. I've got to be the winner on past performance and in the preseason. John's a good kicker who can play in the league. But I have no doubt I'm a better kicker. It's tough for me to swallow the decision."[35]

When Kazor was questioned by the media about the role he played in the choice, he gave a less-than-rousing endorsement of the new man. "Roveto has a chance to get a little better. He has improved a bit from last year."[36] Not satisfied with the answer, Lamb pressed Kazor for more information. "Roveto has a little more strength in his leg at this time," was all the assistant coach added as he turned and walked away.[37]

Even Ditka himself acted as if the choice was somewhat arbitrary. "If I would have seen anything clear-cut either way, it would have made the decision a lot easier."[38] At the start of the competition, Ditka claimed that accuracy would be the most important factor in determining the position, with Kazor concurring that "we'd like to have 70 percent on field goals."[39] But with that logic, the raw data left the cerebral Thomas even more perplexed. "John was 10-for-18 last year. I've been over 70 percent twice in my career."[40]

As Thomas piled his belongings into a plastic bag and exited Halas Hall, he struggled to hold his head high in passing by his friends. In one stroke of the pen, they had become his *ex*-teammates; yet, his unshakable faith permitted him to see the larger picture. He gave a final statement to Pierson while waving goodbye from his car in the players' parking lot. "Your true salt comes out when you are put to the test," Bob said while flinging the plastic bag into the back seat. "I thank God for healing me and allowing me to kick again. I would hope I can kick somewhere this season. My wife and I have talked a lot, and we are believers in the power of prayer. This is such a bizarre ending that maybe God is leading me somewhere else, and I might be better off."[41]

Doug Plank was certain his old roommate would land on his feet. "Bob was a survivor. We all had no doubt he would take his skills to other teams and be successful."[42] Plank and Thomas would indeed meet up on the field again—in the most unusual of circumstances.

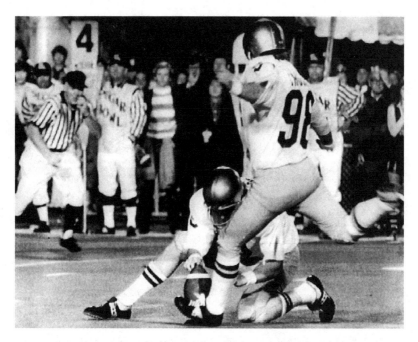

Figure 1. With just over four minutes remaining in the 1973 Sugar Bowl, Bob Thomas connects on a field goal from Brian Doherty's hold to give Notre Dame a 24–23 victory over Alabama and the national championship. Source unknown.

Figure 2. Thomas is mobbed by his Chicago Bears teammates after his field goal in overtime beats the New York Giants on December 18, 1977, sending the Bears to the playoffs for the first time in fourteen years. Courtesy Don Bierman, *Chicago Daily News*.

Figure 3. As Thomas looks on with a smile, Walter Payton plants a kiss on the cheek of Bob's wife, Maggie. Courtesy of the Thomas family.

Figure 4. In the strike-riddled NFL season of 1982, veterans Thomas (right) and punter John James arrived in Detroit to stabilize the Lions' kicking game. Courtesy of the Thomas family.

Figure 5. Thomas notching his 542nd point for the Bears on September 9, 1984, making him the franchise's all-time leading scorer. Courtesy of the Thomas family.

Figure 6. Thomas notching his 542nd point for the Bears on September 9, 1984, making him the franchise's all-time leading scorer. Courtesy of the Thomas family.

Figure 7. Thomas notching his 542nd point for the Bears on September 9, 1984, making him the franchise's all-time leading scorer. Courtesy of the Thomas family.

Figure 8. Thomas returns Maggie's kiss as Payton breaks the all-time rushing record at Soldier Field on October 7, 1984. Source unknown.

Figure 9. Thomas speaks to his players as the head soccer coach at Wheaton Academy, Wheaton, Illinois, in 1995. Courtesy of the Thomas family.

Figure 10. Thomas as the circuit judge of DuPage County, 1988.
Courtesy of the 18th Judicial Circuit Court of Illinois / Mike Lake.

Figure 11. Bob and Maggie. Courtesy of the Thomas family.

Figure 12. Maggie and Bob with his parents, Augie and Anne Thomas, at a campaign stop during Bob's run for the Illinois Supreme Court in 2000. Courtesy of the Thomas family.

Figure 13. Thomas at the microphone with Notre Dame teammates
(including Brian Doherty to his immediate right) for Coach Ara Parseghian's
ninetieth birthday party in 2013. Courtesy of the Thomas family.

Figure 14. Thomas (center) as chief justice of the Illinois Supreme Court, 2005. Through his
years as a judge, he has remained true to a humane application of the law. "There are faces
behind the cases," he once said, "and these cases mean everything to those people." Courtesy of
the Illinois Supreme Court / Greg Daniels.

Figure 15. The Thomas family in July 2019. Top row, left to right, Brendan (holding Lilly), Jonathan, Ashley (holding Sophie), Jason (holding Tyler). Front row, Gus, Gretchen (holding Gretchen, Jr.), Bethenny, Bob, Maggie (holding Molly), Jessica (holding Isaac). Courtesy Maas Photography.

Chapter 7

RESILIENCE

Tomorrow isn't promised to anybody.

—JOE EHRMANN, SPEAKING TO A DETROIT LIONS TEAM BIBLE STUDY, 1982

When Bob learned he had been released, his first order of business was to visit the general manager. "I went in to see Jim Finks, the man responsible for me coming to the Bears. He showed me a list of the final roster given to him by Ditka, and Roveto's name was on it." As Finks handed the list to Thomas, the general manager's face suggested the coaching staff's decision was not one with which Finks agreed—or on which he was even *consulted*.

"And I'll never forget this," Thomas continued. "Bill Tobin was the personnel director. He comes walking in as I'm talking to Finks. He says to Finks while I'm sitting there, 'We just got a call from the Lions, and they want Bob's phone number. What do we do?'

"What do we do?!" Finks replied incredulously, not believing the events that continued to transpire before his eyes. "We give them the number!"

Finks then halted Tobin as the latter was exiting through the through the doorway—and took a moment to fire a sarcastic salvo. "Bill, this is a human-interest story!" he said in derision of the roster move, tossing Ditka's list aside.

The Detroit Lions, on the verge of building a contender in the NFC Central, had been forced to deal with a disastrous 1982 preseason at the negotiating table. Their star running back Billy Sims sat out the entire exhibition schedule in a salary dispute with the club. But the day after Thomas was cut from the Bears, things got worse. The Lions' All-Pro kicker and punter tandem, Eddie Murray and Tom Skladany, were advised by their agent Howard Slusher to walk away from the team on Tuesday, September 7. Skladany led the NFC in punting in 1981 with a 43.5-yard average, while Murray tied Septien for the NFL lead with 121 points after leading the NFC as a rookie in 1980 with 116. "Both of us were coming up on the option year of our contracts," Murray remembered. "I had signed a two-year deal and the option. Seeing how I had performed in the two years, I told the Lions I wanted to renegotiate my contract instead of taking the 10 percent increase with the option. They said no, and they said no to Tom. So, we walked away."[1]

On Wednesday, the call came to Thomas from the Lions, as the Lord had opened another door. That night, Bob made his way to O'Hare to fly to Detroit, while former star Atlanta Falcons punter John James, recently released from that team, was also heading to the Motor City. After the pair booted some trial kicks inside the Lions' home stadium of the Pontiac Silverdome on Thursday, Detroit coach Monte Clark expressed his appreciation that the two veterans were available, especially on short notice. "Thomas looks good," Clark asserted. "We're going to check his medical records and take another look at him tomorrow."[2]

On Friday, Thomas and James were signed to the Lions' roster for their 1982 season opener, taking place forty-eight hours later in Pontiac on Sunday, September 12.

Against the Chicago Bears.

"I hope Bob doesn't kick the winning field goal against us," worried his former holder Baschnagel, who hinted the Bears would have to change the signals for audibles given by their quarterbacks during the game. "We joked about it in the locker room, but we were half-serious. I don't know how much knowledge Bob has stored up, but knowing him, it's quite a bit."[3]

With the game approaching, the editors at the *Tribune* appeared to concur with the sentiment of many around Chicago. As the sports department began its previews of the game in its Friday edition, *"Chance for Revenge"*—with a direct reference to Thomas—was one of the headlines. For his part, Bob tried to remain calm all week. "I can't get real emotional Sunday. It's not like I can go out and run head-on into Doug Plank. I have to keep my cool. Emotions can hurt you."[4]

Football fans in Michigan, meanwhile, could not believe their good fortune with the arrival of the two experienced specialists. "What generous guys those Bears are," mocked Mike Downey in the *Detroit Free Press*. "First, they decide to give a job to John Roveto, a kicker who distinguished himself this preseason by making zero field goals. To make room for the great Roveto, they decide to cut Thomas, who was 2-for-3 during exhibition games and happens to be the Bears' leading kicker of all time. Furthermore, they feel so indebted to Thomas for his loyal years of service that they help him find work with another football team. A team in their own division. A team they play Sunday in the season opener."[5]

Like Thomas, James was adapting to a new environment after a decade with another club. "It was an interesting year," the punter remembered of 1982. "Bob and I had similar careers. In Chicago they had decided to go with a younger guy, and in Atlanta, the same thing happened to me. It was not a *secure* time, as far knowing where our careers were going at that point, but it was an *interesting* and *exciting* time. Bob and I really connected and supported each other in Detroit. We even lived together for a while and shared some laughs. I learned a lot about that Italian temper he has. You'd never know he was Italian until you cross him. I think Thomasini was his original last name."[6]

The fresh opportunity for the pair to extend their careers, however, was on a collision course with a potential business disaster transpiring within the league. With the five-year collective bargaining agreement about to expire, an impending strike by the NFL Players' Association had tossed a shroud over the entire 1982 season. As part of its demands, the union was seeking a guaranteed "wage scale" to be implemented, as well as $1.6 billion of the league's total revenue over the next four years—a figure the team owners were willing to stipulate only over a five-year period. Little progress was seen at the negotiating table since the start of training camp, and as the season kicked off, a stoppage of play appeared likely by the third week of the schedule.

Tuning into the Bears-Lions game on television with extra interest were all sorts of followers of Bob around Chicago—including his brother Rick, who answered his telephone that afternoon with the greeting "Lions' Booster Club!" Rick had recently joined the famous Second City Comedy Club on

North Wells Street in Chicago, where just a few years later, he mentored a novice cast member named Stephen Colbert. "Your responsibilities [onstage] are to see and be seen, to hear and be heard, and to feel and be felt," Rick told the aspiring young performer.[7]

Rick saw his sibling don a strange, oversized, light-blue jersey with the number 12 instead of Bob's familiar navy-blue number 16 jersey as Thomas and Roveto matched early extra points at the showdown in the Silverdome. The game moved into the second quarter in a 7–7 tie as, just before half-time, Bob entered with four seconds remaining and punched through a thirty-eight-yard field goal to give his new team a 10–7 lead at the break.

The Lions' drive had been kept alive on a fake field goal from fifty-three yards away, as Hipple circled out of his holder's position and hit Garry Cobb on a twenty-five-yard pass. The play, called by Detroit offensive coordinator Ted Marchibroda (who served in the same role for Armstrong in Chicago the previous season), had Ditka fuming at Kazor after the game. "The whole world, including me, knows that Bobby Thomas cannot kick a field goal from 55 yards," Ditka later bellowed to the press.[8] Apparently, Ditka had forgotten—or was unaware—that Thomas's fifty-five-yard field goal from 1975 still stood as the team record. "The fake worked because the Bears knew I could make the kick from that distance," Thomas voiced in rebuttal when hearing of the comment from his former coach.[9]

Roveto closed the gap slightly with a late field goal from forty-two yards. But at the final gun, the Lions overcame Ditka in the coach's debut by a 17–10 count. The game was a hard-hitting affair, and, as with most hard-hitting Bears games, Plank was in the middle of it. The game would be his last.

A crunching tackle on Sims in the fourth quarter sent a shockwave of pain down Plank's back as he was helped from the field. Fortunately, tests on his spine proved negative, but the incident would spell the end of his career. Before Plank left the Silverdome, he and another old friend caught up with Thomas. "After the game, Walter [Payton] came across from the other sideline and gave me a big hug—which was a foreshadowing of things to come years later."

Once back inside the Lions' clubhouse, Thomas was presented with a game ball from Clark to the cheers of the other players, as he and John James received an appreciative visit from none other than the team owner himself. "Bill Ford came into the locker room and thanked me and Bob for filling in," James recalled.[10]

In addition to Thomas making all three of his placement kicks, James had a solid day as well, punting seven times for a forty-three-yard average—which gave Clark and the Lions' front office more leverage in their negotiations with Murray and Skladany, the latter of whom was seeking a salary commensurate with the other top punters in the league. "I had just finished out my four-year contract, and had led the NFC twice and made All-Pro," Skladany said in 2017. "When the Lions offered me the 10 percent raise in February, I told them that if I couldn't make what the top five punters were making at that time, then I wouldn't play. Their offer put me sixteenth in the league for a punter's salary. They must have thought I have kidding, because they never got back to me. So, just as I told them, the Wednesday before the first game, I never showed up—so they had to bring in John James to punt."[11]

Clark met with Skladany and Murray on September 13, and they promised not to walk out on the team again. With the Lions slated to play the Rams in Los Angeles the following Sunday, however, Clark was suspicious; with their agent based in the Los Angeles area, the coach was afraid the pair would be talked into sitting out once again. Therefore, Clark extended their suspensions another week. "I want to make sure I've taken care of my responsibility to the rest of the team," Clark reasoned. "Slusher lives in California. I want to make sure we're not into a ballgame and find out we're without any kicking."[12] When the Lions' team plane headed out west, Murray and Skladany were still in the doghouse, as Thomas and James took their seats on the flight.

Determined to make the most of his new chance, Bob hit four field goals at the Rams' new home in Anaheim Stadium. The feat tied his career high from six years earlier, netted him another Golden Toe Award from *Pro Football Weekly*, and made him five-for-five to open the season in leading the Lions past the Rams 19–14. James had again done his part as well, pinning the opponent deep inside the Rams' own ten-yard line three times on punts.

The Bears simultaneously dropped their second game under Ditka, a 10–0 shutout at the hands of the lowly New Orleans Saints at Soldier Field. The Bears' exiled kicker Thomas had now single-handedly outscored his former Chicago team 18–10 after two weeks. "My stay in Detroit has been the most enjoyable two weeks in my NFL career," Bob said after the Rams contest.[13] Had Thomas not landed in Detroit, the Buffalo Bills were rumored to be another potential suitor—where coach Chuck Knox, the man who had released Bob from the Rams long ago, was displeased with the one-for-four season start in field goals by Nick Mike-Mayer.

But just as things were looking up for both Thomas and his new team, the inevitable reared its ugly head on September 21 as the NFL Players Association went on strike. Upcoming games were stricken from the schedule for the foreseeable future.

"Maggie and [one-year-old] Brendan spent part of the time in Chicago, and part of the time in Detroit—because I didn't know what was going to happen," Bob said of the time during the strike as the Lions held player-only workouts. To make matters more complicated, no further decision was imminent from the team about Murray and Skladany—when and if the strike was settled.

Like Thomas, James was looking to make the best of the situation. After rooming together for a while at a Ramada Inn near Detroit, the two went their separate ways as their livelihoods were stuck in a holding pattern. "I rented the basement of a house up on Lake Orion that was next door to Jimmy Hoffa's widow," James continued the story. "The owner of the house had a basement area with pool table, and [Director of Player Personnel] Tim Rooney found the place for me. We worked out on our own with Hipple and Gary Danielson, Doug English, Ray Oldham—getting to know those people was truly great.

"One of the interesting things for both Bob and me was that we both had long careers with one team, and now we got to see how the Lions did things. All teams have different approaches to the same issues—practice, ticketing, training, and so forth."[14]

Nonetheless, the stalemate went on—with neither the incumbent Detroit kickers nor their replacements having an income. "Going nine weeks without a paycheck is tough," Bob added. "At that time, I had joined a Bible study with some other Lions players. One of the group leaders was a defensive lineman named Joe Ehrmann, who went on to become an ordained pastor after his playing days. He gave us a wake-up call about our futures; he said, 'Every football player is afraid that *next* year is going to be his last year; no football player ever considers the possibility that *this* year is going to be his last year. Tomorrow isn't promised to anybody.'"

After fifty-seven days, the two warring sides finally came to an agreement on November 16. The seven games missed from the regular season would not be made up, but an expanded playoff format of sixteen teams would be granted to earn back the interest of the fans—and to make up for lost revenue.

With Murray and Skladany still nowhere to be seen, it appeared Thomas would get a second taste of revenge, with the Lions' first game after the strike slated against the Bears in Soldier Field on November 21. But when the Lions resumed official team practices on Thursday November 18, he and James arrived at the workout to find Murray and Skladany suddenly in uniform, having been brought back off their suspensions by Clark. The following day, Thomas—perfect on all eight of his placement kicks for the year—and James (averaging more than forty yards a punt) were let go.

"The unkindest cut of all," Pierson quoted Shakespeare from afar, watching the events unfold in Detroit while still perplexed with the decision in favor of Roveto in Chicago. "Maybe if Bob Thomas did something like miss field goals, he could keep a job."[15] As when the Bears cut him back in September, Bob had no explanation: "I figured I was doing the main thing they judge kickers by—scoring points. I was one of the leading scorers in the league [when the strike hit], and I won't be playing Sunday."[16]

Another sour note was that, over the eight-week interlude, Thomas had made new friends to whom he would now have to say goodbye. "John [James] and I had stayed in Detroit all during the strike and got to know the players. It was an emotional experience Friday night [November 19], and emotional for Coach Clark. He said he thought we were terrific, but after the roster freeze was lifted, they were going with Murray and Skladany since they had started the preseason with them."

The fill-in punter was humble and grateful. "Getting to know Bob was one of the highlights of my career," James said. "I was able to play thirteen years and in three Pro Bowls, but that was one of the bright spots and fun times—when Bob and I were together. He was very competitive, very disciplined, and always wanted to do the right thing."[17]

Thomas packed his football gear and returned to Lisle, readying himself to continue his law work with Bochte and Kuzniar. Unsure whether he would get another opportunity in Chicago or elsewhere, the weeks grew long. The Sundays dragged by even more slowly, as Bob watched other NFL kickers struggle.

Just before halftime on November 28 in the Vikings' new home, the Metrodome, the Bears found themselves on the short end of a 14–7 dogfight. At that juncture, the offense drove to the Minnesota seventeen-yard line and situated the ball in the middle of the field. Despite the advantageous placement and the stillness of the indoor conditions, Roveto hooked the thirty-four-yard field goal attempt to make him three-for-seven on the season as the team fell apart in the second half in a 35–7 blowout. "Probably the most disappointing thing to me in the entire Minnesota game was the missed field goal," Ditka said, implying the miss had altered the team's morale in the final thirty minutes of the contest. "Everybody tried so hard at that point to get the ball in position to get it through the uprights. And when it didn't work out that way, it affected everybody."[18] Over the next two weeks Roveto was successful on only one of his next three tries, claiming he was playing with a sore kicking leg.

"Don't you wonder why Bob Thomas hasn't been picked up when Mick Luckhurst is missing important field goals in Atlanta and Pat Leahy is missing from the 14- and 20-yard lines for the Jets?" mused writer Curt Sylvester, who had watched Bob excel in Detroit while covering the Lions for the *Free Press*.[19] Back in upstate New York, Augie Thomas was also watching wistfully as Mike-Mayer was finally replaced in nearby Buffalo by Herrera, who had been previously cast off by Dallas and Seattle. New kickers were being contacted—but not Bob.

Nonetheless, faith and patience would ultimately pay off, as news was about to break in the Windy City. On Monday, December 13, Bob received a phone call from Don Pierson at his home. "He told me 'Ditka just had a press conference and said that he is "bringing back a kicker whose name everyone will recognize, and who hasn't missed this year"—and it's got to be you.'" Despite the hopeful news, Tuesday and Wednesday passed by without any word from Lake Forest. "So, I'm thinking, 'Gosh, if Ditka's going to do this, I'd like to take a couple of practice kicks.'" Bob had been keeping in shape in between his law duties, hopeful of yet another shot. "I kicked three days this week," he revealed to the Chicago papers—adding further suspense in the local media that something was about to occur. "One day was in the snow."[20]

By Thursday, Thomas could not wait any longer. He was compelled to find out what was happening and called Ditka's office. "Mary, his longtime secretary, answered the phone. I went through the whole scenario of what Pierson had told me, and she says, 'I'll go talk to Mike.' She comes back and says, 'Mike says to hang loose'—whatever that meant."

In what was perceived by the sportswriters as his last chance, the maligned Roveto got ready to take the field with the Bears the following Sunday, December 19, at Soldier Field against the Cardinals. But because of fan animosity resulting from the strike and the team's 2–4 record, the game was far from a sellout, with just over 43,000 in attendance. The game was therefore blacked out on television in the immediate Chicago area.

With no game on TV, Bob and Maggie were resigned to doing something else that afternoon and started making other plans. Maggie's brother Pat then happened to call, telling Bob that a bar near his home on the south side of Chicago was picking up the Bears game from a South Bend TV station. Appreciative of the suggestion, Bob and Maggie packed up baby Brendan and drove down to the tavern from the western suburbs. "We get in there, and all they have is a nineteen-inch television set in a corner against the ceiling," Bob recalled of the pub. "All of the barstools are taken, so we go to a little room in the back. I could only hear the game from back there."

Eating their lunch away from the bar crowd, Bob and Maggie listened to the first half as CBS broadcaster Tim Ryan reported that Roveto fell short on a field goal into the wind from forty-three yards away. With the score tied 7–7 early in the third quarter, Roveto tried again from thirty-three yards but the attempt was blocked—dropping his field goal performance for the season to four-for-twelve.

With the score still deadlocked and both offenses still struggling late in the third quarter, the Bears provided Roveto another chance to give the team the lead from forty-five yards out. Bob crept into the bar and watched his old holder Baschnagel ready himself, setting his knee down upon the Cardinals' twenty-eight-yard line: "I'm *very* interested now. Maggie, Brendan, and I went up to the front of the tavern near the TV." Maggie held Brendan in her arms a few feet away from the bar while Bob wedged himself in between two customers, "one of whom had about empty twelve beer bottles in front of him."

The snap flew into Baschnagel's hands, and Roveto strode toward the ball. He pulled his third attempt wide as well, now having converted fewer than a third of his field goal attempts on the year and successful on just one-of-five attempts from inside forty yards. But with the blackout around the Chicago area, the bar's disgruntled patrons were among the few who actually saw it. The man next to the Thomas family had just gulped his thirteenth beverage of the day, scowling as he looked up at the TV. "We let that one jerk go for *this* jerk?!?" the man yelled.

With her baby in one arm, Maggie used her other hand to gently tap the guy on the shoulder. She then pointed to her husband: "Here's the *first* jerk." Standing next to the patron was the only kicker in the NFL who was perfect on the 1982 season, yet currently out of work. A circle of well-wishers quickly converged on Bob with laughs, pats on the back, and a round on the house. "The bar then wanted my picture for the wall. I don't know if it's still up there or not." Finally, with twenty-five seconds left, the Cardinals' Neil O'Donoghue kicked one through from forty-eight yards to give St. Louis a 10–7 win.

Shortly after the Thomases returned home to Lisle, the phone was ringing once again. A representative was calling from the New York Jets, who were seeking a possible replacement for Leahy and wanted to know whether Bob would consider trying out for them. Just as Bob and Maggie were later trying to get Brendan to fall asleep, the receiver rang again. The couple figured this time the caller had to be Maggie's brother Pat, wanting to review the funny circumstances of the day. Instead, the man calling was Steve Kazor.

"Bob," Kazor began, "Ditka came into a meeting and asked, 'What do you think of us bringing Bob Thomas back?'" Thomas told Kazor he'd have to think about it, because the Jets had called. Kazor reacted like a toddler not getting his lollipop. "No, *no!*" he cried.

Bob was just letting Kazor sweat it a little bit. "To be honest, I knew in my heart that I wanted to go back to the Bears. I also knew I'd better get into football again pretty soon. There's no way I could watch a game in a tavern again."[21]

On Monday, Thomas was welcomed back at the team offices as Ditka addressed the media. "I've been patient and tolerant, but I want results and they aren't there," he concluded of Roveto.[22] "I thought we had made the right decision. It proves we're not infallible."[23] To some, such as Steve Daley at the *Tribune,* the choice should have been obvious from the beginning. "A sixth grader in Lake Forest with TV privileges could have told the Bears that Bob Thomas was a better kicker than John Roveto. But the mistake was made. Something about kickoffs reaching the end zone, wasn't it? When was the last time anyone got three points for a kickoff?"[24]

As with Hans Nielsen, Thomas wished his latest counterpart well. "You can feel compassion for John, just like you can for any kicker. I hope he does get another opportunity. This is a real tough business. I'm happy I'm back with the Bears, but I genuinely felt for him when he was missing those kicks."[25]

New life had arrived. After exchanging gifts at home with Maggie and Brendan early in the afternoon on Christmas Eve, he found himself in southern California on the night of Christmas Day. When he awoke the next morning, there was another present awaiting him. Just a few miles from where he had his first NFL experiences long ago at the Coliseum—and now on the same Anaheim turf on which he had last appeared in an NFL game a few months earlier for the Lions—he was teeing up the ball on the thirty-five-yard line for the Chicago Bears against the Los Angeles Rams.

With his hand in the air, Bob saw old friends to his left and right as he scanned the Bears' coverage team. Trotting forward, he let fly with a booming kickoff that sailed over the head of Rams' return man Barry Redden and through the end zone, as Los Angeles fans were once again afforded an opportunity to bemoan Knox's 1974 decision on his kicker.

With Payton passing the 10,000-yard mark in rushing, Thomas's two field goals ran his season streak to seven straight while the Rams' Mike Lansford missed a pair of chip shots from 27 and 32 yards. Yet for Bob, all that mattered was the 34–26 win. "All I know is that I'm 3–0," he stated about his season's record.[26]

The Bears dropped their finale in overtime at Tampa, and thus missed the widened playoff invitations. Even so, victory belonged to Bob Thomas at the end in 1982. As the team plane was landing at O'Hare, the other Bears named him player of the game in the 26–23 loss to the Buccaneers, after he had contributed three more field goals and a pair of extra points.

His famous smile was back. He was back home. And his faith had been rewarded.

Chapter 8

COMEBACK

I have a great deal of respect for Bob. Soldier Field is one of the hardest
places to kick—then and now—and to do that for
eight games a season is really difficult.

—Former NFL kicker Eddie Murray

For Thomas, the arrival of 1983 represented a deliverance from the struggles and uncertainties of the past year. In February, he conducted an interview with the Notre Dame–based newspaper *Go Irish!* in which he detailed his experiences from 1982—and how an unshakable trust in God helped him navigate the storm to maintain his career in the NFL. "I was able to tie patience to my spiritual growth," he told the reporter. "For me, patience is merely a matter of waiting on the Lord, believing that He has something better for you down the road." The manifestation of that patience, he noted, had surfaced in a transformational moment that had occurred during the Bible study session with his Lions teammates. "One night we were discussing the Book of James, which addresses the subject of the trials we have in our lives and how we should be patient. It talks about how we should, in effect, *thank* God for the trials because we learn from them. In the midst of humbling experiences, we learn that there are going to highs and there are going to be lows. Reaching the lows enables you to be a little humbler when you're enjoying the highs again. You have to stay level and stay on an even keel."[1]

Bob's solace in his reestablishment as the Bears' kicker also permitted him to focus on off-season work with Bochte and Kuzniar. Looking to grow in his second profession as well, Bob soon came across another opportunity in 1983 that would allow him to pursue his true passion in the law.

While in the courtroom one day that winter, he was arguing a motion against local attorney Jack Callahan, whose firm of Casey, Krippner, and Callahan almost exclusively performed trial work. Shortly after speaking with Callahan, Bob was presented with an offer to join the firm, which he accepted. In addition to taking depositions and preparing and answering interrogatories, the new position also allowed Bob to practice the legal activity he had been seeking—to be in the courtroom on a regular basis.

As Thomas started making arguments more frequently, the judges seemed to enjoy having him in court. "They'll joke with me about kicking for the Bears," he told the *Rochester Democrat and Chronicle* of his first extended forays into litigation. "It's almost always brought up. Sometimes they'll mention it in the courtroom or when they call the attorneys back into their chambers for a discussion. But it's all good-natured, and actually, it's a great ice-breaker. It helps take away my nervousness and reduces the pressure—but I'm used to that kind of pressure. I know some attorneys would rather not be in the courtroom. They'd rather practice corporate law, so that's what they do. But I like the courtroom. That was my image of a lawyer when I decided I wanted to go into the law. I like dealing with people. I like being up in front of people and talking in front of people."[2]

When Bob arrived at the Bears training camp of 1983, he encountered a large crop of rookies—twenty-eight in all, as Ditka sought to reshape the team in his image. Thomas was ready to assert his rebirth as a player and proceeded to lead the entire NFL in preseason scoring with thirty-two points; and in the regular season opener, Ditka was ready to put Bob's leg strength to the test right away. With a twelve mile-per-hour wind at his back, Thomas fell just short on a sixty-three-yard field goal attempt before halftime, a length that would have tied the NFL record. A week later against Tampa at Soldier Field, he easily nailed a fifty-yarder as part of a 17–10 win.

That autumn, sports fans around Chicago were consumed with the pennant pursuit of the White Sox, who were slated to battle the Baltimore Orioles in the upcoming American League Championship Series. As a prelude to the matchup, the Bears traveled to Baltimore on September 25 to play the Colts in the historic franchise's final season in the city before moving to

Indianapolis. But as the game headed toward overtime in a 19–19 tie, friction had surfaced between the Bears' kicker and coach.

Earlier in the contest, Thomas connected on a short twenty-one-yard field goal when a Bears' drive stalled near the goal line. Nonetheless, he was greeted by a screaming Ditka when reaching the sidelines. "He knew I made it, but he thought it was to the right," Bob chuckled about Ditka's anger. "I told him, 'Mike, it was right down the middle.' I think he was just mad because we hadn't scored a touchdown."[3]

More irritating to Ditka, however, was that later in the game, Thomas missed an extra point that would have ended the contest before overtime and given the Bears a victory. When Bob returned to the sidelines this time, the coach grabbed him by the face mask and yanked the kicker's head downward, pointing with the index finger of his other hand to an imaginary spot on the ground. It was Ditka's way of informing Bob that he pulled his head up as he made contact with the ball. "Mike is former a special-teams coach, and besides, he's a good golfer," Thomas said afterwards in graciously accepting the tip. "You don't lift your head in golf."

In the extra period, Raul Allegre hit a thirty-three-yarder to send the Colts away with the win, 22–19. For the second straight week, the Bears lost in overtime by a field goal, having come up on the short end in New Orleans the previous Sunday as well.

The second-straight defeat in overtime was too much for Ditka to bear. Shortly after the team returned to the visitor's clubhouse at Memorial Stadium in Baltimore, he pulled them together and hollered out just two sentences. "I've only got one thing to say to you guys!" the coach screamed. Ditka paused for a moment, trying to find exactly the right words. Turning to one side, he then cocked back his right arm and slammed his fist into a metal locker, not even flinching from the self-inflicted damage. "That thing is," Ditka groaned as he stormed out the door, "is that I think I just broke my hand." The players, each down on one knee expecting a much longer tirade, looked at each other as they covered their mouths. As soon as Ditka left the room, the place exploded. "It was the only time after a loss I can remember a coach leaving 49 guys laughing," Thomas later said.[4]

But for Thomas as well as Ditka, there would be lingering pain from the afternoon in Baltimore. The kicker had exacerbated a chronic sore back during the contest, with the discomfort becoming so intense that Bob could no longer kick off. Big Steve McMichael filled in—a defensive tackle who was given the job of toe-punching of the ball down the field, just as he did at the University of Texas.

On October 16, the Bears held a 2–4 record as the team entered a pivotal contest at Detroit. Beforehand, Thomas greeted Eddie Murray, who had since reconciled with the Lions' front office (Skladany, meanwhile, had suffered his own serious back injury and after a four-game stint with the Eagles in 1983 was forced to retire). Ditka appeared at the team breakfast in the hotel with his arm in a cast from the Baltimore punch and was on edge all the way until the opening kickoff—knowing the game's outcome could keep his master plan on track or derail it. Unfortunately, his team would struggle in the Silverdome for a second straight year.

With the game unraveling for Chicago in the third quarter, the coach could not contain his anger any longer. "For a while on Sunday, Mike Ditka's deportment earned a solid B and maybe an A–," wrote John Husar in the *Tribune*. "But Ditka spent a lot of time with his hands on his knees, staring at the carpet. Soon the steam had to rise; it was that kind of game."[5] When the lid finally blew, Thomas found himself as a pawn in the middle of a Bears-Lions war that would carry through the end of October.

In the fourth quarter, a ten-yard touchdown run by Bears' running back Matt Suhey and a Thomas extra point had closed the Detroit lead to 24–17. After getting the ball back, the Lions drove down the field again. With one minute and eighteen seconds to play, Murray lined up for a twenty-seven-yard field goal to put the game out of reach.

But Monte Clark called for a fake—or so it appeared. "We had 'live' colors for our field goal calls," Murray explained. "Eric [Hipple, the holder] would say 'Green 48,' for instance, if the kick was on, or maybe 'Blue 48' if it was a fake. It was loud in the Silverdome, of course. When we lined up, Eric turned to me and asked, 'Are you ready?' I said 'Yes,' and got set. Then, it got a little louder. He turned to say something else to me—and I couldn't hear him."[6]

When the snap arrived, Hipple paused for a second while holding the ball on the ground, waiting for Murray to do something. After hesitating, Murray executed a feigned kicking motion, following through with his leg and missing the ball on purpose as if it was a fake. "Except it wasn't a fake," Murray added with a laugh.

Befuddled with what was happening, Hipple—hobbling through the game with an ankle injury—picked up the ball, rose to his feet, and gimped untouched around the left end for an eight-yard touchdown. "There was nothing to do but run," the quarterback said. "I had a sore foot, but I didn't want to sit back there and get killed."[7] Trailing behind Hipple on his way to the end zone was Murray, who was seen snickering with his hand covering his face mask. "While Eric was running for the goal line, all I could hear in the midst of the Silverdome noise was him shouting expletives—with my name mixed in among them."

After he booted the extra point for an insurmountable 31–17 Lions' lead, Murray continued to show his amusement when they got back to the Detroit sideline. "Eric was still mad as hell, and he hollered at me again by the bench." Murray, however, could not stop laughing about the miscommunication between them. "The last thing I said to him was, 'Thanks for saving my ass.'"

Watching Murray laugh from across the field was an incensed Ditka, who mistakenly thought the kicker was mocking the Bears. Immediately—and literally—Ditka grabbed ahold of rookie safety Dave Duerson with the coach gyrating angry gestures in full view of the cameras.

"We line up for the kickoff," Murray went on, "and Duerson is right across from me, twenty yards away. He started running up as I began my steps—timing it so he hit me just as I was regaining my balance after kicking the ball." The first-year player from Notre Dame sent the 170-pound Murray sprawling onto the turf. "It wasn't a dirty hit, or even a hard one. It was completely legal," the kicker continued. "But I got hurt when I landed awkwardly on my shoulder, trying to catch myself when I hit the ground."

Murray grimaced while staggering back to the bench with a separated shoulder. As the Detroit medical staff tended to him, his teammates were already vowing revenge. "As the trainer is popping my shoulder back in, I remember Rick Kane and some of our other special teams' guys hollering across the field at Duerson, saying they were going to find him." For his part, Duerson claimed he was just following orders. "He told me go get him, so I got him," the player reluctantly admitted of Ditka's instructions. "I never had that assignment before. I was baffled."[8]

A moment later, the final gun sounded. Husar, gazing down from the press box to gather the final material for his *Tribune* story, noticed something on the Silverdome floor. "A few Bears made a point of crossing the field after the game and apologizing [to Murray]. They let the Lions assume the rookie [Duerson] just got caught up in things, making his mark on the game films.

They probably didn't want them to know the truth."[9] The players who were paying a visit to Murray were Gary Fencik and Bob Thomas.

And while their gesture was out of genuine concern, it was also a practical one for Thomas. "One of the reasons I wasn't crazy about retaliation on the other team's kicker was that they would then send someone after *me*," Bob said frankly of the justice-seeking "code" followed in professional sports, most often seen in hit batsmen in baseball or in a hockey fight. With the Lions scheduled to come to Chicago in two weeks, Bob readied himself for a quid pro quo.

When the writers caught up with Murray in the Detroit training room, he was finished smiling about Hipple's impromptu touchdown run and was now fuming. "Chicago is noted for that kind of stuff," he growled angrily. "Plank used to do it all the time. It's within the rules, but a cheap way to end the game."[10] Murray felt no better when one writer informed him that McMichael's kick-offs during the game had averaged five yards deeper than his own.

In retrospect decades later, Murray was more understanding about that era of the NFL. "That's just how the game was played in those days—there were literal bounties on players' heads. Someone would say in the locker room before a game, 'I'll give you a hundred bucks if you take out this guy or that guy.' A hundred bucks was a lot of money back then."[11]

Over in the visitor's locker room, the Chicago coach made no excuses. "To his credit, he [Ditka] didn't deny sending Duerson to 'block' the kicker," Husar wrote, "which of course is perfectly legal, if a little heartless."[12]

Despite Ditka's clear conscience, he considered the matter far from concluded—and it surfaced again the next morning on WGN Radio in the coach's weekly review of the previous contest. "After the Lions' game," Thomas said, "Ditka stated on the 'Wally Phillips Show' that 'The reason we're losing is because we have wussies on this team, people who go over and apologize to players on the other team.'" Ditka, however, did not mention any names during the interview—and since the television cameras were off when Thomas and Fencik had approached Murray after the final whistle, no one besides the writers covering the game (such as Husar) had seen the gesture. "I get the *Tribune* that day," Bob continued about the events unfolding on the subsequent Monday, "and Ditka doesn't mention any names in there, either. Then, I get the *Sun-Times*, and it mentions myself and Fencik."

When Bob arrived at the Bears' facilities in Lake Forest later on Monday morning, he immediately sought out Fencik. "Did you listen to Wally Phillips today with Ditka on there?" he asked. "Yeah," Fencik responded, "but he didn't mention any names." Thomas then proceeded to show Fencik the *Sun-Times* article. At that moment, the two players decided it was best to be proactive, and go up to the coach's office and clear the air: "So, we cop a plea with Ditka, and he tells us not to worry about it." Thinking the issue had been put to rest, Thomas and Fencik breathed a sigh of relief as they walked into the team meeting. "In the meeting, Ditka then tells the entire team the same thing he said to Wally Phillips—but this time, he *does* mention our names, saying that 'We're losing because of wussies like Thomas and Fencik.' But that was Ditka," Bob reasoned—the same phrase Murray himself used in summarizing the 1983 debacle.

After edging the Eagles 7–6 in Philadelphia on October 23 (in Skladany's last NFL appearance), the Bears hosted the Lions on October 30 at Soldier Field. Bob was ready to resume his kickoff duties as his back had healed; but he wondered whether there was now a bull's-eye on it. "Thomas lumbered into a meeting [during the Lions' game week] wearing the huge shoulder pads and thigh pads of a lineman," Pierson noticed with a laugh. 'I've been lifting weights all week,' the kicker said."[13]

As a Christian, Bob was hopeful he would not be fed to the Lions—and that Clark would instruct his players to turn the other cheek. "I'll remind him about being five-for-five for him [in field goals] in the first two games last year," the kicker planned to say to the opposing coach. "I still have friends in Detroit, but I don't know all the rookies."[14] While some of the Detroit players (such as defensive tackle Doug English) implied that "justice" would be served, Thomas figured it was merely a psychological ploy. And despite refusing to be intimidated, Bob admitted he would be on his toes. "They hope all the publicity will affect my kicking. I'll look around. I'm not going to stand there with a target on my chest."[15]

As Thomas emerged from the locker room for warmups, he glanced over at the Detroit half of the field. All was eerily quiet as he teed up a few practice kicks, with none of the Lions players even looking at him. But as game time approached and Bob lined up for the opening kickoff, he was startled when a voice shouted out to him from the Detroit sideline. It was William Gay, another defensive lineman who played alongside English.

"Don't worry, Bob," he hollered out. "You're safe."[16]

The Lions focused their energy on the game and not on reprisals, demolishing the Bears once again by a 38–17 score. Thomas was left unscathed, and even booted the hundredth field goal of his Bears' career, which sent him past Percival's previous team record of ninety-nine. "I have a great deal of respect for Bob," Murray reflected on Thomas in 2017. "Soldier Field is one of the hardest places to kick—then and now—and to do that for eight games a season is really difficult."[17] Bob had once teased Murray about the differences in their work environments. "In Detroit they had an article in the paper about air conditioning drafts in the Silverdome. I came up to Eddie and said, 'Air conditioning? How would you feel about thirty-mile-per-hour wind gusts?'"[18]

For Murray, the unpredictable weather of Soldier Field made it his least favorite stadium to visit, as it is for many kickers. And after many years of coming to Chicago, one game particularly stood out in Murray's mind:

> The league rules say that the tarp has to be on the field until two hours before kickoff, at which time it needs to be removed for warmups. No matter where we played—Chicago or anywhere—I liked to get to the stadium early so I could go out and check the field, the weather conditions, and so forth. Well, on this one day at Soldier Field, I noticed that the wind was especially bad as I exited the locker room—and it seemed to be getting worse with each passing minute.
>
> I stood there watching as the grounds crew was trying to get the tarp off the field. They were struggling with the wind and could not even grab onto it. Suddenly, a gust blew underneath the tarp and raised it up twenty or thirty feet in the air as the workers were also being blown all around, trying to get a handle on it.
>
> Then, the tarp started traveling through the air, down toward the south end zone. It was quite a sight to see the grounds crew chasing after it. The wind then sent the tarp crashing into the goalpost and knocked it down—so not only did the grounds crew have to get the tarp off the field for the game, but they also had to put up a new goalpost. Just another day at Soldier Field.[19]

The second loss to the Lions dropped the Bears to a 3–6 record, the same mark at which the team found itself at the end of the strike-shortened 1982 campaign. Team spirits were dampened even further on Monday, October 31, when it was learned that George Halas, the architect of not only the franchise but the entire NFL, had died at the age of 88. The players donned "GSH" patches on their jerseys for the remainder of the season, as everyone in the organization seemed to approach his or her job with more vigor and a sudden rejuvenation was felt across the entire Bears family. "The sense of history gave us a renewed pride for what we're playing for," Bob noticed.

One who would not enjoy the new surge, however, was Bob Parsons—the man who had punted the often-stale Chicago offense out of trouble for so many years, but who in 1983 was suffering through the worst season of his career. After struggling against the Packers during a 31–28 loss at Green Bay on December 4, Parsons found himself ranking last in the NFL with a 36.9-yard average. Joining Skladany in the ranks of unemployed punters, Parsons was purged from the roster by Ditka the following day with a team record of 884 punts to his credit.

Despite the one tense moment between them before Thomas's game-winning field goal at New York in 1977, Parsons truly valued the friendship he and Bob enjoyed—a relationship that also developed into one of the longest kicker-punter tandems in NFL history. "Bobby's a great guy with a great sense of humor, but he also took his job very seriously," Parsons noted in 2017. "As kickers, everyone blames us for everything that goes wrong, but Bob always took it well—which is part of what made him a good teammate. I often teased him in saying that he didn't look like a football player, and I was always on him about something else, if not that. But he always took it—and with that great intelligence and sense of humor he has, he always got me back."[20]

For the season finale in a Packers rematch at Soldier Field on December 18, the 35,807 who braved the elements would sit through the coldest Bears game ever played in Chicago, with the temperature at the opening kickoff sitting at a mere three degrees and the wind chill factor at minus fifteen. Under the exceptionally bitter conditions, Thomas decided that, as much as possible, he would place himself near the portable heaters that accompanied the bench area. "I kept trying to get near the heater all day, but all those other guys are bigger than I am," he complained of his teammates.[21] One of them was McMichael—who quickly took Bob's warm seat once Thomas got up and then refused to relinquish it when Bob returned.

Late in the fourth quarter, Green Bay held a 21–20 advantage. On the Bears' sideline, Thomas turned to the Bears' quarterback and offered a confidence boost to McMahon, the team's new leader under center. "With three minutes left, I told Jim, 'This is where you're at your best—in the two-minute drill.' I told him to get me to the 20-yard line. He got me to the four."[22] With ten seconds remaining in the arctic chill, Bob took a moment to say a short prayer with linebacker Al Harris on the sideline. He then jogged onto the icy field, and coolly shot through a twenty-two-yard field goal to beat the Packers, 23–21.

In what he called "the most discouraging loss I've ever experienced," Green Bay coach Bart Starr—who was fired after the game—also labeled the Bears as "the best team we've played, next to the [defending-champion] Redskins. They improved tremendously. And Mike Ditka is the driving force behind that improvement."[23] Thomas agreed. "When we won five of our last six games, it finally became clear what Ditka was trying to tell us all along. The Bears have as much right to win as any other team. In the last ten years, we didn't always understand that."[24]

On the winning play, the reliable Baschnagel had almost muffed the snap from Hilgenberg in the frigid conditions, and he also failed to spin the laces away from Thomas as the kicker made contact with the rock-hard frozen ball. "[It was the] worst hold I ever gave Bob," Baschnagel granted with a smile. "I've been holding for him for eight years, and that might have been the worst. I just slapped the ball down there."[25] The press then asked Thomas if he thought his kick had possibly gotten Starr fired, as had been hinted before the game if the Packers lost and thus missed the playoffs. Bob shook his head. "I wasn't thinking about that. All I know is that it was cold, and in ten seconds after the kick, I would be in the locker room."

Listening from the other side of the locker room with a grin was Baschnagel, who remembered the moment years later. "Bob always had his own way of doing things and saying things, but he always made me laugh. He has a very dry sense of humor. It seemed to be his way of dealing with pressure."[26]

After eight seasons of working together, the holder had become accustomed to Thomas often taking "an unconventional route"—and one story in particular stood out to Baschnagel from early in their careers. "Sometimes we would ride to the airport together. On one such occasion, we were on our way to O'Hare, and suddenly Bob said he needed to go back to his apartment. So, we turn around. I always wanted to be everywhere early, so I got anxious when Bob started putzing around inside the apartment, looking for whatever it was that he needed. Finally, we get moving."

As with Payton, Thomas, and several other Bears, a local dealership had lent Baschnagel a car to drive during the season. Unfortunately, the car was not of the same quality as the one given to the star running back, and

Baschnagel's car picked an inopportune time to malfunction. "The gas gauge was broken. We're going about seventy-five miles per hour down the Tri-State Tollway, and we run out of gas."

As Baschnagel carefully coasted the car into the right shoulder of the expressway, Thomas was now the one getting nervous about being late. "Thinking that we'll miss the flight, Bob jumped out of the car and into the middle of the Tri-State traffic, trying to flag down help." With no Good Samaritans to be found—and the pair still seven miles from O'Hare and wearing business suits—Baschnagel had another idea: "Let's run!"

Bob knew he would not be able to keep up with the wide receiver, so he ignored the request and continued a desperate attempt wave at some help. A handful of startled drivers caught a glimpse of the well-dressed Bears before they were rescued just a few minutes later. "Fortunately Ken Meyer, one of the assistant coaches, happened to go by," Baschnagel said. "He saw me and Bob, and picked us up."[27]

A few weeks after Starr had cleaned out his office in Green Bay, a man named Lee Corso was settling into his own head coaching job. Corso had been selected as the new leader at Northern Illinois University (NIU), an hour west of Chicago. "I owe it all to Bob Thomas," Corso told the surprised media in January 1984. "Wherever you are, Bob Thomas, thank you."[28] Corso's reasoning went as follows: he was replacing Bill Mallory at NIU, who had gotten the job at Indiana University—who replaced Sam Wyche, who had gotten the Cincinnati Bengals' job—who replaced Forrest Gregg, who had gotten the Packers' job in replacing Starr. Corso, however, did not even finish one season in DeKalb. With two games remaining on the schedule, he abandoned the team to sign on as the new coach of the new Orlando entry in the short-lived United States Football League.

With the strong finish to the season, the Bears looked to bigger things in 1984—as did their kicker. In a display of public support, Ditka asserted it would be unfair to criticize Thomas's statistics in 1983, as he had asked Bob to attempt a number of longer field goals that Armstrong typically did not request. Despite a fourteen-for-twenty-five mark, four of his misses were from beyond fifty yards. "Ditka stuck with me through the back problems and the troubles I had in mid-season, and I appreciate it," Thomas said gratefully in looking back at 1983. "It took this team some time to understand his competitiveness and his intensity, but, finally, I think we all kind of understand each other."[29]

With Bob's professional life having been settled, he and Maggie decided in the spring of 1984 that it was time to think about expanding their family again. Two and a half years after welcoming Brendan, they continued to trust in Providence as the guiding role for the direction their lives would take.

> Trust in the Lord with all your heart and lean not on your own under-
> standing;
> In all your ways acknowledge him, and he will make your paths straight.
>
> *(Proverbs 3:5–6, NIV)*

Chapter 9

Hitting New Heights

You can sense that being in the playoffs is not enough for this team.
—Bob Thomas, December 1984

"We decided we would try to adopt again." Knowing it would likely be more difficult and time-consuming to go through an agency if they adopted privately, Bob and Maggie got in touch with the physician who had assisted them in adopting Brendan. "I called him up in January 1984 and said, 'Doctor, I don't want to be presumptuous here . . . it's been a few years and we're thinking of adopting again—and I just wanted to let you know we're interested.'"

The doctor informed Bob he was no longer in private practice, having moved on to a local hospital. From there, all children placed for adoption were sent through the local chapter of Catholic Charities, an organization that the couple had researched previously but that had some problematic stipulations ("We weren't married long enough to qualify," Bob recalled, "but by the time we were married long enough, we would have been too old"). The couple decided to wait; and in the interim, Bob's law career was undergoing a change once again.

The partners in the firm of Casey, Krippner, and Callahan had decided to amicably divide. Before the split was completed, they asked Bob in which direction he would like to go. Having established a relationship with Jack Callahan the longest, he decided to join Callahan's new office—which essentially remained next door to Casey and Krippner. While waiting for adoption possibilities, Bob also spent time in the late winter with Baschnagel heading up the local fundraising drive for the Multiple Sclerosis Society. The pair also joined Ditka, Avellini, and wide receiver Willie Gault on a visit to Stateville Correctional Center in Crest Hill—where they assisted the prison's football team in preparing for its first season in the Metropolitan Semi-professional Football League the following summer.

Despite the doctor promising to keep an eye out for opportunities, Bob felt it was necessary to begin exploring other means: "I told Maggie that it might be a tougher, longer road, but that we had better start contacting some adoption agencies." Winter turned to spring, and still, there was no news. With avenues appearing to be limited, at Maggie's suggestion the couple decided to simply pray and let the issue come to rest in God's hands.

In the meantime, Maggie similarly encouraged her brother Pat, as he and his wife had been trying to have children for nearly a decade. After speaking with Maggie, they decided to pursue adoption themselves. "Adoption is wonderful," she told Pat in a telephone call. "You'll probably have an easier time with an agency than Bob and I did, because our first adoption was private—we didn't go through an agency." The talk with Pat prompted Maggie to say a prayer when she got off the phone: "Lord, if Brendan was meant to be an only child, I accept that. But if you have another child for us, we're ready."

In the very next moment, an answer came. "I remember this like it was yesterday," Bob said. "After Maggie was finished with her prayer, she went to the mailbox. There was a postcard in the mail from the doctor's office." It was from the partner of the doctor who had assisted with the adoption of Brendan. He had written on the postcard, "Please call me at this number." Bob read the brief message and gave Maggie a sarcastic smile from across the kitchen table. "I said, 'This guy either wants an autographed football, or he's got a baby for us—what else could it be?'"

Bob called the number listed on the postcard, and the doctor's voice greeted him on the other end.

"Hi, this is Bob Thomas."

"Is this the Bob Thomas that kicks for the Bears?'

"Yes."

Bob cupped his hand over the phone. With a roll of his eyes, he mouthed silently to Maggie: "Autographed football!" He put the receiver back to his ear, and the doctor spoke again:

"Would you be interested in adopting?'" Stunned at the divine interces- sion, Bob nearly dropped the phone. "God knew that the postcard was al- ready in the mail when Maggie said we were going to pray about it," he stood amazed. "I responded, 'Yes, we are interested.'" The doctor told Bob that a teenager had given birth to a baby boy in late April and had decided to put him up for adoption. Ten days later, Jonathan Thomas came home.

If God's hand in the event was not fully apparent to Bob and Maggie at the time, incontrovertible evidence arrived a month later. "When a car dealer let you drive a vehicle during the football season, one of the things we had to do was go to the Chicago Auto Show in May and sign autographs," Bob said. While Payton had a large, lucrative deal with Buick (which included his own stage and entourage at the show), the table at which Thomas greeted fans in return for the Dodge he was driving was relatively nondescript. "I was a little different from Payton. He would sign five autographs, throw them to the crowd, they would applaud, and then he'd say he'd be back in a while. Well, for me, I had to sit at a card table off to the side for four hours. I just kept my head down and kept signing as people lined up. While I'm signing, this guy comes up and puts his business card in front of me, which causes me to look up." It was the physician who had sent the postcard and then ar- ranged the adoption of Jonathan.

"I just wanted to introduce myself," the doctor said.

"Doctor, I'm sorry, I've been very remiss," Bob replied appreciatively. "It's been so hectic. I know I thanked you at the time, but I should have written you . . ."

"No, no, that's fine. Again, I just wanted to introduce myself."

"It's helpful seeing you, because it's a reminder that I have to also thank your former partner for Jonathan."

"Why would you have to thank *him*?"

Bob went through the whole story. "Well, I called him, and he said that he's no longer with your office but at a hospital, and that the babies he receives go for adoption to Catholic Charities, but that he'd keep his ear to the pavement for us . . . he must have told you about it, and that's how you must have written the postcard. And that must be how we ended up with Jonathan."

The doctor paused, and then shook his head. "You don't have to thank him."

"Why?"

"He never called me."

Bob froze for a moment as a cold shiver went up his neck: "Well, then, what would motivate you to send me that postcard?" The doctor had no explanation. "I don't know," he shrugged. "I was just sitting in my office one day, and it came to me that you had adopted a couple of years ago. I thought maybe you might be interested in adopting again."

> "For I know the plans I have for you," declares the Lord, "plans to prosper
> you and not to harm you, plans to give you hope and a future."
> *(Jeremiah 29:11, NIV)*

The Bears moved preseason practices to Platteville, Wisconsin, for July 1984 after having been in Lake Forest since 1975. As had Pardee and Armstrong, Ditka again brought in challengers for Thomas as six other kickers joined him for camp. Included among them was former English soccer player Vince Abbott, who scored eighty-two points for the Los Angeles Express in the United States Football League (USFL) in 1983; American college soccer player Dean Carpenter, formerly of the University of Chicago and Maine West High School outside the city; and the barefooted Mike Bass, who at the time was the career-scoring leader at the University of Illinois with 212 points.

Along with Bob's regular workouts, Bears strength coach Clyde Emrich had Thomas doing "Russian shock jumping" for the first time to help continue Bob's resurgence—an exercise in which one leaps onto a thirty-two-inch-high table as many times as possible until failure, sometimes while toting twenty-pound dumbbells in each hand. The results were readily apparent; by the second week of two-a-days, Thomas had made thirty-six of the thirty-eight placement kicks charted by the coaches, with a long of fifty-three yards. "I've been kicking better than ever," he confirmed. "The only thing to explain it is that weight program. I'm never going to be Lou Ferrigno or Arnold Schwarzenegger, but if I can see the fruits of my labor, it's been worth it to me."[1] Earlier in the summer, Bob had also impressed another coach—his very first—when he made a trip to Rochester for Augie's camp. "Even my dad said I'm kicking better, and he's one of my toughest critics."[2]

Thomas had so outdistanced himself from the competition that by August 8—after only one preseason game—four of the six other kickers were cut. In the week following the second exhibition contest, a fifth would be dismissed, as only Abbott remained. But despite having a strong camp, Abbott was released on August 21 as well, as Bob had already secured his job with another preseason game left to go. Ditka, with his usual demonstrative assuredness, then uttered a phrase that would carry great irony down the road. "I explained to Vince that, even though he kicked very well, you don't take a kicker's job away from him unless he is beaten out," the coach proclaimed. "No one beat Thomas out."[3]

In late August, the team emigrated south from Wisconsin to get ready for the start of the regular season. Just as he was settling back home, the lives of Bob and Maggie took yet another dramatic turn. Back to their weekly in-season schedule (but with the players still staying at the Lake Forest facility), the team was granted Wednesday nights off from meetings. On one such Wednesday, Maggie called Bob from Lisle and suggested they meet for dinner at the Deer Path Inn in Lake Forest. Arranging for two friends to watch Brendan and Jonathan overnight, she made the drive up from the western suburbs and found Bob at the restaurant. As he rose to greet her, she delivered some startling news: "She told me she was late, which she never was."

Excited at the prospect of another addition to the family, Maggie got a room at the inn that night while Bob returned to the Bears' offices and had the team physician order her a blood test, which was conducted at the hospital that night.

The next day after the morning practice, Bob skipped the team lunch and went to pick up Maggie. But first, he found a pay phone so he could call the hospital and get the results of the test. "Congratulations," the nurse told Bob. "Your wife is pregnant! I understand you're just about to adopt?"

"Just *about* to adopt?" Bob responded. "We just *did* adopt!"

Maggie returned to DuPage County and called her ob-gyn to inform him of the news. The doctor, who was also a fertility expert, was shocked. "Do you know what a miracle this is?" he responded with amazement. He then offered a word of caution. "You're at greater risk, Maggie, so don't tell anybody." When she got off the phone, she was puzzled. Maggie and Bob had trusted in God to this point, and He had delivered—so why doubt things now? "Wait a minute," she reasoned to herself. "He said it's a miracle, but not to tell anybody . . . If it's a miracle, why shouldn't I tell anybody? I'm going to tell *everybody*!"

After routing Tampa at home 34–14 on opening day, the Bears next hosted the Denver Broncos in Soldier Field on September 9—and mauled them by a 27–0 score. All twenty-seven points were scored in the first half, as Payton broke Jim Brown's NFL career record of combined rushing and receiving yards with 15,517. The record on which everyone was focusing was Brown's all-time rushing mark: Payton now stood only 447 yards shy of Brown's 12,312 total.

But that day, a Bears' team record also fell to another individual—the pursuit of which had fallen under the radar as football fans had been more closely following Payton's exploits. When he lit up the scoreboard with a thirty-eight-yard field goal at the 10:05 mark of the first quarter to give the Bears a 3–0 lead, Thomas tied George Blanda as the team's career leading scorer with 541 points, a record that had stood for twenty-five years. A short time later, after the speedster Gault hauled in a sixty-one-yard bomb from McMahon, Bob's ensuing extra point separated him from Blanda's figure and into the top spot all by himself. "I'm just happy to be part of the Bears' tradition," Thomas told the *Tribune*'s Cooper Rollow after the game. "I thank Mike [Ditka] for bringing me back to Chicago. My chances of breaking the record had to be astronomical a few years ago when I was in Detroit."[4] Then, with a smile, Thomas revealed that the team's confident quarterback had shared an accurate prediction in the locker room: "McMahon told me I'd break it in the first quarter."[5]

Bob extended his record with another field goal later that day. But keeping pace with him was Payton, who posted a seventy-two-yard touchdown run in the whitewash—as both men recorded six points that afternoon, with Payton thus remaining nineteen points behind Thomas for the Bears career lead. Bob, however, was not intimidated, and issued a warning to the press: "I told Walter if he breaks my scoring record, I'm going after his rushing record."[6]

After three Thomas field goals in a 9–7 win at Green Bay, the Bears were 3–0 for the first time since 1978. With the kicker often being the barometer for any football team's success or failure, the victory in Green Bay cast a new light on Thomas. He was quickly moving toward the top of his game, as were the rest of the Bears—with no limit on what they might achieve. "There's a little less pressure when you're going out there quite a few times each game, as opposed to maybe one time every eight or ten quarters, as was the case in some of the years I was here. Every kick in some of those years was a pressure kick because it might be the last chance you'd have for points. That's not the case now."[7]

As another sign of his growing self-assuredness, Thomas by 1984 had stopped practicing his unique habit of flexing his leg before kicks—his trademark since his days at Notre Dame. "I did it in high school and then college as a nervous habit. And by 1984, I stopped doing it. I just found it to be a little distracting by then, and didn't have a need to release that nervous energy anymore."

But after the hot start, the Bears weathered a two-game losing streak while Bob also hit a cold spell. He missed both field goal attempts in a loss to Ditka's previous employer, the Cowboys, as the embarrassed coach made it a point to say "I've got a lot of kickers' resumes' on my desk this week." Bob took the threat seriously—and even suddenly considered that the end may be at hand in an instant. "I knew he wasn't joking; he'd cut me once before. I'd seen him cut other players for less serious offenses than missed field goals. I prepared for our next game against New Orleans [on October 7] with the thought in the back of my mind: 'If I don't do well against the Saints, this could be my last game with the Bears.'"

As he pulled into the players' parking lot on the lakefront, a deep introspection hit Thomas that Sunday:

I told myself, "If this is going to be my last game in Soldier Field, I want to remember exactly what is was like." So as the team walked out onto the field, I paused at the end of the tunnel and tried to soak in all the sights, sounds, and smells of that old stadium. As I stepped out onto the field I felt my cleats sink into the green artificial turf beneath my feet and noted the clouds drifting across the rich blue sky overhead. I listened to the sounds of football in Soldier Field that day—the cheers of the crowd, the echo of the PA system, the pop of shoulder pads as opposing lines collided on the field, the grunts and groans of my teammates, and even the raucous rhythms of the Big Bear Band. I inhaled the odor of analgesic, and I think I even caught a whiff of popcorn and Polish sausage wafting out from the stands. I experienced professional football in way I'd never experienced it before in my ten NFL seasons.

Thomas rose to the occasion and hit from forty-six and forty-eight yards while the defense authored another supreme performance in holding Richard Todd, the former Alabama quarterback, to seven-of-twenty-six passing. Nonetheless, the 20–7 victory over New Orleans at Soldier Field belonged to one man, and to one man only.

As the Cubs were being eliminated from the National League playoffs by the San Diego Padres out on the West Coast that afternoon, Payton took a pitchout from McMahon on the first play from scrimmage in the second half and made a quick scamper around left end for seven yards to pass Brown's rushing record. Later, when Payton crossed the century mark in the fourth quarter, he broke another of Brown's records with the fifty-ninth hundred-yard game of Payton's career.

Having joined the team together as rookies ten years earlier, Thomas and Payton had a mutual respect that had grown with each passing season. Many of the powerful moments of both athleticism *and* humanity that Bob observed from Walter were far removed from the public eye. "When people talk about Payton, everyone saw his greatness on Sunday," Thomas acknowledged. "But as great as that was, one really had to witness the things he did in *practice*— for it is really something when you see someone do those things *six* days a week instead of just one. He could do it all. He could kick (I always said I was glad he chose not to be a kicker), he could punt, he could throw the ball— he had all those abilities. It's well documented in the record books what he did on the field. But among the Bears' players, we had the privilege of seeing the totality of his skills, and how he worked on a daily basis. Those were the sorts of things people *didn't* see. He worked as hard, or harder, than anyone in practice. He did a lot of his own training at home, and he was so gifted physically. I used to say that other guys would go into the weight room to *get* strong—but Walter would go in the weight room to *see* how strong he *is*."

While Bob was there to celebrate Payton's grand moment on October 7, 1984, another player who had toiled with Walter for the same number of years unfortunately missed the event by a matter of days. When McMahon was injured in the week three win over the Packers, his absence set in motion a stream of contestants who attempted to stabilize the quarterback position. First up was Avellini, who was assigned his first start in two years against a vastly improved Seahawks team in Seattle on September 23. Facing a staunch defense, the veteran endured a horrible afternoon in a 38–9 loss; but to make matters worse, a public feud with Ditka led to Avellini being released on October 1—the Monday before Payton, his longtime teammate and the recipient of so many of Avellini's handoffs, had his glorious day the following Sunday.

While the defense was thriving, the Bears' offense was also growing more diversified under Ditka with new skill-position players having arrived. And as with Avellini, a residual effect had been the dwindling role assigned to Brian Baschnagel. Starting all but two games as wide receiver from 1980 to 1982, the veteran Baschnagel found himself mostly on the bench by 1983, catching only five passes and watching his accomplished work as a kick returner from past years go by the wayside as well. And in 1984, Baschnagel dropped two field snaps in the same game for the first time ever in his career. Still, Thomas trusted no one else when it came to holding for placement kicks, particularly with Avellini—the only other viable option—now gone. "Bob was very sensible; he kept things in perspective," Baschnagel said in 2017. "If I had a bad day, he would come up to me and say, 'Remember that great catch you made in practice a couple days ago?' He knew how to pick his teammates up."[8]

After a surprising 20–14 loss to Green Bay on December 9, the Bears traveled to Detroit looking to secure its first ever NFC Central Division title. Late in the fourth quarter, they found themselves ahead by an insurmountable 27–6 margin and on their way to the playoffs. With the seconds winding down, another Chicago drive stalled short at the Detroit twenty-five-yard line. Despite no need for another three points, Ditka dismissed the idea of running a play on fourth down. Instead, he sent Bob into the game for his third field goal attempt of the day—thanks to the lobbying of Payton, as Bob stood at ninety-eight points scored for the season at that juncture. "If I reached one hundred points, there was a clause in my contract that I would receive a bonus of ten thousand dollars," Thomas said. "Ditka was unaware of it—but Payton was on the sidelines for that last drive, and went up and told him that 'Bob has a bonus on the line!'" Thomas claimed it was one of the most pressure-filled kicks he faced all season: "I heard that, up in the stands, general manager Jerry Vainisi was joking to himself, 'Don't go for the field goal!'"

Bob split the uprights from forty-two yards out for a team-leading total of 101 points to close the season (in the fifth time he had paced the club in that department), far ahead of Payton's second place finish with 66. Knowing the bonus was now his, Bob reverted back to his Notre Dame days of jumping up and down after a good kick as he was congratulated by his team-mates.

"You were really jumping high out there when you got your hundred points," noticed a rookie on the sidelines who did not know Thomas very well. "I don't jump that high for *points*," Bob informed him.

Thomas's last field goal also made for a team record of eleven straight, as he had not missed since a fifty-three-yard attempt on October 28 against Minnesota. But while achieving the postseason for the first time in five years, Thomas and the Bears were not about to rest on their laurels. "You can sense that being in the playoffs is not enough for this team," the kicker said.[9] Although they had dismantled the defending Super Bowl champion Raiders earlier in the season, the Bears were nine-point underdogs in the opening playoff round against the reigning NFC titlists, the Washington Redskins, which had evolved into an even more powerful outfit than the one that had claimed the Super Bowl victory after the 1982 season.

Upon arriving at RFK Stadium in Washington for a team practice on Saturday, December 29, Thomas noticed the sod was so thick that one could barely step through it. It was later deduced that Washington officials had ordered the grass to be grown taller in an effort to slow down the Chicago platoon, as Payton, Gault, and the rest of the Bears' offense relied more on speed than the plodding Redskins (with fullback John Riggins and their stalwart offensive line). "The grass was four or five inches high," Bob said, in contrast to the razor-thin Astroturf of Soldier Field, where it was easier for the kicker to locate his striking point of the football. "You knew the bottom of the ball was down there somewhere, but you couldn't see it."

After Mark Moseley opened the scoring with a field goal—the only kicker in the league to have been with his team longer than Thomas—Bob matched him with his own. While the three points had tied the game, the field goal would also turn out to be a significant one individually for Thomas in looking back upon his career.

The Bears ultimately held on a for 23–19 triumph, putting them one step away from the Super Bowl. Ditka had the team clicking on all cylinders; and Thomas discovered that the man in charge would go to any length to get what he wanted.

When the team was flying to San Francisco for the NFC Championship Game against the 49ers, Bob arrived weary at O'Hare, having endured a sleepless night due to little Brendan being up with an ear infection. As one of the veterans, Thomas was typically afforded a wider, more comfortable seat in first class. Once aboard, he looked forward to napping on the three-hour flight.

Ditka, however, loved playing cards—and was in the back of the plane wishing to play gin with Bob, who had been taught the game as a youngster by Augie. The coach ordered one of the rookie players to retrieve the kicker. "Coach wants to see you," the rookie told Thomas. "I'm tired," Bob informed the messenger as he turned over in his seat. "I think I'll catch a nap instead."

A couple minutes later, the stakes were raised as it was now Baschnagel who awoke Thomas, tapping him on the shoulder: "Mike says he wants to play some cards with you." Thomas did not even open his eyes. "Tell him I just don't feel like it today," Bob grunted while shooing Baschnagel away.

A few minutes later, it was one of the team's secretaries. "Bob, Mike's getting pretty upset back there. He wants someone to play cards with." Sensing he should not deny Ditka three times, Bob rubbed his face and pushed himself up. "I dragged myself out of my plush first-class accommodations and walked back to sit next to Mike—not in a cramped coach seat, but worse—in one of those tiny fold-down spots normally used by flight attendants. For the next three miserable hours I yawned almost continuously while we played cards in complete silence, because Mike never talked unless he felt like it. When he was doing anything competitive, even playing cards, he was usually too intent on the competition to want to make conversation."

Despite his fatigue, Thomas was able to win several hands—a run of success that caused an enraged Ditka to *tear the entire deck of cards in half.* Yet, without missing a beat, the coach pulled a brand-new set of cards out of his pocket, shuffled them, and began dealing the next round as if nothing happened. "Growing up as I did in a blue-collar Italian community, I had seen and experienced my share of emotional outbursts," Bob granted. "But there's still something intimidating about playing gin with a guy who responds to your good luck by ripping the deck of cards in half."

The team's magical run was halted, as they were shut out by Walsh's team 23–0. Nonetheless, the future looked bright as Chicago looked to take the next step up football's staircase in what would be Bob's eleventh season in 1985.

With the off-season once again upon them in January, Bob and Maggie took the opportunity to get together with Baschnagel, Terry Schmidt, and their wives for dinner. On occasion, they met up at the famous Second City Comedy Club, where Rick was still performing. "Rick would usually get me, Bob, and our wives seats near the front, and they would sometimes work us into the skits," Schmidt remembered. "And the storyline of the skit was always something like, 'Schmidt runs an interception back for a touchdown to tie the game, and Thomas kicks a fifty-five-yard field goal as the Bears are world champions!'"[10]

As the friends got together after the 1984 season was over, laughs and memories were shared as usual, but there was also discussion about the team being on the verge of the biggest prize of all—and the veterans were hopeful they could hold on and see it. While enjoying their dessert and coffee, Schmidt finally expressed something that had been troubling him. "My biggest fear," he confessed to the group, "is that after playing twelve years, I'm going to get cut the year the Bears win the Super Bowl."[11]

A few months later in early April 1985, Schmidt had been working out at the Bears' facilities when he was clocked in the forty-yard dash by an assistant coach. Both he and the coach were dismayed at his slow time. Schmidt and the staff agreed that he could not compete with the younger defensive backs any longer. Schmidt announced his retirement and, like Bob, would begin the next chapter of his life by enrolling in graduate studies at Loyola— on a full-time basis in the School of Dentistry. "I hate to quit, but it's okay," Schmidt told Pierson on April 17. "It was a mutual decision and an amicable parting."[12] Long underrated as a cornerback, Schmidt had once gone three straight seasons without being beaten for a touchdown (from 1978 to 1980) and had corralled twenty-six career interceptions, twenty-one of which came with the Bears—the tenth-most in team history at the time.

In 2017, Dr. Schmidt spoke with gratitude about finding a fulfilling occupation beyond football. "I've had two careers in which I've been mostly known for giving pain," he laughed after performing a root canal.[13]

A month prior to Schmidt's news, the longest-standing Bear of them all, defensive tackle Jim Osborne, had announced his retirement as well, ending a career in Chicago that began in 1972. Thus, heading into 1985, Thomas, Payton, and Mike Hartenstine remained as the senior team members, all from the bountiful 1975 rookie class.

Welcoming a baby girl for the first time, proud parents Bob and Maggie brought Jessica Thomas home on April 15 to join Brendan and the recently added Jonathan. Bob decided to celebrate the event by offering cigars to his teammates, as well as hoping to catch Schmidt before he left Halas Hall for good. On April 30, Thomas went up to Lake Forest to conduct his workout, planning to bring the cigars back with him the following day. He would not, however, be in a celebratory mood.

While driving home to the west suburbs, he turned on the radio. "I still remember that day," he said in 2017. A broadcaster on a local station repeated what NFL Commissioner Pete Rozelle had announced in New York, where he was overseeing the league's 1985 draft at the Omni Park Central Hotel. "With the 105th pick in the fourth round, the Chicago Bears select kicker Kevin Butler of the University of Georgia."

Chapter 10

Faith Rewarded

Take up your cross and follow me.

—Matthew 16:24

Bob refused to believe what he had heard. "I nearly went off the road. Because of the great year I had in 1984—the best year of my career—I was actually waiting for them to say the announcement was a mistake." Even Butler himself was caught off guard when asked for his own reaction: "I was surprised. I didn't know the Bears were in the market for a kicker."[1]

The next day, Thomas drove back to Lake Forest and managed a smile as he handed out the cigars. After doing so, he made his way up to Ditka's office to get some answers. The coach assured him that everything would be fine—and even seemed to dismiss the move Vainisi and his personnel staff had made. "They can draft whoever they want," he told Bob, "but I'm still going to make the decision on who's going to be my kicker."

Rarely were kickers drafted so highly, especially in the wake of an exceptional season by the incumbent such as Thomas had produced in 1984. However, as a result of the skyrocketing improvement of the Bears as a whole—something that Thomas acknowledged was a factor in his own increasing success—the team had thus been able to spend a higher draft pick on a "non-need area," as Vainisi explained.

Butler did not arrive without credentials. He ended his career at Georgia as the all-time leading scorer in the Southeastern Conference (SEC) with 353 points and also kicked the longest field goal in SEC history (to that time) at sixty yards, beating Clemson with eleven seconds to play. Playing with wider goalposts and the block tee for placement kicks in the college game, Butler had been 23-for-28 on field goals in his senior year while Thomas was 22-for-28 during the same autumn under NFL conditions.

When Ditka met with the press at the conclusion of the draft, he was predictably noncommittal about the impending decision he would be forced to make. "If Thomas kicks like he did last year, it could be tough. I told our people in the draft room they might lose a fourth-round choice. Butler has to learn to kick off the ground. But competition is good."[2] In addition to Butler, another accomplished kicker from the collegiate ranks was also brought in to challenge Thomas—undrafted free agent Bruce Kallmeyer from the University of Kansas, himself the holder of six Big Eight Conference records. Nonetheless, Thomas was not fazed by the presence of either one of them. "There are all sorts of stories about veteran kickers trying to play around with the minds of the rookies. Some have gone as far as to steal rookies' shoes. If you expend mental energy trying to psych out the competition, you're taking energy away from concentrating on your own job."[3] But while Bob was accustomed to competing with other kickers in camp each summer, few over the years—if any—had been as talented as Butler or Kallmeyer.

Ignoring the big-leg reputations of the newcomers, Thomas proceeded to drill ten of his eleven kickoffs into the end zone on the first day of practice, while Butler did not reach the goal line and Kallmeyer did so just once. "I was rusty," Butler told the writers. "I'm not worried about that. I know I can do it, but it wasn't a good start."[4] After a couple of days in Platteville, however, Bob discovered something occurring behind the scenes that threatened to undermine his efforts on the field.

As the kicking duel wore on and the results were charted, Thomas sensed a lingering animosity aimed at him from certain corners of the Bears' coaching staff. "I remember that, when I got to training camp in 1985, Buddy Ryan was completely in favor of Butler and not me," Thomas said. "He accused me of being a 'brown-noser' because I played cards with Ditka." After Butler had been drafted, the assistant coach made his feelings clear first time he encountered Thomas in the corridors of Halas Hall. "Looks like you've been playing gin with the wrong guy, huh?" Ryan told Bob before strutting off—as if Ryan implied he was running things. "Even when I would out-kick Kevin in a drill," Bob continued, "Ryan would praise Butler and say nothing of me. I remember finally going to Ditka and telling him, 'This just isn't right, the defensive coordinator acting this way.' And Ditka once again said that 'I'm going to be picking this football team'—so not to worry." Yet, Ryan was not the only one of whom Thomas became suspicious.

Other instances suggested that the data compiled in the kicking race were not being objectively recorded and analyzed. "There was one time in camp when me, Kevin, and [special teams coach] Steve Kazor went to an upper field, where there was always a huge wind blowing. Kazor said to us, 'Let's see how far back we can go without somebody missing.' We started at about 40 yards, and we both made it from there. At 45 yards, I made it, but Butler missed. I keep going back to 50, and I made it from there, too. I kept going back, and I made one from 65 yards—granted, with the wind at my back. And it was just the three of us there. Nothing was ever mentioned of it."

The three kickers continued to make their cases, with Butler and Thomas getting most of the publicity but Kallmeyer working to keep himself in the mix as well. On August 9, the team headed south to St. Louis for the first preseason game, with Ditka planning for Butler and Kallmeyer to handle the kickoffs and Thomas to take the field goals in the first two quarters and for the trio switch roles in the second half. Butler launched the opening kick-off six yards deep into the end zone and later provided the Bears with the team's only points on a twenty-one-yard field goal, while Bob missed a forty-six-yarder in a 10–3 loss to the Cardinals.

A new, gnawing tension started to grow within Thomas—an anxiety now directed not at Butler nor at any malcontents on the coaching staff, but at some segments of the media. In the second week of August after passing his thirty-third birthday (making him the oldest player on the roster), an unknown reporter from an Iowa newspaper asked Bob whether, in light of what happened in the preseason opener in St. Louis, he was already worried about losing his job.

With visible annoyance about the presumption being repeated time and time again since Butler was selected in the draft, the kicker paused and looked around at some of the more veteran writers who were also assembled. "Thomas turned to my familiar face," wrote Ray Sons in the *Sun-Times*, "as if appealing for a change of venue to a judge who understood the injustice of it all." Bob's response revealed his frustration. "Nobody comes up to Jimbo Covert, who had an All-Pro type of year last year, and asks him if he's going to be a starting tackle," Bob argued. "I had the same type of year. I kicked about 80 percent. I'm going into this season with eleven straight field goals, the longest streak in the league. It's a little ironic to be asked about keeping your job."[5] Bob continued his summation by adding other exhibits of evidence. "There are certain things a training camp can't show. The wind in Soldier Field, or the winters, or how a guy responds after missing a couple of kicks in a league game. I've been through all that."[6]

Butler, meanwhile, had been relatively free of questioning from the sportswriters and, despite suffering from recurring headaches, was generally enjoying himself in training camp, embracing the freewheeling attitude of McMahon and some others. Quietly confident he would be given the job, Butler was reported to have phoned his fiancée, Kathy, from Platteville and instructed her to move their planned wedding date of January 25, 1986, which coincided with the weekend of the Super Bowl—as Butler was certain he and the rest of the Bears would be there.

The following week, in the home opener on the exhibition schedule against the Colts, Thomas struck a blow with a forty-one-yard field goal in the second quarter. Butler countered with a thirty-five-yarder in the third period, while Kallmeyer watched the entire game from the bench with the exception of a lone kickoff assignment that resulted in a touchback. In the course of the Bears losing 24–13, both Thomas and Butler had sent kickoffs out of the end zone as well—but Butler shanked his second attempt off the tee, inadvertently sending a curving line drive down the field in overexerting himself. "I was a little too pumped up," he admitted about the growing intensity of the competition. "The ball was carrying really well. There was no reason to try and kick it that hard."[7]

Thomas and Butler were neck-and-neck by the time of the third preseason game at Dallas on August 26, as Pierson characterized the two as "indistinguishable" with both excelling at a comparable level.[8] On the nationally televised Monday night broadcast, the Bears fell to the Cowboys 15–13 as Thomas and Butler again made field goals in the second and third quarters respectively, and both survived the required roster cutdown to fifty afterward.

With just one exhibition game remaining and five players still having to be released to get down to the league's maximum, Ditka was pressed further by the writers for an answer on who had the edge. The coach revealed nothing but again acknowledged that a difficult decision was near: "I would feel comfortable with either one. And I'm going to feel uncomfortable getting rid of either one. It's tough to cut, period. Not that we're going to cut Thomas, but like Coach [Tom] Landry once said, when you've got to cut veterans or people you've had around for a long time, it is *really* tough." The implication was that, among the five to be shown the door on the final release day, it was inevitable that not all of them would be rookies. "We're going to have to cut some veterans," he concluded frankly.[9]

Making Ditka's decision even more troublesome was that other teams, whose kickers were clearly injured heading into the regular season, were stonewalling the Bears' front office; when Vainisi proposed trades of either Thomas or Butler, other organizations responded that their kickers were *not* injured and therefore they did not want to make a deal. Yet, in reality, several such teams were indeed interested in either one and were just waiting for the other [kicking] shoe to drop in Chicago. "They say they don't have any problems, but they know we have to let one of our guys go," Ditka added. "The decision will be fair to one, and it will be unfair to the other. They are both excellent competitors. They conducted themselves as professionals. I'm happy about that. I'm not happy I have to cut one of them. I wish I could keep them both."[10]

Even as the preseason ended on August 31 with a 45–14 destruction of the Bills at Soldier Field, little appeared to be solved. Thomas was given the first half by Ditka, who told the veteran, "You're done for the night," after Bob was successful on all three of his extra point tries. Butler was assigned the second half and made his three conversions as well, while the rookie also added a short field goal from twenty-one yards away.

Outside the locker room after the game, Maggie was waiting for Bob. Payton was the first player to emerge; and when he saw her standing there, he gave her a big hug. "He's going to be here," Payton assured her during the embrace. As Thomas, Butler, and the rest of the players showered and dressed, Vainisi was at the podium in the media room. With final deliberations at hand, the general manager provided no more insight than Ditka had offered—but did present a frank and balanced assessment. "There is no clear-cut way to go. Whichever decision we will make will be the wrong one, as far as a lot of the public is concerned. We're a contending team in a division in which a lot of games are decided by a couple points, so do you go with a rookie placekicker? But, to be a contender and improve, do you stand still and let a real talent like Butler get away?"[11] Vainisi and Ditka would discuss the decision until 11 p.m. that night.

The scribes then caught up with Thomas at his locker. Before the verdict was to be read the following morning, Bob had one final statement to make to the court.

> This team has a good chance to go to the Super Bowl, and I'd like to be part of it. I have my wife, my friends, my faith in God. I never thought going to Detroit would be a positive experience for me, but it was. It made me stronger.
>
> This has been the longest training camp in my life, but I'm not going to feel sorry for myself if it doesn't work out the way I want it. Maybe it's unfair, but it's what a factory worker feels when he's let go. That's as real to him as this is to me. What Mike Ditka might have to do, in the end, is close his eyes and see that snowy day in December when the Bears need a field goal to maybe finish first or make the playoffs. If he sees Kevin Butler, he should go with Kevin Butler. If he sees Bob Thomas, he should go with Bob Thomas. One of us is going to win, and one of us is going to lose. If it's not me who wins, so be it.[12]

As Thomas and Butler headed home that night, neither man knew where he stood.

When Bob made it back to Naperville, he asked God for a sign of what would happen. Going up to his bedroom, he slid open a dresser drawer and looked at his Bible. The first passage he saw was "Take up your cross and follow me."

The sun rose on the morning of Monday, September 2, on what would be a blazing hot day in the suburbs. Upon getting to Lake Forest, the kicker for the Chicago Bears was summoned by Mike Ditka up to his office on the second floor of Halas Hall. "Bring your playbook," Kazor told Thomas—a phrase no player wants to hear.

As Bob made his way upstairs and sat down in a chair across from Ditka's desk, the coach could not even look him in the eye. "We're going with the younger guy," Ditka mumbled to him, fiddling with the eraser on a pencil. Then, the coach added words Thomas would never forget: "Bob, it isn't fair, and it isn't just."

They were the exact same words Thomas was thinking at the time. "I had toiled in obscurity for the Bears all those years," he summarized decades later, "and now, I wasn't going to be on a team which was destined for greatness." He was the only player being cut from the 1985 Bears during the preseason with more than two years of service to the team.

Ten years after being told by Chuck Knox that the talented Los Angeles Rams were keeping their veteran kicker instead of a rookie in the hope of a Super Bowl run, Thomas was not afforded the same consideration in Chicago.

It was 8:50 a.m. on Labor Day, and Bob Thomas was out of work.

Knowing that a team meeting would begin at the top of the hour in the basement of the building, Bob waited before heading back down to the locker room on the first floor to clear out his stall. He did not want his teammates to see him in his distraught state; anyway, he figured there would be time later for goodbyes. He also wanted to make sure he collected all his shoes and other gear before leaving the premises, as he wanted to get right to work on finding another team for which he could kick. He was not ready to become a full-time lawyer just yet.

As Ditka departed from his office to go down to the team meeting, Bob wandered around the second floor, trying to kill some more time. Ultimately, he found himself in the office of the team's public relations director, Ken Valdeserri—the son of Roger Valdeserri from Notre Dame, who long ago had "disappointed" Thomas in informing him of his selection as an academic All-American. "I went into Kenny's office just to wait for a few more minutes, to make sure all the players were down in the meeting room. When Kenny saw me, he started crying—because he knew I had been cut."

Early that morning, Valdeserri thought he had been the first to arrive for work—but he found Payton already there waiting at the front door of the building, which was highly unusual. The player had a single issue on his mind in approaching Valdeserri as he walked up from his car.

"What's going to happen to Bob?" Payton demanded to know.

"Walter, I can't tell you."

Payton got his answer. "Well, you just did."

After sitting idly in Valdeserri's office for a while longer, Thomas finally made his way downstairs to the locker room at 9:15 a.m.—as he figured even the stragglers would be at the team meeting in the basement by now. "I walked into the locker room, and it was just as I expected. It was completely empty and so quiet you could hear a pin drop—unlike the lively, active place it normally was."

Thomas gazed upon the rows of cavernous, wide spaces afforded to the players in what he imagined might be his final time in an NFL clubhouse. But as he turned toward his own stall, Bob discovered that one player remained behind from the team meeting, unconcerned about being late. Trying to get Bob to laugh, the player was actually sitting *inside* of Thomas's locker—and *on top* of his shoes.

It was Walter Payton. Payton had been prepared to wait for Bob as long as it took, knowing he would have to come downstairs at some point. Thomas managed to crack a smile and shook his head in disbelief in greeting his friend. "I forgot they would still let *you* play, even if you were late for a meeting," he told Walter. Payton smiled back. He got up out of the stall, gently took Bob by the wrist, and pulled him toward the door. "Let's step outside," he suggested.

The two found a seat on some railroad ties that adorned the side entrance to Halas Hall, adjacent to the equipment room. They sat quietly for a few seconds. Then it burst forth. All of the pent-up anger, frustration, loyalty, and love Bob Thomas had for the Chicago Bears poured out of his eyes. He flung himself on his teammate's chest and sobbed uncontrollably, as Payton sat there and held him for nearly a half an hour. "He let me soak my tears into his shirt. As I'm crying, *he*—in my opinion, the greatest football player of all time—tells *me* what a privilege it had been for him to play with *me* for ten years."

To Bob, that gesture of kindness and comfort far transcended any euphoria that a game-winning kick or a Super Bowl ring could possibly provide. Instead, he considered it one of the greatest highlights of his career: "My most memorable moment in football was the day I got cut. Walter's act was a great example of Christian servanthood."

Whether in soothing Hans Nielsen in 1981 after his missed kick in Minnesota, supporting Thomas in being released the first time from the Bears in 1982, or now once again in 1985, that was Payton—always wanting to make others feel better with the thrill of a long run, a compassionate word of friendship, or with one of his famous pranks to keep the stressful life in professional football loose, fun, and in perspective. And in time, the sympathy Payton distributed would indeed come back to him. In a reversal of roles, the man of unbreakable strength would soon need others supporting *him*.

Cast your bread upon the waters, for you will find it after many days.

(Ecclesiastes 11:1)

Finally, the two friends clutched each other tightly one last time, as Payton headed downstairs for the last few minutes of the meeting while Thomas returned to the clubhouse to clean out his locker.

When he emerged from the building to head to his car, Bob found all the writers from the various papers—including Don Pierson, Kevin Lamb, Cooper Rollow, Ed Sherman, and others—lined up along the sidewalk, wanting to shake his hand. "He left with the same class that characterized his tenure," summarized Pierson. "Thomas stopped to talk to every newspaper, TV, and radio reporter who wanted an interview. He expressed no bitterness. 'It's a little puzzling,' Bob granted as he waved goodbye, 'but I pray that God's will be done in this matter, and I think He wants me someplace else. I think I can leave with the knowledge I wasn't beaten out for my job, and the knowledge that I did come off a terrific year, and also the knowledge that it seems there was nothing I could have done that would have let me stay.'"[13]

As he reached for his car door, someone shouted one more question: "How would you like to be remembered by Bears' fans?" Thomas did not hesitate in his reply. "I'd like to be remembered as someone who persevered."

He exited still holding the mantle as the team's all-time leading scorer with 629 points, having lengthened his lead by 41 over Payton as the 1985 season began.

Bob headed back to Lisle as the reporters got to work on finding a definitive answer. Only Butler's solid performance in training camp kept the media from staging a complete mutiny in defense of Thomas, as Pierson confronted Ditka immediately. "Reminded that he had said the decision would have to be clear-cut," the writer mocked of the head coach's earlier assertion, "Ditka responded, 'I lied.'"[14]

Uncertainty appeared to linger in the coach's mind. "I'm not sure we did the right thing," Ditka said to Kevin Lamb. "We've been wrong before. We might be wrong again."[15] Pierson probed further to understand the thinking. "Economics was not a reason for Ditka's choice. Thomas's salary of $150,000 was about the same as the Bears will pay Butler this year, including the signing bonus he got as a fourth-round draft choice"—a bonus the Bears would have been forced to consume if they had cut Butler.[16] Nor was age an issue, at least from what Thomas could conclude. "When I mentioned [to Ditka] that Jan Stenerud is ten years older than I am, Mike said he feels I'm in the best shape of my life and I can play another five or six years. In light of that comment, I guess that wasn't the determining factor."[17] (Stenerud was still kicking for the Vikings in 1985 at the age of 43, having earlier set Green Bay records for the longest field goal of fifty-three yards and season accuracy of 92 percent at the age of thirty-nine.)

Another theory circled back to Buddy Ryan. In the first round of the 1985 draft, the Bears selected behemoth defensive tackle William Perry out of Clemson—whose well-stretched orange jersey can be seen in the middle of line during Butler's sixty-yarder at Georgia. The acquisition of the 330-pound Perry had been called a "wasted pick" by the irascible Ryan (who quickly dubbed Perry with the nickname "Fatso"—despite Ryan being rotund himself). Some wondered whether Ditka and Vainisi had to justify keeping other draft choices on the roster for the combative Ryan—especially a fourth-rounder that was spent on a kicker.

A concern Vainisi held about releasing Thomas was that the waiver wire was offered to teams in the reverse order of their records—and thus, a struggling team in the NFC Central like Tampa Bay or Green Bay could sign the kicker and have him hurt the Bears directly, as Thomas did in Ditka's debut against the Lions in 1982. "I fear he is going to end up in this division," Ditka admitted. "The shape he's in, Bob can probably go on kicking for six more years."[18]

Thomas himself was not so certain. Afraid his career might indeed be over, he called his brother Rick to get some solace. "I just can't believe that I might never kick again," he shared with his sibling. Rick paused for a moment, and then responded.

"You know what you should do, Bob?"

"What?"

"You need to go out to a field and just kick a ball, and remember how it was when you were a kid, before kicking became your living. You'd go out to a field with Dad and kick for hours. You did it not because you were getting paid, but because you enjoyed it."

The older brother listened to the advice. With lots of free time on Tuesday, September 3, Thomas got up out of bed, stuffed eight footballs inside a bag, and left the house to make his way across Lisle and Naperville to the football field at North Central College. There, he kicked for an hour by himself—no snapper, no holder, no coaches, no Matt Blair from the Vikings trying to block it, no questions from reporters, no legal work to do. He took out his frustration on the ball, pounding eight field goals at a time. After kicking eight from one distance, he jogged to the area behind the goalposts, gathered the balls, jogged back to the field, and slammed eight more from another length, repeating the process again and again until afternoon had turned into dusk.

"Rick was right. I relished the satisfying feeling of solid contact of shoe leather on pigskin. I loved the beauty of flight as the ball soared into the sky and then tumbled through the uprights. And as I kicked, I remembered . . . I thought of Dad and all the time we spent together. I recalled the thrill of discovering my talent and the sense of pride that resulted from seeing the slow but steady progression of my skills. I thought—without regret—of all the sweat and effort invested. I recaptured a small measure of the joy and satisfaction I had experienced over the years learning to do something, even if it just was kicking an oblong ball, very well."

When Thomas returned home, he was disappointed—but not altogether surprised—to find there were no messages from other teams interested in his services. The only call had come from yet another *Tribune* reporter. "How long before you just say, 'Forget it?'" he responded to the interviewer when asked about giving football another shot somewhere else. "I was thinking that today. I just don't know the answer. I do know one thing. If this is it, I'll be the first guy to retire having made his last eleven field goals."[19]

WGN Radio also called the Thomas home a couple of days later, asking whether Bob would be interested in hosting the pre- and postgame Bears broadcasts along with Chicago radio personality Chuck Swirsky and football analyst Hub Arkush. Thomas agreed to do it. "But don't get comfortable," Swirsky told him encouragingly the first time they met, "because I know you'll be picked up by another team real soon."

The pain remained firmly entrenched. It would take the perspective of time—well beyond 1985—for healing and understanding to fully take root. "When I was cut from the Bears, I kept thinking of the *injustice* of it all—which is how we, as human beings, largely look at life," Bob said in 2017. "Whether it is trouble with our jobs, relationships, finances, or whatever, we tend to look at the world in terms of justice and fairness. Fortunately for me, God looks at things in terms of *mercy* rather than justice—otherwise, none of us would be in heaven one day."

His faith, once again, would be rewarded. Within a week, a new suitor in the NFL came calling, from faraway San Diego, California. A lingering injury to Rolf Benirschke had sent the Chargers' kicker to the sidelines, and the bitterness of seeing others perform his longtime role was similar to the pain Thomas was experiencing. "The week after I was hurt, they brought in different kickers to try out, and I had to watch them do my job for a team for which I had spent nine years playing for," Benirschke recalled. "It was a difficult situation."[20]

On Wednesday, September 11, Thomas was among three possible substitutes, along with Dean Biasucci and Eddie Garcia. Twenty-four hours later, the longtime Chicago Bear was offered the position. "Thomas did the best job out there in the trials, and has the best track record by far," San Diego coach Don Coryell proclaimed.[21]

Rather than animosity arising between Thomas and Benirschke, the two instead developed an immediate kinship in discovering they had much in common. "Bob was just one of those guys who understood my situation," Benirschke said in an appreciative tone. "He was a veteran, he had been through his own challenges, and he was really very gracious about where I was and recognizing that it was difficult for me. We became good friends through it all."[22] After Thomas signed his contract on Thursday afternoon, September 12, the two even hung out together at Rolf's home that very evening, watching the Raiders-Chiefs game on television.

As they did so, the two began sharing memorable moments from their long careers. "He was a fun storyteller," Benirschke continued. "We'd talk about our previous experiences and about playing under different coaches. I don't think anyone quite understands what a kicker goes through except another kicker. And a lot of things you go through, you really can't share with anyone else. We've all had different experiences with different snappers and different holders, and all a kicker can do is really bite your tongue—you really can't be perceived as passing the blame. Only another kicker is empathetic to that sort of feeling."[23]

As for Thomas, he did not see himself as permanently supplanting Benirschke; rather, Bob sounded much like John Roveto in 1981, cautiously optimistic about the new opportunity. Also like Roveto, Thomas had been promised nothing long term by the organization. "I still look at Rolf as the Chargers' kicker," he told the San Diego press. "I just have to contribute in the next four weeks. I hope and pray Rolf gets well. He has been through so much hardship. You wonder how much someone has to be tested. I'm not pulling against him, because I think the world needs more people like him."[24]

Thomas spent time on Friday refamiliarizing himself with the grass (and baseball dirt) in San Diego's Jack Murphy Stadium, where the previous December he was part of a Bears team that dropped a 20–7 decision to the Chargers.

While extending his regular season field goal streak to twelve in his Chargers' debut against the Seahawks in San Diego on September 15, Thomas had two extra points blocked and missed another when his plant foot slipped on the dirt portion of the field. Seattle ended the day victorious by a decisive fourteen-point margin, 49–35, but many fans directed their main displeasure at the stranger. "Thomas had to come in and adapt to a new center and a new holder," reminded Dave Distel in a piece for the *Los Angeles Times*, "and replace a popular fellow [Benirschke] who champions the cause of endangered animals, visits orphans, signs autographs in the middle of dinner and even had his picture in the paper escorting Brooke Shields to some black-tie affair. Thomas was greeted as an interloper, who [in the fans' minds] had probably hired a hit man from Cicero to put Benirschke out of commission. Fans actually took time out from booing the defense and booed the kicker instead."[25]

Having just exited from a pressure-filled competition with Butler in Chicago, Bob was already feeling the tension rise once again. Just after Maggie and the kids joined him out in San Diego, Thomas traveled to Cincinnati the following week for his first road game with the Chargers. Augie came in from Rochester to meet him, sensing his son needed some extra support.

As they left the hotel in downtown Cincinnati on Saturday evening for dinner, Bob's mind raced with thoughts about his football future, both near and distant. It was even possible that, by Monday, he would be back full-time at the Callahan Law Firm. "I'm again thinking that I'm going to be on the street if I don't have a good game tomorrow," he recalled of that night.

The Thomas men walked several blocks to get to the restaurant. At one point along the way, Bob noticed a homeless man leaning against a pole. Turning to say something to Augie, he looked back once again at the man— who had suddenly vanished. On the pole behind the man, Bob noticed that someone had vertically painted the words "Trust God."

> For it is by grace you have been saved, through faith—
> and this not from yourselves, it is the gift of God.
>
> *(Ephesians 2:8, NIV)*

An incredible afternoon ensued at Riverfront Stadium the following day. "Ten years of pro football couldn't prepare Thomas for the things he saw and heard Sunday," penned San Diego writer Chris Cobbs. "He had spent most of his career in Chicago, where 44 points used to be a season."[26]

In another high-scoring AFC affair, the Chargers found themselves tied with the Bengals 41–41 late in the fourth quarter. "With a couple minutes to go, [quarterback Dan] Fouts asked me, 'Should we win it with a touchdown, or have the drive stall so you can kick the winning field goal?'" Bob recalled. "I told him, 'Let's have the drive stall so the people in San Diego will remember my name—one way or another.'"

Fouts marched the team into scoring position at the Cincinnati seventeen-yard line. "When we got in field goal range, Dan just told me, 'Okay, we're ready for you. Hit it.' I just went out, hit it, and that was that. Everything went so smooth. Perfect snap, perfect hold, great blocking. I knew I wouldn't even have to look up to make sure it was good. It felt dead center when I hit it."[27] Bob's field goal with four seconds left—his third of the day—beat the Bengals, 44–41.

The team traveled to Denver on November 17 with a 5–5 record, still in contention in the AFC West against the host Broncos who were sitting in first place at 7–3. Winter weather was already striking the Rockies, and Denver fans were gaining a reputation for hurling snowballs at opponents' field goal attempts. With no snow to work with at practice back in San Diego, Chargers' special-teams coach Marv Braden—a former Broncos assistant—had an idea. During the Chargers' first workout that week, Thomas went through his steps to kick—but was stopped in his tracks when Braden began firing rolled-up pairs of socks him in an effort to simulate the missiles he might encounter on Sunday.

When the hard-fought struggle came to pass on Sunday, the contest ended in regulation tied at 24 as the teams got set for overtime. When the Chargers took over, they drove to the Broncos' twenty-eight-yard line as Thomas lined up for a game-winning try from forty-five yards away, fighting a head wind.

The end man on the line of scrimmage, Dennis Smith, got to the ball and blocked it; fortunately, a penalty on Denver gave Bob another chance. But Smith also deflected the do-over out of the air, and it was scooped up by fellow defensive back Louis Wright, who sprinted sixty yards down the field for a touchdown and a critical Broncos' victory.

Watching on television back in San Diego, Chargers' fans blamed Thomas once again. Nonetheless, the game film showed the fault was with missed assignments by one of the team's legendary figures. "Post-mortems revealed that Smith twice broke through the left side of the Chargers' line after tight end Kellen Winslow failed to block him," wrote Clark Judge in the *San Diego Tribune*. "Neither of Thomas's attempts had a chance."[28] Winslow, positioned by Braden where Doug Buffone had performed so well for Thomas in Chicago, was seen weeping in the locker room after the game, realizing his responsibility. He had mistakenly blocked the "outside" man on both occasions and not the "inside" man (Smith) as he was supposed to do.

Despite Winslow's private admission among his teammates, the story was not made public as Judge had been the lone writer to defend Thomas. Other observers had chosen to castigate the substitute kicker and not the sacred cow. "In the papers the next day, I'm taking all the abuse," Thomas recalled. "There was not one mention of Winslow's responsibility, even by the coaching staff."

Only two weeks earlier against the Broncos in San Diego, Thomas had been perfect on all six of his kicks—three field goals and three extra points—as the Chargers easily disposed of Denver 30–10. But in the "what have you done for me lately?" world of professional football, the performance had been quickly forgotten. With Coryell and rest of the staff seemingly unwilling to address the situation openly and honestly, Bob turned to the one coach he felt he could trust. "I go in to see Braden and I said, 'What is this? I'm just going to ask for my release.' But he says, 'No, don't do that—you're not that kind of guy.'"

Braden, a devout Christian with whom Bob had developed a strong relationship, convinced Thomas to stick it out as Bob turned to his faith yet another time. "I know God has me in San Diego for a reason, even though it's a bit hard to figure out after what happened in Denver," he told the Rochester papers by phone the following Thursday. "I figure His plan is better than mine, and someday I'll know why I'm where I am."[29]

Compounding his angst, however, was the scene unfolding back in Chicago. As Thomas and the Chargers were kicking off in Denver at 4 p.m. eastern time, the rampaging Bears had just finished terrorizing the Cowboys in Dallas earlier that afternoon, 44–0. The team followed up on November 24 by also shutting out the Falcons in Soldier Field, 36–0, holding Atlanta to minus-22 passing yards. Ditka and his team had streaked out to a perfect 12–0 start—a fact not escaping Bob's attention as each week of the season elapsed. "I had my feet on the turf of Jack Murphy Stadium in San Diego, but my eyes were on the scoreboard as I watched the Chicago Bears of 1985 roll over opponent after opponent after opponent. And with each win by the Bears, the unfairness, injustice, bitterness, and resentment of what happened to me in Chicago just built up inside."

All he could control, he figured, was his own situation. While the Bears were beating Atlanta, Thomas desperately sought to make amends for the ugliness in Mile High Stadium by helping the Chargers against the Houston Oilers. But his lone field goal attempt hooked left of the uprights in the Astrodome and was the difference in another heartbreaking loss, 37–35.

A 38–34 defeat to Kansas City ended the Chargers' season on December 22, leaving them out of the playoffs with an 8–8 record as Thomas led the team with 105 points—nearly doubling the figure of 60 posted by second-place finishers Wes Chandler and Tim Spencer. Upon reflection, the slings and arrows of southern California once again made him stronger as he looked forward to kicking again in 1986. "In light of the obstacles here," Thomas judged, "this was probably one of my most rewarding years."[30]

Maggie and the kids preceded Bob in leaving San Diego, heading back to Lisle in early December to get the house ready for Christmas. When Bob arrived home on December 23, Maggie told him WGN Radio had called once more, saying they wanted him to again join Swirsky and Arkush on the air as the 15–1 Bears went through the playoffs. Being only one year removed from the team, the station figured, Bob would have valuable insights to share with listeners as the team pursued its long-awaited crown. The ultraconfident team was having so much fun destroying the opposition that it released a brash rap video entitled "The Super Bowl Shuffle"—three weeks before the regular season had even ended.

The initial round of the postseason was set for January 5, 1986, at Soldier Field against the New York Giants, the first time the two teams had met since Thomas's dramatic field goal had ended the 1977 regular season eight years earlier. Bob's duties with WGN required him to be at a portable studio at the stadium three hours before the opening kickoff to provide some pregame commentary, offer further perspectives at halftime, and then answer call-in questions from listeners after the game. Bob was happy to do so—but not entirely for the altruistic purpose of sharing valuable insights. "I thought that in some small, vicarious way," he confessed, "I could be involved with this team that was destined for greatness."

Butler had excelled while feasting on the Bears' offensive efficiency and defensive dominance in 1985, becoming the first Chicago player in twenty years to lead the league in scoring with 144 points. In the process, Butler was a perfect 51-for-51 on extra points and had tied Thomas's year-old team record of eleven consecutive field goals, while Butler's 83.8 field goal percentage (31-for-37) had also surpassed the team mark of 78.6, which Thomas had also set in 1984.

Nonetheless, problems surfaced for Butler against the Giants in the blustery cold of the Chicago lakefront, where the temperature at the opening kickoff was twelve degrees and the wind chill stood at minus thirteen. In what he would call his "worst day in football," the Georgian missed three field goals while his teammates shut out the Giants, 21–0. The wind at Soldier Field, Butler noted, was unlike that in any stadium where he had ever kicked, college or pro; and the powerful bursts of wind on this day even caused the Giants' punter Sean Landeta to nearly miss the ball entirely. "Big as it is, it's low," Butler said the following day about the structure. "I can't think of any pro stadium, or maybe a college stadium that size, where the stands don't extend any higher. But I'm not using that as an excuse. I just didn't get it done.

"Some people are going to think that it's playoff pressure and all that. But it's not. Pressure came for me months ago, just making this team, going through that thing with Bob Thomas at training camp. I understand he was at the ballgame, on the radio. It's not Bob's style to rip, but he'd have had plenty of material watching me yesterday."[31]

When Butler got home after the game, he realized he had left his house keys back at Soldier Field and was thus stranded on his front doorstep. "I'm standing out there in the cold and I'm thinking, 'I know I can at least kick in the door. I can't miss that *too*, can I?'"[32]

In the week following the playoff opener, multiple letters appeared in the local papers opining that Thomas would have been better suited to handle the worsening winter weather around Chicago in the postseason, worrying that Butler's lack of such experience could be factor in the Super Bowl run with one more hurdle yet to overcome.

Happy with his performance on the airwaves, WGN once again hired Thomas for the Bears' NFC Championship Game against the Rams at Soldier

Field on January 12. After the pregame show at the stadium, Bob was permitted to conduct his halftime and postgame duties from the warmth of the WGN building, watching the contest in the comfort of a recliner in the station's basement and coming upstairs to the microphone when needed. As kickoff neared and Bob seated himself in the easy chair in the WGN cellar, he immediately spotted his old chess opponent on television—the flags atop Soldier Field. The pennants were giving him their familiar taunt, pointing stiffly eastward toward the frosty shores of Lake Michigan. A west wind had been gusting up to twenty five miles per hour during the afternoon. Even without the wind chill, the temperatures were nearing the freezing mark as Butler took the field an hour before kickoff to begin his warmup drills.

In the first quarter, McMahon scrambled around left end for sixteen yards, diving inside the pylon for a score as Butler's extra point gave the Bears a 7–0 lead. Regaining his confidence, Butler soon added a thirty-four-yard field goal for a quick 10–0 halftime advantage.

Heading upstairs to the WGN broadcast studio, Thomas forced himself to provide a few comments at the break; but tension was mounting within him. When he returned to his private viewing area in the station's basement as the second half kicked off, his solitude only exacerbated his stress. Every play, every second, every minute that fell away was bringing *it* closer—*the moment*. As the Bears marched toward the Super Bowl, the game soon evolved into a coronation, in what would be one of the most difficult and lonely moments of Thomas's life.

The Bears showed no mercy to Los Angeles on either side of the ball in the final thirty minutes, keeping the foot on the gas with a diversity of play-calling on offense and constant blitzing on defense. After McMahon found Gault for another touchdown in the third quarter to lengthen the lead to 17–0, the Rams made their last desperate push midway through the fourth period—a final, doomed charge against a Chicago defense that had been on a path of devastation hardly ever seen in NFL play.

On third and eleven from the Chicago thirty-seven-yard line, quarterback Dieter Brock dropped back to pass and was quickly engulfed by Richard Dent, who had become the most feared defensive end in the game. Dent jarred the football loose as it skidded back toward midfield, where linebacker Wilber Marshall scooped it off the turf with snow flurries swirling.

As Marshall took off in the other direction with the ball, a lone Los Angeles player remaining in the vicinity made a feeble grab at the back of Marshall's jersey: running back Eric Dickerson, who had just rushed for a playoff-record 248 yards against the Cowboys a week earlier and set the league's regular season mark of 2,105 yards in 1984. Nonetheless, he looked less than ordinary against Ryan's indomitable defenders that freezing afternoon.

Clinging to the back of Marshall's shoulder pads with one arm, Dickerson's strong fingers ultimately gave way. Looking like a man surrendering to his demise, he dropped to the ground and could only watch as the second-year linebacker sprinted to the south end zone, giving the Bears a 23–0 lead before Butler added the final point of the game—the first time any NFL team had ever posted back-to-back playoff shutouts. As Marshall crossed the goal line, WGN play-by-play announcer Wayne Larrivee canonized the moment for the team as "the crowning jewel in their NFC championship."

With any doubt of the game's outcome now erased, the CBS Television cameras started panning the Chicago sideline as the celebration began in earnest. Younger players such as Butler, Thomas Sanders, and Jim Morrissey leapt excitedly into each other's arms, while veterans Singletary, McMichael, and Dan Hampton simply exchanged quiet, stoic nods and clenched fists of satisfaction. A broad smile was seen on the face of Evanston native Emery Moorehead, who battled as a skinny wide receiver for the Giants against the Bears on the frozen field of the Meadowlands in 1977 but now had grown into a formidable 230-pound tight end for Chicago.

Still, there were other veterans who shed tears of joy—tears that washed away a decade of frustration, pain, and struggle. For those present who had helped build the team through the trials and tribulations over the past ten years—Payton, Fencik, and Hartenstine in particular—the surreal nature of an impending trip to the Super Bowl was almost too much to comprehend as the Soldier Field clock expired. The same tears of joy also flowed from long-suffering Bears fans who were watching on local television.

But perhaps across all of Chicagoland, there were tears of *sadness* from only one viewer, who was sitting in the basement of WGN. "I sat literally paralyzed in that recliner. I couldn't get up," Bob said of watching the revelry unfold. As he glared angrily at the TV, the scene was composed of faces he knew well but also of some rookies and free agents he did not recognize at all. A bitter voice whispered to him. *The strangers did not deserve to be there.* "The injustice and the unfairness of it all suddenly took the form of tears."

Swirsky entered the room and found Thomas overcome by his sadness. "Come on upstairs when you're ready," he told Bob as softly as possible. "We need to do the postgame show." After Swirsky departed, Thomas still could not get himself to move.

Over the previous few weeks, Bob's friends had offered advice on how to capitulate to the likelihood of a Bears' Super Bowl trip. One had told him to pick up a copy of *Sports Illustrated* from five years earlier and see how many faces he recognized (attempting to point out how fleeting fame can be); another buddy reminded him of a quote from the former Cowboys' running back Duane Thomas. "If the Super Bowl is the ultimate, why do they play it every year?" Bob tried to take comfort in those thoughts; still, nothing could get him up from the chair. He continued to sit there, immobilized by his resentment. He was being shut out of football's biggest stage.

His tears were not only for himself. They were also for Parsons, Plank, Osborne, Avellini, Schmidt, Harper, Sorey and the many others who helped lay the foundation of the team over the past decade—but especially for his friend Brian Baschnagel, whose shot at a Super Bowl appearance wound up even closer to the pin than Thomas's. Baschnagel, Bob's long-time partner on placement kicks, had torn cartilage in his knee in the preseason as Thomas and Butler were waging their battle. He was put on the injured reserve list but was able to return later in the season to practice with the team. Baschnagel, however, was not activated for any games in 1985; a similar fate befell Jeff Fisher, who had also been injured, as both missed out on the postseason. Baschnagel and Fisher could be activated for the Super Bowl only if someone else had gotten hurt in the earlier playoff rounds. "He's not the type of person to wish for that kind of thing," Thomas said of Baschnagel to Skip Myslenski the week before. "I'm sure it's killing him."[33]

Suddenly, Bob's tears stopped flowing. His tight grip on the armrests of the chair slightly loosened and the stress was released as a jolt of faith had entered his mind.

"While I was in San Diego that season, we had a Bible study on Tuesday nights with our wives," Thomas said in 2017. "Some of the San Diego Padres baseball players and their wives would join us as well. On one particular Tuesday, the minister leading the study asked how many people had watched the *Monday Night Football* game the previous night. It was a sports crowd, so nearly all of the hands went up. At halftime of that particular game, ABC devoted all of its coverage to a ceremony honoring Joe Namath at midfield. The crowd erupted, and everyone was giving him a standing ovation. The minister said, 'In that moment, I wanted to *be* Joe Namath.

Eighty thousand people were on their feet for twenty minutes straight, and millions more were watching on television.'"

But just as Bob had been trapped in his recliner, the minister had a similar conversion experience that Monday night. "The minister said that he closed his eyes while sitting in that chair, watching that game—much as I closed my tear-soaked eyes in the basement of WGN—and said to himself that he would give up all that fame and acclaim that Namath was receiving if, when he died, Christ would clap His hands just *one* time and say, 'Well done, my good and faithful servant.'" Jolted by the memory of that moment, Bob willed himself out of the recliner. He climbed the stairs up to the WGN microphone and took part in the postgame show. "Maybe the only reason God had me in San Diego in 1985 was to learn this lesson."

Life was indeed good. "I've tried to be philosophical about the whole thing. I have a lot to be thankful for. I come home to my wife and three children every night and realize how fortunate I am to have them. If not going to the Super Bowl is the worst thing that happens to me in my life, then I'll be a very blessed man."[34]

But a week after the Bears' Super Bowl victory over New England, Thomas's contract with the Chargers expired on February 1 as Marv Braden was fired from the coaching staff. Once again, Bob was uncertain which turn his life would take next.

> You will keep in perfect peace him whose mind is steadfast, because he trusts in you.
>
> *(Isaiah 26:3, NIV)*

Chapter 11

Boot Camp—and Moving On

He handled the pressure of a forty-eight-yard field goal on a windy day, so
I knew he could handle a court case that is much more important for
somebody's life.

—John Skibinski on Thomas, 2017

Thomas acknowledged the inevitability of Benirschke returning at some point to compete for his old job; but even if Bob was not in San Diego come September, he did not foresee such a contingency as the end of his career. "I think both Rolf and I deserve to be kicking in the NFL next season," he said the week before the Super Bowl, "and I think we will be."[1]

Although the Chargers' long-time kicker was indeed on his way back—a fact bluntly reinforced to Thomas by Al Saunders, a San Diego assistant who was about to become the head coach with the impending resignation of Coryell—the team still expressed an interest in negotiating a new deal with Bob. But in deference to Benirschke, Thomas declined the team's qualifying offer in April and requested his release. "I notified them that I wanted the offer withdrawn. I really felt with Rolf being healthy, this was the best move for both of us. This gives me the opportunity to test the waters and go where there's the greatest need. I am appreciative they granted the request, because a lot of other teams could have sat back and said, 'Why accommodate him?' I'm thankful to the Chargers.

"When you talk of San Diego, Rolf's been there a long time. If we had kicked even, or even if I was a little better, he would have had the edge because he means so much to the community, and that's rightly so. I'm really happy with the decision."[2]

In parting ways, Benirschke and Thomas once again reflected upon their commonalities. Both were sons of immigrants who escaped tyranny in Europe to begin better lives for their families in the United States; both had been part of the second wave of soccer-stylers who redefined the role of the place-kicker in the NFL; both had overcome injuries later in their careers to reclaim their positions with their teams; and both traced their short football roots back to the latter halves of their high school days, when a long relationship with the sport seemed far from a possibility. "We were both 'accidental' players," Benirschke said. "We never dreamed we would be kickers in professional football. We appreciated the opportunity to get to do something we loved, to have an impact on the game, and to be counted on by our teammates in important situations.

"What I remember about my time with Bob, really, was his kindness. He was a mature guy, and he was well-rounded. He wasn't just an athlete—he was bright and well-read. Obviously, he has gone on to be successful way outside of football, and we both appreciated such a quality. When you have someone who is intelligent and worldly, the conversations go way beyond football—and I think we had a kinship because of that."[3]

It was time for Thomas to head back to the western suburbs of Chicago and resume his law work with the Callahan firm, while also keeping in shape in the hope that another chance would come. "I thought I was kicking well enough to play. When I left San Diego, I also realized how blessed I was to play ten years for one team with the Bears—because I knew that, to keep playing, I had to now get acquainted with yet another new team and another new city."

And in mid-June, a most unexpected team and city came knocking on his door. Early in the summer Thomas heard from John Hilton, Bob's first special-teams coach in the NFL more than ten years earlier under Pardee with the Bears. Hilton was now working in the same role for Forrest Gregg with the Packers in Green Bay—the team for which Hilton caught the last touchdown pass thrown by Bart Starr on a snowy day in Pittsburgh's brand-new Three Rivers Stadium in 1970. Hilton convinced the Packers' front office to sign Thomas and bring him to training camp at St. Norbert College in De Pere, Wisconsin. "Hilton obviously knew about me, and he seemed excited for me to come out there," Bob recalled. "I thought it would be a good competition with the returning kicker, and I wouldn't have signed if I didn't think I had a good chance of winning the job. But once I got there, it became evident I was going to get little chance in practice—let alone in games."

As opposed to the situation with the Chargers, Thomas was not arriving to a team in need of a kicker. Rather, it was Gregg's plan to have Thomas provide a challenge for third-year man Al Del Greco—which he did. "I hit a sixty-yard field goal the first day here," he told Herb Gould at the *Sun-Times* back in Chicago. "It was wind-aided, but I can't remember many times where I have done that, wind or not. The book on me was always: 'Accurate, but not long distance.' Wouldn't it be ironic if I beat out somebody because my kicks were longer?"[4] Gregg held off on any live field goal drills until two weeks into camp, when on July 31, Thomas was once again thrust into the arena for another duel with a younger kicker. With the ball spotted at the twenty-seven-yard line and the defensive rush coming, Thomas made two of his three attempts while Del Greco was one-for-two.

On the surface, both men appeared to be on equal footing by the time of the first exhibition game on August 9, in front of the largest home crowd ever to watch a Packers game (73,959—at Camp Randall Stadium in Madison). After seeing a steep decrease in his opportunities at camp during the week, Thomas booted two extra points in a 38–14 win over the Jets, while Del Greco was given the remainder of the placement kicks. A week later, both men succeeded on a lone extra point in a 22–14 loss to the Giants in Milwaukee's County Stadium. However, Bob could sense that he was not getting a fair look from Gregg.

When the contest against the Giants was completed, the frustrated Thomas spotted the New York head coach, Bill Parcells, walking across the field toward the visitor's locker room: "I knew they had problems with kickers, and I yelled to Parcells, 'Get me out of here!'" On Monday, Thomas sat down with his position coach and vented his grievances. "I said to Hilton, 'Why don't you just have them release me? They're not even letting me kick in practice.'" The request was granted, as Thomas was waived by the Packers that afternoon. When questioned by reporters about the departure, Hilton's vague response sounded a lot like Ditka's explanation of the Thomas-Butler saga from a year earlier. "Bob has a little bit stronger leg, but not by a big distance. Overall, Al was better or even. I wouldn't want to let Al go now. He's at the point where he's going to become a pretty doggone good kicker."[5]

For the fifth time in his career, Bob gathered his belongings from the locker room once again and set off for destinations unknown, still wishing to ply his trade for a team in need. With resilience being a prime requisite for the itinerant life of a kicker, he knew he had to be ready for the next opportunity. "If I didn't feel Bob Thomas is the best kicker he has ever been, I'd probably hang it up," Bob said to Gould. "But I really enjoy it. And mentally, I know I'm better, because you get better mentally in this position with experience. And that's coinciding with being better physically."[6]

> Consider it pure joy, my brothers, whenever you face trials of many kinds, because you know that the testing of your faith develops perseverance.
>
> *(James 1:2–3, NIV)*

Bob's plea to Parcells across the County Stadium grass had not fallen on deaf ears. Impressed by what he had shown them in the exhibition game forty-eight hours earlier, the Giants claimed Thomas on waivers on Tuesday, before he had even left Green Bay. A fairer opportunity appeared to exist for Thomas in New York than in Green Bay; as in San Diego, he was now being called upon to possibly replace an injured player.

Bob landed at the Giants' training camp facilities at Pace University–Pleasantville a day later, throwing his gear into his sixth NFL locker, which twenty-four hours earlier had been occupied by wide receiver Phil McConkey. Thomas had essentially traded places with McConkey, as the receiver had been sent to the Packers on Monday (in a further irony, McConkey had also caught a touchdown pass in the game against Green Bay—but would return to the Giants in a matter of weeks). The Giants had been hoping that their fourth-year kicker, Ali Haji-Sheikh, would reclaim the form he displayed as a rookie in 1983 when he made thirty-five field goals, the most ever in an NFL season to that time. The former Michigan star had stumbled in 1984, making just over half his field goals before going two-for-five in 1985 while missing fourteen regular season games (as well as the Giants' playoff loss to the Bears) with a pulled hamstring. Now, nearing the end of August 1986, Haji-Sheikh had kicked only once in the preseason, as he suffered a new injury to his groin in the August 16 game against Thomas and the Packers.

From the moment Bob took to the practice field, his momentum from the past two years continued as he was still kicking as well as ever. "When the Giants brought me in for the tryouts, I didn't miss one kick, not even in warmups," he said. Watching him do so was Tim Rooney, the Giants' director of pro personnel. Back in 1982, Rooney had been the director of player personnel for the Lions—where he watched Thomas excel during his brief time in Detroit. In watching kick after kick sail through the uprights at Pleasantville, Rooney turned to the people next to him on the sidelines and exclaimed, "I've never seen this kid miss!"

While Bob was glad to have another opportunity, Maggie was not getting the best vibe about the situation. Having to quickly look for another place to live in yet another new part of the country, the couple searched for rental possibilities in the area surrounding Giants Stadium in East Rutherford. They discovered a house in Franklin Lakes, New Jersey, that seemed to meet their needs, and they signed a lease. But on entering the house, Maggie told her husband that she had a bad feeling about it. "We walked around to the back of the house and noticed a ladder going up to a second-floor window," Bob described. "Shortly thereafter, the owner asked if it was OK if her adult children could still come over from time to time and play 'Dungeons and Dragons' in the basement. I said, 'No, that is not OK.'"

Living conditions notwithstanding, Bob was the kicker in New York's season opener on September 8 in Dallas in a Monday night game against the Cowboys, as the Giants looked to topple the Bears in the NFC in 1986. Thomas joined the Giants at the team's final full workout on Friday, September 5, in advance of heading to Texas. Just before the field goal unit was called out to the turf by Parcells, Bob took a few warmup swings with his leg over on the sidelines—as he had done on thousands of occasions. Going through his stance, steps, and kicking motion one last time, his foot suddenly scraped a raised chunk of earth. "There was some uneven ground on the Giants' practice field. I hit a clump of dirt as my leg went through—and I blew up my ankle."

Collapsing in misery, Thomas had to be helped from the field and into the training room. The injury seemed to be worsening by the minute, as the foot and ankle continued to balloon larger. "They gave me an automatic boot to wear," Bob recalled, "which was supposed to put pressure on the bursa sac and get the swelling down." Not wanting to surrender what might be his final opportunity in the NFL, Thomas spent the next thirty-six hours trying to forget about the immense pain as the team physician prescribed round after round of painkillers.

On hearing of the injury, Augie drove down from Rochester. He took his son to a nearby sporting goods store where he purchased a pair of high-top basketball shoes to support the ankle as Bob tried to remain ambulatory. "I had some ankle injuries playing soccer as a kid, but nothing like this. I think my dad was trying to be hopeful that I could come back, but I knew it was bad."

Hobbling into his seat on the team flight, Bob accompanied the Giants to Dallas and took the field in Texas Stadium. There, he got ready to begin his twelfth season under the Monday night lights and in front of a national television audience. With his kicking foot heavily bandaged, Thomas willed himself through the agony alongside his new teammates in a game that became a back-and-forth struggle. The Cowboys finally seized control late in the fourth quarter after USFL refugee Herschel Walker, making his NFL debut, darted into the end zone from ten yards out to make the final score 31–28 in favor of Dallas. Over the course of the evening, Thomas gritted out all four of his extra points but pushed a thirty-six-yard field goal attempt wide of the goalposts in the second quarter. "When I hit the ball that night, I just saw stars. The pain was so bad that I couldn't even follow through with my kicks, and I left the field goal off to the right."

Convinced the ankle was not going to improve anytime soon, he saw the club physician on returning to New York, with the team scheduled to play Benirschke and the Chargers in Giants Stadium the following Sunday. "I asked the doctor how long it was going to take to heal—and I could tell by the look on his face that it was going to be a while." Soon after, Bob met with Parcells once again—who told Thomas he was displeased that Bob had asked the doctor how long the injury would take to heal, presuming the kicker to be contriving a contractual strategy. "What are you—some kind of clubhouse lawyer?" the coach snipped at him. Parcells then informed Thomas that he was being put on waivers. "I knew the ankle was severely damaged," Bob said, "but I was angrier with Parcells' reaction than I was about being released."

Before leaving town, Thomas had one more discussion with the organization. The New York newspapers reported it was the first time the Giants had ever placed anyone on waivers who was injured; therefore, they were required to provide him with an injury settlement. The Giants offered Thomas a half-year's salary plus a half of a playoff share if the team made the postseason. After listening to the proposal, Thomas got up from the table and went into another room. From there, he phoned the NFL Players Association to see what they thought of the proposal. A union representative provided advice on the other end of the line.

"Hey, that's a great deal," the representative said. "They don't even have to give you a playoff share—so take it." Bob then returned to the room where the negotiation had taken place. "OK, I'll take it . . ." he started to tell them. But even before he had finished that brief sentence, a Giants' staffer raised his hand and interrupted. "We don't have to give you a playoff share," he interjected, "so you're not going to get that." Thomas sank back into his chair, startled by the abrupt shift in terms. "Either it was very coincidental," he said years later, "or they had overhead what I was talking about with the union."

Performing his last act as an NFL player, Bob walked out of the room, out of the Giants' building, and out of the league forever. "I knew then I would be going back to my legal career at the Callahan firm full-time."

In November, Thomas's name surfaced as a possible replacement in Cleveland for the Browns' Matt Bahr, who had torn ligaments in his knee while attempting to make a tackle on a kickoff. But with a further diagnosis of Bob's injury revealing his own torn ligaments in the ankle and facing a minimum of a yearlong recovery, he had no plans to return to football and made his peace with the game.

Nonetheless, as he watched other kickers go through the 1986 NFL playoffs, he found himself stranded in the most painful of ironies as the Super Bowl matchup was set for January 25, 1987, at the Rose Bowl in southern California. The Bears and Giants had matched each other with 14–2 records in the regular season, but it ultimately proved to be New York's year. In Chicago, injuries to key personnel finally caught up with the Bears as their season ended in the first round of the playoffs. The Giants, while not the dominators the 1985 Bears were, claimed football's title with a 39–20 victory over the Broncos in Pasadena. Thus, for the second straight year, a team that had cut Thomas early in the season marched on to a world championship, tantalizing him with a Super Bowl ring that was not meant to be. There would not be another chance. There would be no such jewelry in the Thomas home.

As he was sitting in the Newark Airport awaiting his flight back home to Chicago, Bob struck up a conversation with a man from the north suburbs named Steve Lesnik. Lesnik was the cofounder and chairman of Kemper Sports Management in Northbrook, and by the time the flight attendant had announced the first boarding call for their planes, Lesnik was already interested in having Thomas leave Callahan's firm and become Kemper's in-house counsel and a sports agent. Lesnik and Thomas hammered out the details of the agreement in a later phone call. "It was a corporate type of setting at that firm," Thomas said. "I really didn't want to go into athlete representation, but that's what they wanted to do, so I did some of that for them."

However, if football was truly going to be in the rearview mirror for him, Bob figured it was time to begin making plans to pursue his ultimate passion within the law. Thomas's goal had been confirmed during his days with Callahan, in a discussion the two men had: "I talked to Jack about how, to be fair, I could see the other side's point of view in a case. In a pleasant way, he said, 'We aren't about *fairness* here; you have to look at it *our* way, and our way *only*.' But I wanted to look at it both ways. I wanted to be able to examine a case on its merits and make a decision based on what was right. Jack was right—you can't necessarily do that as an attorney, because it's an adversarial system. The only time you look at the other side is when you're trying to head off something that will hurt your client. But on the bench, you look at what is fair and just. That's what a judge does, and that's why I wanted to become one."[7]

Even Callahan himself did not discourage the idea. "You *should* be a judge," he had once told Thomas. Or, as the former kicker added with a laugh, "I wanted a job where people wouldn't boo in front of me anymore."

The idea of him pursuing a seat on the judiciary made perfect sense to his former teammates. "Bob was very astute about the game, and very intelligent in how he approached it," said Robin Earl. "That is how he has approached his law career as well. None of us was surprised when he decided he wanted to be a judge. We all figured he'd be good at that, too. He's good at everything he tries."[8]

Toward this objective, Thomas left Kemper after a six-month stint and became a partner in the Wheaton firm of Guerard and Drenk, a position that provided him with more litigation experience. As at Kemper, his new employer also wished to make use of Bob's connections in sports, sending him (along with another attorney) to a special seminar in Washington, D.C., on athlete representation to steer him into that line of work. After representing the Bears' Keith Ortego and a few others, Thomas found that such pursuits still did not interest him. "When I first went in, I told them, 'I am going to be honest with you. I want to be a judge.'"

After ten days on the job, Bob took a planned vacation to Rochester when he got a call from his new office. "Over the phone I was told that the firm was splitting up, and I was asked which partner I wanted to go with. That was a big surprise, having just gotten the position. I wound up going with Richard Guerard." And shortly after Bob started with Guerard, an associate judgeship opened up in early 1987.

Appointed by sitting circuit court judges, Illinois associate judges typically handle high-volume dockets such as traffic offenses, misdemeanors, divorce, and other such cases. Thomas was among twenty-three attorneys who applied for the opening but was not selected: "Nobody really knew me at the time. The DuPage County Bar Association recommended me, but somebody else got it." He resumed his work as a civil trial lawyer for Guerard, keeping his eye out for other possibilities on the bench.

After leaving the courthouse one afternoon in May 1987, Bob took time out to drive up to Lake Forest and drop in at the Bears' mini-camp. Wandering along the sidelines, he caught sight of Butler on the other side of the field, twirling a football on his fingers. Thomas next ran into a familiar face in Skip Myslenski from the *Tribune*, as he admitted that the memories from Halas Hall—both sweet and bitter—were swirling back as he heard the cracking of the shoulder pads. "It's funny; it's like I never left," he told the writer. "It helps that I've been to other places, even in packing up the family and going to San Diego and then getting hurt in New York last year. But this is the one place where nostalgia has set in."[9]

Despite not getting the assignment to the associate bench, it was possible Thomas could bypass that level altogether and land a circuit judgeship through the electoral process. While working for Guerard throughout the rest of 1987, Bob laid the groundwork. "I went around and talked to the various circuit judges. One of them, John Bowman, said, 'You seem like a good guy, and I think you would make a good judge. There's a number of people ahead of you that I'm committed to supporting as far as an assignment to an associate position is concerned. But with your background and name recognition, why don't you run for a circuit spot? You might win—and if you don't win, people will take you seriously.' It wasn't too long after that that there was a circuit vacancy."

In 1988, Helen Kinney—the first woman ever elected as the circuit judge of DuPage County—retired from the bench, having served in the role for twelve years. Thomas acted on Bowman's advice and sought the Republican nomination for the position, with the primary to be held in March and the general election scheduled for November. Despite his enthusiasm, he was essentially going after it on his own: "I hadn't been involved with the party, and I had no affiliations with anyone. I knew one precinct committeeman—the precinct where I lived—and that was it. I had no political support."

Moreover, Thomas was competing in the primary against two individuals who were already associate judges and who also seemed to possess friends in high places. "When I and the two associates stumped at local appearances in the campaign, I usually introduced myself last—I guess we went in alphabetical order. When the first associate got up to speak, he was able to claim, 'I was appointed by the Illinois Supreme Court.' The second associate then boasted, 'I was recommended by a blue-ribbon committee, and the committee recommended me *over* the previous gentleman who was appointed by the Supreme Court.'"

When it was his turn at the microphone, Thomas began with a shrug of his shoulders. Unable to drop names or claim any such backing, instead he appealed directly to the citizenry. "I'm confused," he told the gathering. "All I know is that the next circuit judge of DuPage County is going to be elected by the people, not the party. So, the confusion should end after the election."

To power his campaign, Thomas put together a group of friends, lawyers, and their spouses who embraced the project as an exciting adventure with the slogan, "A New Kind of Upright," to showcase his commitment to an ethical campaign and judgeship. "It was a lot of fun. I assembled some people who maybe did not have extensive political connections, but they believed in me—and I don't know if we knew what we were doing, but we prayerfully went into it. We prayed before every meeting and asked God to bless our efforts."

As he and his committee disseminated his message to the voters, one of the other candidates ultimately approached Bob and invited him to lunch. The other candidate proposed something to Thomas: "During the meal, he told me that if I withdrew from the race, he would make sure that, down the line, I would become an associate judge."

No deal.

"I don't know why I would do that," Thomas told the opponent, "because I'm going to win."

"Well, you had *better* win," the other candidate said. "Because if you don't, you'll *never* be a judge.'" Undaunted by the warning, Thomas was only ignited with a further drive to succeed—a drive that was proving necessary in the absence of political clout. He was, in effect, a rookie in a new league all over again. But amid Bob's diligent efforts, one engagement had slipped his mind. When he came into his office on a Monday morning, he was greeted by his secretary, Stephanie. "How was the Lilac Day Parade?" she wanted to know.

"*What* Lilac Day Parade?"

Stephanie issued a shivering reminder after the fact. "You were supposed to be the grand marshal in the Lilac Day Parade yesterday!"

Thomas's jaw dropped. Running to his desk and quickly shuffling through his chock-full calendar, he realized he had overlooked the function, which was an important yearly Republican organizing event. "I still get freaked out about it, even thinking about it now," he admitted later in life.

Bob immediately got on the telephone to the man who had oversaw the parade, attempting to make amends. The reception he received was the one he expected: "If that phone could have possibly turned into a chunk of ice, that's how cold the guy was on the other end." Thomas expressed his most humble regrets, as well as an offer of restitution. "Is there anything I could possibly do?" he asked. The man relented a bit, grumbling that his organization would soon be having a steak-fry social and that perhaps Bob could come speak to the members at that time. Thomas graciously accepted, giving his assurance to be there for the makeup date.

When he was finished with his remarks to the group, the organizer pulled him aside for a private word. "We were going to do everything in our power to see that you didn't get elected," the man revealed about the members' subsided anger, "but after having met you, we can see where this mix-up could happen. We're happy to go out and work for you." Thomas drew a deep sigh of relief. At the end of the dinner, the leader called Bob back up to the podium one more time, and presented him with a humorous token of "appreciation" to show that all was forgiven—a cowboy hat with an inscription that read, "1988 Lilac Day Parade Grand Marshal."

When primary day finally arrived in March, Thomas was certain there would be no more surprises. It was now just a matter of waiting to hear the results and seeing how far his work, the work of his committee, and the relatively scanty $50,000 in campaign funds they had raised could take them. But at the eleventh hour, Bob uncovered a bombshell: "I was sitting in the courthouse cafeteria on election day. Somebody walked up to me and showed me an oversized postcard produced by one of my opponents. It was a negative campaign piece." While it was too late to do anything about the postcards and their effect on the voters, Thomas decided he could at least find out where the postcards had been delivered. "Since I lived in the Naperville area, I figured that's where they had been sent, and indeed they were—ten thousand of them, I discovered."

Disturbed by the development, Bob struggled to put it out of his mind as he watched the election returns, hoping that the gamesmanship by the other candidate would not alter the outcome. "I was fine up until tonight, because I could always do something," Bob said of his nerves. "I could always go to another speech or go to another train station, but after the polls closed at 7:00 p.m., I couldn't do anything else."[10]

A total of 82,000 ballots were cast. At the final count, by a mere 271 votes, Thomas was victorious in the nomination for the Republican Party's ticket come November. Shortly thereafter, he received a congratulatory phone call from a supporter—after which Bob was convinced that his faith in God had, yet again, been rewarded.

"We knew you were going to win," the supporter boasted in an easy tone.

"How did you know?" Thomas wondered.

"I was working for Bob Dole," the supporter explained, "and at our headquarters, we not only knew how many precincts were outstanding, but we also knew where the votes were coming in from—and at the very end, we knew the votes were coming in from Naperville Township. And at the very last minute, we flooded Naperville with 10,000 postcards for Dole, and we also put in a piece for you with each one."

It was the *exact same number* of postcards Thomas's opponent had sent out.

Like his triumphs in securing spots on football rosters and kicking game-winning field goals, victory for Thomas and his supporters came through a combination of skill, hard work, perseverance, and trust in Providence—which became evident to others as he prepared for the general election in the fall. "I remember going to an event in 1988 with Jim Ryan, who was running for reelection as DuPage County State's Attorney. He came to my office to meet with me after I became the party's nominee. He saw the committee I had assembled—which, again, was very loyal but didn't have much political experience. Ryan said, 'Let me get this straight—*this* is your committee? No politicians, no political experience, you spent only the fifty thousand that you raised—and you won that race?!?' He was flabbergasted."

On November 8, 1988, as GOP nominee George H.W. Bush was winning the U.S. presidential election in a landslide over Massachusetts governor

Michael Dukakis, the young lawyer and former NFL kicker was simultaneously soundly beating his own opponent. Without the endorsement of a single newspaper and lining up against Downers Grove attorney Gregory Freerksen, Robert R. Thomas harvested more than 70 percent of the vote with 204,811 tallied and was elected judge of the 18th Judicial Circuit Court of DuPage County. "Our campaign exhibited the fact that you don't have to talk about your opponent to win," Bob told the *Tribune* in an acceptance statement shortly after Freerksen conceded at 10:30 p.m. local time. "We're very happy."[11] While occasionally attempting to play on his opponent's athletic notoriety as a negative talking point during his candidacy, Freerksen was gracious in defeat. "I congratulate Mr. Thomas. He's a very personable individual with a quick wit, and I wish him the best as a circuit court judge."[12] Staying loyal to DuPage County, Freerksen returned to his local private practice and started hosting a blues music show on the College of DuPage radio station—a role in which he served for twenty years until his death in January 2017.

By December, Thomas cleared out his office at the Guerard firm and was ready to begin his position at the DuPage County Courthouse. Chief Judge Carl Henninger assigned Thomas to the Law Division, where his duties would mainly consist of presiding over civil jury trials. "First, we will have a vacancy there," Henninger explained of his decision to place Thomas in that slot. "And second, I want to make a practice of assigning judges to areas where they have the most experience, and where they will feel the most comfortable."[13]

While the adjustment from attorney to judge can be a seismic one, Thomas took the first few steps in stride—but he also knew he would need to gather wisdom from others' experience. "I had a lot to learn. I was willing to learn, and I wanted to talk to judges who had been there a long time. The presiding judge in the Law Division, Bill Black, was a good man, and I considered him one of my first mentors. He was more than willing to share his expertise, and if ever had questions, I would go in and talk to him."

Thomas was also aware that, in a certain sense, he would have to build his legal reputation all over again, and in a different context. "I knew I was going to be looked at as not having been an attorney very long," he recalled about his first time on the bench, "even though I had applied for the associate judgeship before I ran for the circuit court and had received a 'Recommended' rating from the Bar Association. I also knew that I had run against two popular associate judges, and that I would have to do a good job." The early returns were positive, as Thomas received strong review grades after handling his initial cases. "I don't think it took long to get the respect of the attorneys presenting in front of me."

The respect of his superiors came quickly as well. Within a few months, Chief Judge Anthony Peccarelli asked Thomas to serve as acting chief judge of the Circuit Court (making Thomas able to sit in the position if Peccarelli was unavailable for certain cases), as Peccarelli had taken over for Henninger in 1989 and would serve as the chief judge until 1993.

With the strain of the campaign behind him, Thomas took a step back in the summer of 1989 and enjoyed some recreation time—which included returning to South Bend for his fifteen-year reunion with other Notre Dame grads. While there, he took part in the alumni soccer game. "I got in shape and worked out," an incentivized Thomas recalled about his preparation for the event. "I've played in front of eighty thousand people as a Chicago Bear, and now we've got a handful of wives in the stands watching a bunch of old guys play soccer." Bob stood out among those on the pitch, scoring three goals in a 4–1 victory for his side—although the attention level among the sparse crowd was not what the players had been hoping for. "So, I'm feeling great," Bob said about the moment when the final whistle blew. "I walk off the field and Maggie says to me, 'Good game. Didn't you score a goal out there?'"[14]

Five-year-old Jonathan had made the trip as well—a journey that launched a yearly tradition he would share with his father into adulthood. "When I was six, my dad took us down to the Notre Dame Blue-Gold [spring football] Game, and then I started going to Notre Dame games with him for the past twenty-five years or so," Jonathan said. "That's something we do every fall. And every time, I drag him around campus and have him tell me old war stories. A few of his college buddies have been there for our most recent trips, and it's something that's really special for us."[15]

After being elected, Thomas heard more than a hundred jury trials as a circuit court judge over the next six years. In doing so, he finally understood what the quest for fairness and justice in the courtroom really meant. "Two attorneys approach the bench on a motion, and one of them is going to walk away unhappy," he reflected in 1993, five years into the new role. "That's the nature of my job, and you can't worry about it or else you'll never make a decision. It's like kicking. You've got a job to do. You try to do it to the best of your ability, you try to do what's right, and then you move forward. If a kicker was so concerned about what people thought, he would go out and miss the kick every time."[16]

He also returned to McQuaid that March, where he was recognized by his high school in receiving the Father Richard Noonan Distinguished Alumnus Award. Soon to follow were inductions into the Academic All-America Hall of Fame by the College Sports Information Directors of America and the NCAA Silver Anniversary Award, presented to distinguished student-athletes twenty-five years after their graduation.

Then, in early 1994, a new opportunity presented itself. An election would be held that November to fill a vacancy on the Appellate Court of the Second District of Illinois, housed in Elgin. The appellate court had nine members, some chosen by voters and others appointed by the state supreme court. An assigned appellate court judge does not have to run in an election; yet, despite this courtesy, one of the sitting judges decided to throw his hat into the ring and run. Thomas nonetheless won the primary by an even wider margin than he had in the 1988 election. "It was very different from the circuit court race," he recalled. "I think I got 85 percent of the vote." Even more impressively, the victory had once again occurred without Thomas having the local Republican endorsement. Instead of seeking the approval of one group or another, he decided to stay true to his principles. "Every time I would run, I would go to the DuPage County Republican Chairman [and president of the Illinois Senate] James 'Pate' Phillip, and ask, 'Could I have your support?' And I never got it, because according to him, I never 'carried enough water to the elephant.' I wasn't a precinct committeeman, and I wasn't really involved with Republican Party politics.

"Well, before the appellate primary, Pate writes a letter to the township chairman of DuPage County, saying that he's throwing his support behind the other candidate—who wasn't even from the county."

In the wake of Thomas's resounding victory in the primary, however, Phillip's office decided to reach out to him. "As the general election approached, the Republican Party put out its usual 'book' for the voters, which contained brief biographies of all the candidates—[Governor] Jim Edgar was in there, Phillip was in there, and others." The party requested that candidates "donate" $5,000 to be included in the publication. During the summer of 1994, another party official called Thomas. "I see where you haven't sent in your $5,000 to get your name in the book," the caller prompted in a friendly tone.

"Well, I'll talk to my committee and think it over," Bob responded.

A few more weeks passed, and Bob had forgotten about the phone call. Pate Phillip then personally followed up with one of his own.

"Bob, I see that your committee hasn't put up the $5,000 to get your name in the book."

"Yeah, Pate, that's right."

"I don't think you understand the book," Phillip countered.

"Well, why don't you explain it to me."

"The book has *staples*."

"Staples?" Bob asked, perplexed.

"Yes. You see, there are pages on all the candidates in the book. The precinct committeemen aren't going to take time to tear your page out of the book."

There was silence for a moment. Phillip then tried to reinforce his point. "You are *in* the book."

"Oh—*because they're all stapled together*," Bob said with a chuckle, feigning an enlightened attitude.

"Yes—now you get it!" Phillip answered with hopeful excitement. "So, you'll pay the $5,000?"

"No, I won't," Bob informed him, "staples or no staples." Thomas, believing Phillip simply wanted his name recognition from his NFL days, had one more parting thought: "You know what, Pate? I think it was unprecedented that you sent out a letter to the DuPage County township chairman that supported my opponent—who was from *another* county. I figured that that little maneuver cost me more than $5,000. If you want me in the book, you pay the money and have me in the book. If you don't want me in the book, don't put me in the book. But I'm not paying the $5,000."

"You football player!' Phillip hollered as he slammed down the phone and hung up.

Thomas had remained true to himself and his constituency. "He was not willing to make any deals," remembered Bob's friend Dr. Charlie Ireland as Thomas was in the midst of the appellate campaign. "His allegiance was to the people of Illinois, and his integrity proved it."[17]

Even without political support, the Notre Damer marched on to victory yet again. Running unopposed in the general election, Thomas received more than 517,000 votes as he took his seat in December 1994 on the bench of the Second District Appellate Court. In doing so, Bob would be reunited with Bowman, the man who had first suggested he run for circuit judge back in 1988.

Over the next six years, Thomas heard nearly 2,500 cases at the appellate level—appeals spanning the entire legal gamut, ranging from traffic tickets all the way to felonies in which life sentences hung in the balance. It was another exciting new chapter in his second career, a fresh challenge to be tackled that also reinvigorated his love for the law. Yet, while rising quickly through the judiciary, Thomas held steadfast to a moral premise he maintained from his first day in circuit court   that every legal decision handed down, from the most innocuous to the most complex, can have a drastic impact on any number of people. He made it a point to balance firmness for procedure in the courtroom with a compassion for the litigants involved. "There are faces behind the cases," he made a point to say, "and these cases mean everything to those people."

His former coworkers continued to be impressed but not surprised. "He handled the pressure of a forty-eight-yard field goal on a windy day," said his former Bears teammate Skibinski, "so I knew he could handle a court case that is much more important for somebody's life."[18]

Nor did Thomas lose sight of his personal priorities. While rising in the legal field he simultaneously returned to his sports roots, sharing with his own children the athletic foundation that Augie had provided Bob. By the time of his election to the appellate court, Bob had already coached Brendan, Jonathan, and Jessica in soccer for several seasons. In blazing a trail for his two younger siblings, the sport was initially (and admittedly) force-fed on Brendan, while Jonathan would play in high school and Jessica through her college years—a battle Brendan recalled with a laugh.

> With my personality, it's been an interesting combination with my dad. I basically have no interest in sports, and I'm not very emotional, so that's in stark contrast to him—as he obviously has a strong interest in sports and comes from a very emotional Italian background.
>
> He had me playing park district soccer for several years, up until the age of eight or so. During my games, I'd usually be in the back on defense. Anytime there would be any action in the front of the field, I would just sit down and relax. So, I really wasn't much into playing—and I remember him getting kind of frustrated that I wasn't more interested in it.
>
> When I was in the second grade, I remember telling him, "I really want to quit soccer"—and he didn't take it well. I remember having a little fight

with him about it in the garage. It was time to go to practice, and I didn't want to put the cleats on, and we're getting into it. Finally, my mom comes out and says, 'Bob, you should just let him quit!' So, he finally gave up on me playing soccer.

Even so, his father instead strove to learn and appreciate things that were important to Brendan. "As I continued in school, I took a strong interest in math and science. It wasn't necessarily my dad's strong suit, but he saw it was an interest of mine, and he encouraged me to excel in those areas." The efforts paid off. In 1995, Brendan's eighth-grade science project won first place in the regional fair. The achievement allowed him to proceed on a trip to the University of Illinois for the state competition—a crusade on which Bob gladly accompanied him, as Brendan remembered.

> When we got to U. of I., we discovered that the state committee had been looking for more judges for the science fair, so my dad volunteered, and they enrolled him.
>
> I ended up getting third place. My judges were really tough—they were laying into me with some hard questions. My dad was on the opposite side of the building, so he wasn't judging my project. I met up with him afterwards and told him what had happened. He thought my judges had been unfair to me. I asked him, 'How about the projects you saw?' He said, 'Oh, everyone did a great job. I gave everybody first place.'
>
> He had a great time that day. He's a generous guy, he's very friendly, and he was just happy to be down there, spending time with me. But whoever had him as a judge that day was having a great day, too—that's for sure.[19]

At other times, however, Bob proved that his competitive juices were still flowing—on behalf of his kids, anyway. One day in the spring of 1993, he and Maggie attended Jonathan's third-grade field day at his school, in which the students enjoyed a wide range of friendly games. Jonathan was anointed by his class as its representative in a "mud-eating" contest in which each blind-folded contestant, armed only with a small spoon, attempted to be the quickest to down a cupful of ice cream, crushed Oreo cookies, and gummy worms.

While the teachers were getting the gladiators ready, Bob snuck up behind Jonathan for a little last-minute coaching. "Try to get one of the spots on the end," he offered, "where you won't get bumped so much by the other kids." Immediately, the embarrassed judge felt as if he were in contempt of court.

"I think maybe I'm taking this a little too seriously," he confessed to Maggie back on the sidelines. "I can't believe I did that."

With Brendan getting ready to start high school, Jonathan and Jessica were displaying a greater interest in athletics as they neared middle school. With the idea of perhaps coaching one or both in the future, Bob leapt back into soccer and became the head coach at Wheaton Academy, a nondenominational Christian high school of just over 350 students in the nearby town of West Chicago. Beaming with pride when hearing the news was Bob's own coach back in Rochester, as Augie was still following the sport and still tutoring football kickers at the age of seventy-five.

The opportunity resulted from a random conversation Thomas struck up with school administrators: "I had been talking to them about perhaps just helping out with the soccer program. But when I had spoken to them, they had just released their soccer coach—so they asked if I would step in and take over as head coach." Thomas accepted, although he wondered what he had gotten himself into. "I wanted my kids to play soccer rather than football, so I became involved locally," Bob told the Chicago suburban paper, the *Daily Herald*, upon landing the job. "It was very encouraging to be asked to coach at Wheaton Academy."[20]

Designing creative and challenging practice sessions for his players, Thomas even jumped into his grueling thirty-minute, three-on-three scrimmages when an extra player was needed. While practice was an enjoyable release for Bob after a long day in court, the student-athletes appreciated his time with them even more. "We respect him for being on the Bears, but we just look to him as a coach and a leader," senior midfielder Aaron Lunt said. "We understand he has experience on the professional level and he knows what it takes to win."[21]

The results were immediate. After the Wheaton Academy Warriors hovered around the .500 mark the previous season in 1994, Thomas posted an 11–6 record in his first year, including a 6–0 conference record in the Private School League (PSL), giving his players confidence they could compete against larger institutions. "This team would get on the field against bigger schools and feel they wouldn't have a chance," Bob said to a *Tribune* reporter who came out to watch a late-season practice in 1995. "I had to change the pattern. I had to make them believe that they could win against big schools, some of which we've done this season. Hopefully one of my strengths is motivation. I've been around enough motivators like Ara Parseghian and Mike

Ditka."[22] Thomas indeed succeeded in making the players believe in themselves. "He instilled a sense of confidence in us that we could compete against bigger schools," recalled the Reverend Patrick King, the Warriors' all-state goaltender and four-year starter at the time and currently a church pastor in San Diego. "We had a graduating class of about a hundred people, and we would go play against some of the biggest public high schools in our area—some schools with five thousand students—and beat them."[23] After claiming the PSL postseason tournament, the Warriors advanced to the sectionals of the state playoffs before a 3–0 loss to West Chicago High School. The following season, the team performed even better with a sparkling record of 16–4.

The Warriors' biggest fan was a retired professional soccer player from out east. "We sometimes live vicariously through our children—I don't think that stops when we're older. So here I am coaching, and that was one of my dad's desires. If I'm emotional, he was super-emotional. He wasn't particularly thrilled with the referees in one particular game I was coaching. He was so animated that the ref came over to the sidelines—remember, my dad was about seventy-five at the time—and said, 'Hey, are you one of the subs here?' He had to go and stand the other side of the field. When we played for the conference championship game, my dad was again in the stands. You would have thought we won the Super Bowl. And he was equally excited when my kids played as well."

After the soccer season, Bob also found time for golf; teaching a trial practice course at Loyola's law school; and, most important, spending more time with Maggie after leaving the courthouse each day. He also kept in touch with Baschnagel, Fencik, Schmidt, and other former teammates. But in early 1999, Bob and the rest of the Bears family would be struck with stunning, saddening news.

On February 1, it was made public that Walter Payton—one of the finest physical specimens ever to be seen anywhere in professional sports—had been diagnosed with a rare liver disease known as sclerosing cholangitis, a sickness that struck only three people in every hundred thousand. After comforting Thomas in the most difficult moments of Bob's career, Payton would now reach back out to Thomas, other friends, and God for the strength to accept the handoff in the toughest run of Payton's life.

Chapter 12

Justice Tempered with Civility

Thomas would bring the best mix of legal ability and
political independence to the high court.

—*Chicago Tribune*, March 5, 2000

The last time Thomas saw Payton was in fall 1998, as the two watched Payton's son Jarrett play soccer for St. Viator High School in a game against St. Charles. Bob recalled his former teammate showing a slight loss of weight at the time, but the full effects of the disease were not yet noticeable. Payton's system would be mercilessly ravaged over the next year. On November 1, 1999, Walter Payton passed away at his home in South Barrington, Illinois— nine months to the day after he went public with his condition.

Mourners prayed for him, and countless church services were offered in his memory. But since the latter part of his career with the Bears through his retirement after the 1987 season, Payton appeared to have been "on the outskirts of faith issues," according to Thomas. "I used to go to Bible studies with Mike Singletary and some other players. Walter was always, literally, on the outside looking in. When we would come out of a study session, he would ask us what we talked about, and he seemed interested."

A few months later, Thomas caught up with Singletary. "I said, 'Mike, did you share the Gospel with Walter?' He said, 'Yes, I did—and Walter accepted it. He trusted in Jesus alone for his salvation.'" As Singletary gave Thomas the good news, Bob had a flashback to 1985. On the fateful day when Thomas was cut from the Bears, Payton allowed Bob to soak his tears into Walter's chest outside Halas Hall. And now, Bob was comforted in knowing that Walter could rest his own head on the chest of Jesus.

The indestructible man—with physical training habits few could match and observers could not believe—had stunningly withered away and was now in the loving arms of God. As one observer suggested, it was as if the Lord had completely broken Payton down to build him back up for His kingdom. "The whole ordeal was a reminder that even the great Walter Payton was the *created*, not the *Creator*," Thomas continued. "Compared to eternity, this life we have of 70, 80, 90 years—let alone the mere 45 years Walter had—is a blip on the radar screen."

For those who had been in Payton's daily presence for years, such as Thomas, the reminder of one's own humanity was even more stark in consideration of Payton's demise. "When I was flying with the Bears to an away game and we would experience turbulence on the plane, I would look around and make sure Walter was on the flight," Bob said. "Then I'd say to myself, 'God's not going to bring this plane down—we've got Payton on board.' But we're all destined to that reality one day. And when someone bigger than life succumbs to death, it's a wake-up call for all of us. In the end, we have to ask ourselves: What do we have to trust in? *Whom* do we have to trust in?"

After a private funeral for family members, a public memorial service for Payton was held at Soldier Field on November 6. Bob had to miss the ceremony, as the Wheaton Academy soccer team was in southern Illinois playing in the "Elite Eight" of the Class A state tournament. In readying the Warriors with his pregame speech, Thomas described the greatness, the will, and the drive of his departed friend. "While I wanted to honor Walter, I knew in my heart that I had to be there with my team, and I could hear Walter saying to me, 'You really have to be there with your players—you owe it to them.'" In the school's first state quarterfinal appearance since 1980—when it was then known as Wheaton Christian School—Wheaton Academy lost a tough overtime battle to St. Joseph, 2–1, as the goalie King finished his career with 51 shutouts, one shy of the state record.

Payton's death also reminded Thomas that, as a person, he comprised the sum of his interactions—his many encounters with different individuals over the course of his own life. "We are all victims of our experience, I suppose.

I had the wonderful experience of my parents, of Ara Parseghian, of playing ten years with Walter Payton, and learning from so many other people. Those things are all part of my background. But I don't think we realize that these people become such an integral part of our fabric and makeup." For Thomas, Payton's ordeal was another example of all roads ultimately leading back to the oasis of faith. Bob himself had experienced many ups and downs; yet through the vicissitudes of football, law, the loss of friends, the loss of jobs, and the myriad other things the world dumps in one's lap, his reliance on God had been the immovable constant. Specifically for Bob, his and Maggie's trust had manifested itself three separate times in the miracle of adoption and the miracle of childbirth. "God really uses adoption as an example of his love for us," Bob reflected. "When you think about it, we are adopted into His family."

As Brendan, Jonathan, and Jessica grew through their school years in the 1990s, the Thomas clan encountered many challenges typical of the American family, as well as some unique to the circumstances of adoption. The uncertainty that a child can feel in an adoptive household and an adoptive world—regardless of the love that surrounds him or her—can be all-encompassing. "Not all kids respond to being adopted in the same way," as Bob pointed out.

On an occasion when eight-year-old Brendan was in a foul mood one night at home in 1989, Maggie had sent him to his room.

"What's the problem?" she asked after coming upstairs to talk with him. "Who are you angry at?"

"Mom and Dad," Brendan sharply replied.

"Why are you mad at us?"

"Because you adopted me."

In that emotional moment, faith was once again called upon for solace. Maggie understood his confusion but also challenged him to embrace her: "Well, Brendan, do you think we just took you away from your birth mother eight years ago? Because we didn't. We adopted *you*—and now, I think it's time for you to adopt *us*."

She gave him a moment to consider what she had said. "Do you want me to pray with you?" she asked.

Brendan softened a bit. "No, I'll do it," he replied.

From that moment, Brendan's parents noticed a complete change in his approach to their relationship. "He became the most affectionate kid,"

Bob said. "A few years later, when Brendan was in junior high, Maggie would go into his school as a room mother and he'd go right up to her and put his arm around her—at an age when kids are usually embarrassed to do so."

As Brendan was fully turning his heart over to them, four-year-old Jessica was starting to figure things out—and she wanted in on the deal as well. With the family sitting around the dinner table one evening, Jessica posed a question to her parents. "Brendan 'dopted?" she asked between sips of milk.

"Yes," Bob and Maggie responded, "Brendan was adopted."

"Jonathan 'dopted?"

"Yes, Jonathan was adopted."

"I'm 'dopted?"

"No," the mother and father said, "you were not adopted." Jessica suddenly burst into tears. "I wanna be 'dopted!" she cried.

With his loving, growing family to come home to every night, Bob had the inspiration to tackle his next goal. A few weeks after Thomas caught up with Payton on the St. Viator sidelines in the fall of 1998, big news about the state's judiciary came to his attention. On December 11, Illinois Supreme Court Justice John Nickels announced he was retiring from the bench, with plans to return to his family farm outside of St. Charles in Kane County. Nickels stated that his departure would be immediate, thus leaving him two years short of completing his ordinary ten-year term. With the election to fill his position not scheduled to take place until November 2000, an appointment was necessary to fill the vacancy in the interim.

To do so, a majority (four out of seven) of the sitting justices on the Supreme Court, including Nickels, could approve any lawyer or judge from Nickels's region, the thirteen-county Second Appellate District of Illinois. The district included Thomas's home of DuPage County, a county from which no one had ever made it to the bench in Springfield. "There has long been a strong push by Republican County regulars to have an individual from DuPage on the state Supreme Court," Janan Hanna of the *Tribune* noted in the aftermath of Nickels's announcement. "Political insiders say only one name has surfaced for the appointment: Appeals Court Judge S. Louis Rathje, who has a long political history in DuPage and money to spend for a strong campaign in 2000. Bonnie Wheaton, a DuPage Circuit judge with ambition for higher office, would also likely throw her hat in the ring for any vacancies on the appeals court or Supreme Court, sources say."[1]

Thomas wished to be considered as well—and also had an eye on the election two years down the road: "I was up for retention after six years on the appellate court at that time. But regardless of Nickels's decision, I had pretty much made up my mind that I was going to run for it when the election came around. It was a natural progression from the appellate level." As predicted, Rathje was selected to fill the slot—and displayed an intention of running in the Republican primary in March 2000 to keep it. When the appointment was announced, Wheaton began making her plans to oppose him in the primary. And on Monday, September 13, 1999, Bob Thomas announced from the steps of the DuPage County Courthouse that he was entering the race as well.

As Thomas was speaking to the crowd of twenty-five or so that had assembled for the news, a passing pedestrian smiled and raised both arms above his head, signifying a made field goal. "I like that sign!" Bob yelled through the cheers from the throng as the unknown supporter made his way down the street and out of sight.

While Thomas understood that his name recognition could once again work to his advantage, he was quick to disperse attention away from his NFL celebrity when he noticed another backer unfurling a banner in the orange-and-black colors of the local football team. "I am proud of my decade with the Chicago Bears," Bob said to the group. "But this race for the Illinois Supreme Court is about more than life experience. It should be defined in terms of judicial experience and integrity."

With all three primary candidates coming from DuPage and therefore likely "splintering the vote," as the *Tribune* predicted, it was imagined that a fourth individual from outside the county might try to get in the race—a strategy that had served Nickels well in his own victory in 1992.[2]

Now, more than ever before, Bob would be relentlessly hitting the campaign trail nearly every night, requiring the understanding and cooperation of those closest to him. "The actual job of a judge—whether it's circuit, appellate, or supreme—actually gives you *more* time with your family than practicing law," he said years later. "I think that's why a lot of people want to pursue it—to get out of the late hours, to get out of the 'rat-race.' That's why there's no shortfall of attorneys applying for associate judgeships or circuit and associate judges making their intentions known to a Supreme Court justice of having an interest in a circuit or appellate appointment. There's more of a sense of normalcy of being a judge than being an attorney. The hardest part, however, is running for it."

In his most difficult race of all, the support of his loved ones remained strong and unwavering. Each Thomas family member made sacrifices toward the success of the effort—including Bob himself, as he decided to give up his coaching position at Wheaton Academy. Brendan was on his way to college at Cedarville University in Ohio, while Jonathan was beginning high school and Jessica finishing up junior high. "I think they [the kids] understood, and they knew I would still get to their activities if I didn't have a campaign event," Bob said in looking back at the 1999–2000 school year. "Having Maggie organize everything was the best, as she made it all so seamless."

Herself getting more active in sports, Jessica appreciated that her father not only continued to make her a priority on his long list of responsibilities but also continued to make sure that the Thomas household remained a favorite neighborhood place. "My dad was never too busy for me," Jessica recalled fondly. "Despite the fact he is a judge, I don't think he ever missed one of my soccer games. He also has such a great sense of humor and is such a great storyteller. My friends were never intimidated in high school to come over to the house and spend time with my dad."[3]

The road to Springfield would not be an easy one, as Bob had to overcome new challenges presented by new opponents in the Republican primary. Although he might have finally gained a measure of political capital during his time on the bench, Thomas was now facing two competitors who were deeply rooted in the area.

By 1999, Rathje had been an attorney for thirty-six years and had spent the previous twenty-eight years as a partner of a DuPage County firm, while his wife Maria Rosa Costanzo had built her own considerable reputation as a heart surgeon. He had deep roots in DuPage, as his father (Bertram) and grandfather (Sylvanus) had been judges in the county as well.

The other candidate, Wheaton, was an accomplished cellist whose in-laws had even deeper roots in DuPage County than Rathje—and perhaps the deepest of anyone. The ancestors of her deceased husband, Ralph Wheaton, had established their hometown under its surname, and in 1867 convinced the county to move its seat from Naperville. A top-of-her-class graduate from the Northern Illinois University College of Law, Wheaton had first appeared on the bench as an associate judge in 1988 and was now attempting to bypass the appellate level on her way to a seat on the state's highest court.

Bob and his team got to work once again, with new and old friends ready to join the fight. Among the endless campaign events were several fundraising dinners, one of which was sponsored by Doug Buffone. Another occurred out in Boone County near Belvidere, where Thomas took part in a meal attended by some five hundred people and sponsored by the local Republicans. Being as proactive as possible, Bob was certain to get there early and place his biographical "walk card" on every single butter plate. When he was finished doing so, he hustled over to the front door to personally greet the guests when they walked in. As Thomas was shaking hands with everyone, an elderly gentleman paused for a moment when it was his turn. He looked the candidate over with extra curiosity. "Are you Bob Thomas?" the man asked

"Yes, sir, I am."

"Were you elected as the circuit court judge in DuPage County in 1988?"

"Well, yes, sir, I was."

"For the last six years, you've been the appellate court justice for the Second District in Elgin—isn't that right?"

"Yes sir, that's right." ("At this point," Bob recollected, "I noticed two things about this man—one, that he didn't have a walk card in his hand with all this information on it, because he had just entered the building; and two, he wasn't a relative—so I didn't know how he knew all this. I was impressed!") The man continued with yet another question. "Now you want to be the next Supreme Court justice from the Second District, is that right?"

"Yes, sir, that's right," Bob answered confidently. The old man took another step closer, his face now inches away from Bob's. The proximity gave him a revelation.

"You're the guy who missed all those field goals for the Bears!" the man exclaimed.

Thomas laughed. "Well, sir, you must be very happy now—I'm no longer the Bears' kicker."

"Oh, I was happy *then*," the man said. "I'm not a Bears fan."

Hanna, in covering the race for the *Tribune*, noticed that Thomas carried himself with a unique charisma that was distinctive from the other two candidates. "He never misses a note in his rhythmic stump song—never an 'um' or 'like.' He stays on the message, raising his voice and wagging his fingers in the air to drive home a point . . . yet he rejects contentions that he is a natural politician, probably because he is running on the message that he is a political outsider. 'He's the prosecutors' choice,' said one assistant state's attorney who asked not to be identified, citing Thomas's relatively low reversal rate of criminal convictions."[4]

The support for his message kept growing, from everyday people and notable individuals inside and outside the district. In January, a Rockford radio station began airing an advertisement that Singletary had produced. "Be part of the team that scores a victory for Illinois," the former Bears linebacker advised the audience, "in placing Bob Thomas, a conservative Republican judge, on the Illinois Supreme Court."[5]

On February 28, Bob's old boss—the man who had fired him twice—officially entered his corner as well. Mike Ditka hosted his own fundraising dinner for Thomas at the coach's downtown Chicago restaurant, with the *Tribune* reporting that attendees had included "DuPage prosecutors, defense lawyers, high-profile trial lawyers and a huge Notre Dame alumni contingent. . . . According to Ditka, Thomas 'embodies the values of the Republican Party—God, family, and country. He knows the Ten Commandments, knows right from wrong and won't get lost in a lot of legal gobbledygook.'"[6] Many other Chicago sports celebrities were in attendance, such as the recently retired Denis Savard from the Chicago Blackhawks. The luminaries' appearance served as another way in which Thomas could differentiate himself from his opponents. "I have the only fundraiser," he joked when addressing the banquet, "where people come to see the guests."[7]

Nonetheless, the state's GOP VIPs remained slow to embrace Thomas. Jim Ryan, elected twice as Illinois attorney general in 1994 and 1998 after his stint as the DuPage County state's attorney, became yet another high-powered Republican to throw his endorsement behind Rathje in the second week of March. "Justice Rathje is an exceptional student of the law and the Constitution," said Ryan, who had once marveled at Thomas's accomplishments with a limited staff and budget, in a prepared statement. "It would be in the state's best interests to retain his services on the Supreme Court."[8] Rathje also had garnered "the support of Illinois Senate President [Pate] Phillip," Hanna wrote, "which means he has a legion of Republican volunteers at his disposal."[9]

While accumulating a massive war chest, Rathje had mostly lain low during the campaign, appearing to rely on the blessing of old-guard Republican allies such as Ryan and Phillip along with a smattering of nonthreatening advertisements—such as a voter's booklet entitled "Holiday Recipes for a Happy Heart" compiled by his cardiologist wife.

Thomas remained undeterred from the power lineup backing Rathje. Like the opposing kicker hitting a go-ahead field goal at the two-minute warning, Bob knew he would get a shot at the game-winner before the final gun: "We kept at it, kept working very hard, and we kept getting our message out. And, we got some breaks along the way."

Aided by a strong appearance in an interview on WGN Radio, Thomas grabbed the momentum with a clear message for the voters. He insisted the media end its preoccupation with his storied past as a Notre Dame and Bears placekicker; with the press having been quick to discuss his athletic exploits at every campaign stop, Thomas pointed out, there had been little mention of the fact that he was indeed an experienced judge, having written nearly 550 dispositions in the past five years on the appellate court. He underscored his platform as an independent man of the law beholden to no one and his record as a successful attorney before attaining a position on the circuit and appellate bench, thus making him the person best suited for the available seat on the state's high court.

One of the higher-profile cases in which he and Rathje were both involved was that of Eric Robles, an Elgin High School student who was convicted in the 1993 killing of his parents in the town of Bartlett—an act that Robles's attorneys argued he committed to actually *save* his mother, as well as himself, from the abusive hands of his father. "While on the appellate court," Hanna noted, "Rathje wrote the majority opinion overturning the conviction, ruling that the 'guilty but mentally ill' verdict was unconstitutional. Thomas dissented. The Supreme Court later reversed Rathje, upholding the conviction. The Robles case is, in large measure, what swayed many GOP prosecutors in DuPage to support Thomas [in the primary]."[10]

The tide continued to turn. Bob won the endorsement of the *Tribune* on March 5, pronouncing that "Thomas would bring the best mix of legal ability and political independence to the high court . . . Thomas, an excellent public speaker, would be an excellent public representative for the court at a time when the credibility of the court has come into question."[11] A week later, on March 12—in spite of Rathje's picking up the endorsement of the *Sun-Times* on the same day—Thomas had suddenly gone from two points behind Wheaton to thirteen points up, with Rathje trailing even further.

When the day for the primary arrived, and through a stressful night of watching the returns, the numbers from the most recent poll would hold. Thomas won the nomination by twelve points with 42 percent of the vote—a considerable margin in a three-way race (as Wheaton pulled in 30 percent and Rathje 28 percent). "What made the difference, I think, was that I did very well on WGN," Bob concluded, "and I think we used our money more wisely than Bonnie or Louie did." The *Tribune* concurred. "Thomas finished a distant third in spending but first in votes."[12]

Come October, the newspaper would tab Thomas "an easy choice" for its endorsement in the general election to take place a month later against Larry Drury, a class-action attorney from Highland Park in the northern part of the Second District who had run unopposed in the Democratic primary. "His [Thomas's] legal skills and collegiality are sorely needed," the editors wrote. "Thomas has considerable bench experience that his opponent does not."[13] On November 3, he received another endorsement—that of the Political Action Committee of the Illinois Civil Justice League, a group that had supported Rathje in the primary. "Don't We Deserve Better Judges for the Illinois Supreme Court?" read the headline for their advertisement, which touted Thomas as well as First District candidate Thomas Fitzgerald and Third District nominee Carl Hawkinson.

Following tradition in the Republican-laden Second District, the primary proved to be more of a challenge than the general election itself. On Tuesday, November 7, Thomas was overwhelmingly elected to the high court, having received 63 percent of the tallies (more than 630,000 votes). When the news traveled east and reached Rochester, Augie and Anne Thomas could not contain their pride. "He's really a great kid," was Bob's mother's response about his latest achievement. "He's down to earth, and if you could see him at home, you'd never know he was a judge. He has a lot of integrity, he's fair, and he's honest."[14] The Bears commemorated their long-time kicker's victory as well, inviting Thomas to serve as an honorary captain for their game against Tampa Bay on November 19 at Soldier Field along with former teammate Alan Page, himself a Notre Dame grad and a justice on the Supreme Court of Minnesota.

Thomas was settled into his position by the spring of 2003, having learned the ways of Springfield. He was sitting at his desk in his Chicago-area office on May 15 when a reporter from the *Daily Herald* called him: "He told me there was an article in the *Kane County Chronicle* I should see."

Chapter 13

INTEGRITY

I believe he is of the highest moral character.

—ILLINOIS SUPREME COURT JUSTICE CHARLES FREEMAN IN SPEAKING OF
THOMAS, NOVEMBER 1, 2006

After the *Daily Herald* reporter informed him of the contents of the article, Thomas hurried out to the parking lot, got into his car, and drove west from DuPage County. Upon crossing the Kane County line on Route 64, he pulled into the parking lot of a donut shop and picked up a copy of the *Chronicle* from a bin outside the door. On the front page was the story of which the *Daily Herald* writer had spoken.

The article, written by a fifty-eight-year-old part-time columnist named Bill Page, told the story of Mary Elizabeth "Meg" Gorecki, who had been a rising star in the Illinois legal community. Three years earlier, in 2000, at the age of thirty-three, she became the first female state's attorney for Kane County, having upset incumbent David Akemann in the March primary and gone on to triumph in the November general election. In advance of the primary, however, it was revealed Gorecki had left a recorded phone message for a friend back in 1998 in which she suggested political appointments were available in return for campaign contributions to a particular Kane County official.

Despite her victory in both the primary and general election, the Illinois Attorney Registration and Disciplinary Commission (ARDC)—an arm of the Supreme Court assisting in supervision of lawyer conduct in the state—decided Gorecki had committed ethics violations. The ARDC thus recommended to the Supreme Court a two-month suspension of her license to practice law.

In his column, Page claimed Thomas originally wanted to pursue a much steeper penalty for Gorecki—up to and including disbarment. Yet in the end, Page contended, Thomas pushed a four-month suspension in return for the Gorecki camp assisting one of Thomas's appointed judges, Robert Spence, in an upcoming election. Page—a "former restaurant owner-turned-freelance publicist" who had since left the *Chronicle* and moved to Gainesville, Florida, according to the *Tribune*[1]—was accusing Thomas of official misconduct, which was tantamount to a felony. "Word is the Illinois Supreme Court is close to deciding Meg Gorecki's fate," Page had written on May 15.[2]

However, the Supreme Court did not mention Gorecki's name in its deliberations in Springfield until three days later, on May 18, and, contrary to Page's declaration, Thomas was not even in Springfield at that time. Just a couple of weeks earlier, Augie, age eighty-three, had undergone quadruple bypass surgery at Good Samaritan Hospital in Downers Grove. Despite a new Supreme Court term about to begin, Bob had remained behind in the Chicago area to help Anne with Augie's recovery process.

Scanning the article with shock and disbelief, Thomas felt a wave of emotions. He returned to the office and immediately called the Supreme Court's press secretary, Joseph Tybor. "This is total nonsense," he told Tybor. "Where did this come from? I want the paper to issue an immediate retraction—and not the typical retraction that's on page ten in a little box." Tybor, himself a licensed attorney and a former *Tribune* reporter, contacted the *Chronicle* and relayed Thomas's request. Not only was Tybor's phone call dismissed by the editorial office at the *Chronicle*, but another article followed from Page on May 20 reiterating his accusations against Thomas.

Tybor then phoned the *Chronicle* once again, this time speaking directly to the managing editor, Greg Rivara—who informed Tybor a retraction would not be forthcoming and that he was standing by his writer and the columns. His anger building to a crescendo, Thomas called Chicago attorney Joseph Power, Jr. and suggested they consider filing a defamation lawsuit. "I'm just not going to put up with this," Bob said in exasperation. Power, however, cautioned Thomas against any heavy-handed legal action at the outset. "'I understand why you're so upset," he responded. "It's a small paper, and it's a small story right now. But if you file a suit, it will become a *big* story—so give it some thought."

In addition to the national coverage such a case would likely bring, Thomas and Power also knew that defamation lawsuits were rarely successful, as the burden is on the plaintiff to prove that the defendant acted with actual malice. Power instead suggested they first attempt to resolve the situation out of court to elicit Page's (and the newspaper's) public and personal apology to Thomas. The newspaper obstinately stood its ground. There would be no retraction, and there would be no apology.

Backed into a corner, Thomas was left with no alternative. He would not be able to uphold any semblance of moral authority—as a judge, as a man of the law, as a man of Christ, as a husband, a father—if he permitted the libelous statements to live. Justice was necessary for him to keep working *as* a justice. An unconditional exoneration through litigation, he knew, was now the only way to retain the confidence of attorneys. "What type of Christian witness would I have if I allowed this to stand?" he decided. "Once they refused to print the retraction, I knew we had to go through with the lawsuit." As in other times of personal crisis, Thomas found his inspiration through prayer: "My faith helped me decide to do it; and then, my faith helped me deal with the trial when the time came."

The defamation suit was filed on January 16, 2004, naming Page, Rivara, and the Shaw Suburban Newspaper Group (which owned the *Chronicle*) as defendants. "He plans on seeking his day in court, as any regular citizen would do," Power told the press. "Someone took liberties and wrote about something that didn't happen. He [Thomas] was forced to resort to the court system."[3] As in response to Tybor's and Power's phone calls, the newspaper was undeterred with the filing of the lawsuit—and instead dug in its heels even deeper. "The *Kane County Chronicle* categorically denies Mr. Thomas's assertions," publisher Mark Sweetwood stated in response.[4]

Power, whose own father was a longtime judge, reflected in 2018 on the early days of the case. "Because of judicial ethics, judges can't always directly respond to allegations—so they're an easy target for the press. We tried to get the paper to issue a retraction. They weren't willing to do that—and in fact, they basically 'doubled-down' [with Page's subsequent article]. Bob felt that in order to get his integrity back, he needed to go through with the trial.

I told him that a lawsuit may get more attention than the actual columns. And with Bob being a public figure, it was going to be a high burden of proof. If we lost the case, it could have serious ramifications for him. But to him, it was a risk worth taking, because he knew it was false—and he wanted to show that it was false."[5]

The pursuit of justice, however, would have to wait. The trial would not begin for nearly another three years until the fall of 2006, and an ultimate decision in the matter would not come for another eleven months thereafter; nonetheless, there was much to keep Thomas busy in the interim. Brendan, Jonathan, and Jessica would all graduate from Cedarville University in that time, while their father was selected by his peers in 2005 to serve as the chief justice of the Illinois Supreme Court and had been named as a possible candidate to replace Jack Ryan in the 2004 race for a seat in the United States Senate against Illinois State Senator Barack Obama. "I had a family, a busy job, and other things to keep me occupied," he remembered about the hiatus. "But the long wait gave me a new appreciation for what litigants have to go through—because now, I was one."

Finally, on Wednesday, October 25, 2006, at the Kane County Courthouse in Geneva, the time had come. As the trial was about to begin, Thomas received a phone call from the *Sun-Times*. The reporter wanted to know why he would file suit against such a small newspaper with a limited circulation. "Let me ask you a question," he responded to the reporter. "If you had a neighbor who accused you of committing a crime and you didn't do it, would you go down and talk to that neighbor in person? Would you want to have them know the truth and get it right, if that's what they thought? Well, that's what I'm doing. I just can't have my integrity impugned like this."

Maggie and the growing kids were also enduring the daily stress; but the family took it all in stride. "I read the material, and knew what had happened," Maggie recalled of first seeing the articles by Page. "I went over to Geneva for most of the days of the trial. It was really something new to sit through a case and see how it works. The whole thing really didn't shake me that much; Bob and I trusted God for protection and for the truth to be revealed. I was busy with all the kids' activities, and Bob was busy with work. He didn't dwell on it when he got home; he chose to spend that time with our children. He would share with me what was happening each day, but we didn't let it take over our lives."[6]

Just before the proceedings were launched, an extra impediment surfaced for Thomas's legal team to overcome. "For trial lawyers, we always look at jury selection as one of the most important parts of the process," Power said. "In the jury selection for Bob's lawsuit, the judge had issued a time limit. When the allotted time had ended, there was a fellow who had been sworn into the jury who said he loved Bill Page—that Page was his favorite columnist, that he wished Page was back at the paper, that he reads the paper every day, and so forth—but the juror was claiming despite all that, he could still be fair."[7] Power noticed the juror had even been smiling at Page while in the courtroom. "We had run out of [juror] challenges—so I either had to get him off the jury for cause, or we were going to have a problem."

Still unsure of what to do a couple of days before the trial was to begin, Power went home after a long day of preparation and tried to relax by turning on the television. He caught the closing moments of the World Series game that evening between the St. Louis Cardinals and the Detroit Tigers.

Power stared at the TV screen for a moment. He took notice of the pitcher, the batter, and the man in blue behind the plate who was calling the balls and strikes. He had an idea: "Something just snapped in me. I said to myself, 'You know what we're looking for here—we're looking for a fair umpire.'" When Power returned to the courthouse the following day, he approached the juror with a question. "What if," he offered to the man, "there was a die-hard St. Louis Cardinals fan who loved the team and followed them every day, and who just happened to be the umpire calling the balls and strikes in the World Series between the Cardinals and the Tigers. Would that be a fair World Series? "No," the juror responded.

Power had instantly made his point. "This is important to all parties here," he sternly reminded the man. "You said that he [Page] is your favorite columnist, and that the *Kane County Chronicle* is your favorite paper, and that you read it every day. Wouldn't you agree that, since you're a fan of the paper and the defendant—and that you have been looking over at him and smiling at him in this very courtroom—that you shouldn't be the 'umpire' calling the balls and strikes?" The man paused and considered the logic. "I think you're right," he answered. "This isn't the right case for me."[8] Cook County Circuit Court Judge Donald O'Brien, who had been summoned to Kane County from outside of Thomas's district to preside over the trial, ordered the man off the jury for cause.

As the witnesses began testifying, Tybor was among the first called to the stand by Power. "I told him [Rivara] there was not one ounce of truth in that column," the Supreme Court's press secretary said of his May 15, 2003, phone conversation with the paper's editor after the first article had appeared. Tybor said he finished the phone call by informing Rivara that Page appeared to be "making up facts." "I told him I thought he had a runaway reporter," Tybor testified.[9] Yet, despite the clear directive by Tybor to cease and desist, the *Chronicle* nonetheless followed with the second article from Page on May 20.

When it was time for Thomas's colleagues to answer questions, they were universal in their unqualified dismissal of Page's claims. "Several Illinois Supreme Court justices involved in the Gorecki case testified Tuesday [October 31] that Thomas never pushed for disbarring Gorecki," wrote Dan Rozek of the *Sun-Times*. "The justices also said they saw no evidence Thomas weighed any political concerns during their discussions of the case. 'I saw no factual basis for what I saw asserted in those columns,' said Justice Thomas Kilbride, who at one point in his testimony described the columns as 'outrageous.' Justice Charles Freeman praised Thomas for his character and integrity, saying he never saw Thomas act improperly during proceedings involving Gorecki. 'I believe he is of the highest moral character,' Freeman said of Thomas."[10]

Before the trial was over, each of the other six Illinois Supreme Court justices involved in the Gorecki case took the stand on behalf of the seventh—including Thomas's predecessor in the chief justice chair, Mary Ann McMorrow. "The justices said that, contrary to Page's columns, the court had not even deliberated on the matter at the time the first column was published," added Russell Working in covering the trial for the *Tribune*.[11] "It was troubling to all of us on the bench," said Justice Rita Garman, who had joined the court a couple of months after Thomas in 2001. "We knew Bob was really struggling and hurting."[12]

In later years, Thomas reflected upon the powerful moment of seeing his fellow justices addressing the courtroom. "All six of my colleagues came in with their 'red books,' where we put our impression votes [an initial vote taken by the chief justice during early deliberations on a case to see where the other justices stand], and every one of them said I never acted as the reporter had claimed."

Finally, it was Thomas's turn on the stand. Power asked his client to de-scribe his feelings when he saw the first article. Before opening his mouth to speak, Thomas turned his head slowly toward the other side of the court-room. He pointed at the poster-sized copies of Page's columns on display for all to see. "I don't know if there's a word bigger than outraged, so I'll just say outraged. I was stunned, devastated, hurt, humiliated, embarrassed. Bill Page has hung a 'justice for sale' sign around my neck. Bill Page said I can't be fair. He's taken away my integrity and my good name. I'm here to get it back."[13]

"Is your reputation important to you?" Power asked Thomas.

"It is."

"What have your parents taught you about reputation?"

"That your word is your bond," Bob said, thinking of Augie and Anne. "That integrity is everything."[14]

For a total of nearly eight hours at the trial, Thomas also responded to questions from defense attorneys and was never impeached, while Page "no less than 15 times was impeached by prior testimony," according to the court transcript.[15] Page had participated in a deposition before the trial, providing statements hardly exculpatory for him and the newspaper. At one such de-position, he stated on videotape he did not know whether the story about Thomas was true, nor did he even *care* whether it was true. "Joe [Power] probably played that twenty times during the trial," Thomas later said.

Before being excused by O'Brien, Thomas reminded one of the defense lawyers that the primary purpose of disciplinary hearings such as Gorecki's is not to punish the offender but, first and foremost, to preserve public faith in the legal system. When Power had rested, the defense team called its wit-nesses. No one from *Chronicle* could affirm that the information Page had penned was legitimate; even in his own testimony before the court, Page—whose daughter worked for Gorecki's office—"acknowledged he never wit-nessed any unethical conduct by Thomas," Rozek noted. "Taking the stand, Page testified that he had no firsthand knowledge of any political bias or deal-making by Thomas during the 2003 disciplinary proceedings against Gorecki. 'You never witnessed him stating one negative thing about Meg Gorecki?' Power asked. "'Personally, I did not,' Page replied."[16]

Page also admitted on the stand he made no attempt to contact Thomas before publishing the articles (a procedure advisable according to the ethics of the Society of Professional Journalists, an organization of which Rivara initially denied having any knowledge—despite being the past president of his college's SPJ chapter). As the proceedings continued, it became clearer that Page could not base his writing on *any* form of proof, empirical or otherwise. "Power asked Page repeatedly whether he had 'a shred of evidence'— based on either personal observation or media articles—that Thomas was biased against Gorecki or had publicly stated he was out to get her. "'Based on my firsthand observations, no,' Page said."[17]

Yet, despite having no evidence of the actions he was accusing Thomas of committing, Page pushed forward in the wake of the articles by also issuing a series of ominous warnings to a variety of individuals related to the case. "At one point," Eric Herman of the *Sun-Times* wrote in compiling the testimony, "Page sent the Supreme Court an e-mail promising a 'nightmare of bad publicity' if Thomas didn't withdraw from the Gorecki case."[18] When ARDC Chief Counsel James J. Grogan took the stand, he testified that Page had called him and threatened to "ruin" him after the commission recommended only a temporary suspension of Gorecki's law license in 2002. While Page denied the conversation had ever taken place, Grogan proclaimed in court that "Page identified himself in the call. . . . So finally I said to him, 'Do you have a question for me?' And he said he was going to destroy me."[19]

Not getting an answer, Grogan—a professor of ethics at the Loyola University School of Law—repeated himself. "Do you have a question for me?" he said again. "I am going to wreck you. I am going to ruin you. I am going to destroy you," Page responded. Grogan hung up the phone—the first time, he testified, that he had ever hung up on a journalist in the hundreds of reporters' calls he had fielded during his career.[20]

The testimony harmful to Page continued to pile up. When questioned by Power, Page's editor also showed no concern about the articles' veracity. "[Rivara] said he was not worried about the column's accuracy, and that because it was a column rather than a news story, it could be held to different standards," reported Matt Hanley of the *Aurora Beacon-News* from the courtroom. "According to Rivara's testimony, after one of the columns ran, he told Page: 'They're mad down in Springfield.' To which Page allegedly responded, 'Good.'"[21]

In his closing argument, Power claimed that Page, for some unknown reason—perhaps ill-pursued professional gain—was "out to get" Thomas from start. "That's Bill Page, the bully on the block," as Power pointed at the defense table. "The guy who was allowed to [go] after public officials who are trying to do their job. It's really sad that you're seeing the underbelly of that kind of journalism."[22]

Attorneys for Page and the newspaper argued that Thomas had not really suffered all that much from the articles, noting that he been "promoted" to chief justice (despite that honor being bestowed upon him by his peers on the Supreme Court—which, perhaps unwittingly to the defense, may have strengthened the justices' testimony) and had received awards from various bar associations since the articles appeared. The jury was sent to deliberate at 4 p.m. on Monday, November 13. At 8:03 p.m., the twelve members broke for the night.

When the jury returned at 9 a.m. the next day, they were sequestered for another four and a half hours. Bob spent much of the time pacing up and down the hallway outside the courtroom. Every few minutes, he would join in one of the conversations going on among those who had assembled, including Maggie, Power, various attorneys, and some friends. Despite his extensive experience in judicial proceedings and even though he had immense support, a feeling of helplessness overcame Thomas. He did not know which answer to expect and had little idea of when the answer would come.

What he *did* know was that a verdict for the newspaper would be a de facto verdict against him on the accusations Page had made. "I realized if they [the jury] came back and let the newspaper off, the next news story would not have been that we did not prove actual malice—the story would have been that I *did it*."

With each minute dripping slowly by with excruciating uncertainty, Thomas finally stepped into the empty courtroom to sit by himself. From the gallery, he silently gazed out on the things so familiar to him from the bench, objects he normally saw from the opposite view on the other side of the room—the counsel tables . . . the jury box . . . the witness stand . . . the gavel.

Suddenly, in the stillness of his solitude, a sharp sound resonated from the corner of the vacant courtroom, echoing throughout the hall. The noise startled Bob out of his pensive state. A knock was coming from the jury room door. "Having been a trial judge for six years, I knew what that was. It was the foreman seeking the bailiff. They had a verdict."

As when he sat frozen in the basement of WGN watching the closing moments of the Bears' playoff game, Bob clenched the armrests of his chair with heightened anxiety. He took a deep breath, forced himself up, and went back into the hallway to inform Maggie and Power that the jury was returning. He felt as if everything for which he stood was hanging in the balance. Life would change forever in the next instant—in one direction or the other. Once again, he turned to God.

> Commit your way to the Lord;
> trust in him and he will do this:
> He will make your righteous reward shine like the dawn,
> your vindication like the noonday sun.
> Be still before the Lord
> and wait patiently for him.
>
> *(Psalm 37)*

People gradually filtered back into the courtroom as Judge O'Brien had it come to order. He instructed the litigants to rise as he read the verdict: the jury had returned a judgment in favor of the plaintiff. In gratitude, Bob leaned forward, put his face in his hands, and wept. "He later shook hands with jurors and thanked them for their service," reported the *Sun-Times*. "Their decision marks the first time in 15 years that a Chicago area court has ordered a newspaper to pay damages in a libel case."[23]

To compensate for damages the defamation could have caused to Thomas (such as harm to his ability to seek a federal judgeship or a partnership in a law firm), the jury awarded an amount of $7 million. The figure was ultimately reduced by O'Brien to $4 million, but it was still a penalty the newspaper could have easily avoided. "Thomas would have dropped the case if the paper had admitted the columns were false," Power said minutes later when encountering the media outside the courthouse. "All they had to do was print some type of retraction."[24]

Ken Sotern was among several jurors questioned by reporters on exiting the building. "Everybody's entitled to their integrity," Sotern stated. "We saw no reason at all to doubt Mr. Thomas's integrity."[25] O'Brien provided his own summary of the case in March 2007. "The jury could—and did—find that Mr. Page constructed the columns out of whole cloth," the presiding judge wrote.[26]

Thomas offered to settle with the *Chronicle* for O'Brien's reduced judgment in the days following the trial. But attorneys for the newspaper, who vowed to appeal the verdict, refused. "Twelve jurors from Kane County decided this was false and done by clear and convincing evidence with actual malice," Power told the *Tribune* on November 27 after the *Chronicle*'s lawyers sought to continue the fight. "We wanted to bring an end to it, and instead, they persist down Defamatory Road."[27] Nearly a year after the trial was concluded, the *Chronicle* finally agreed to a lesser settlement while publishing its retraction and apology to the chief justice on October 12, 2007.

The integrity and faith of Bob Thomas, in both a very public and private manner, had been put to the test—a test that lasted nearly five years. And, as in his previous life trials, his integrity and faith had triumphed.

Chapter 14

Looking Ahead

Bob is a class act. I knew he would be a success in whatever he chose
to do after football.

—Mike Ditka, 2018

On November 10, 2011—thirty years after his father graduated from the
Loyola School of Law—Jonathan Thomas was admitted to the bar and was
sworn in by Illinois Supreme Court Justice Robert Thomas at the Hemmens
Center in Elgin. With his proud eyes occasionally landing on his son in the
audience, from the podium Bob gave some last-minute advice to Jonathan
and the other 220 new attorneys as they ventured out into their legal careers.
His remarks encapsulated the testing of his own principles he had experienced during the lawsuit. "Remember that with every choice you make, you're
building your reputation within our profession," he instructed the beginning
lawyers, "and ultimately it's not your education, your talent, your credentials
or your position that will make people take notice. It is your *integrity* that
will make people take notice."[1]

A full year before his defamation trial against Page and the newspaper
was to begin (and two years after the lawsuit was filed), Thomas started his
three-year stint as the chief justice of the Supreme Court in September 2005
after being chosen by his colleagues to follow McMorrow. Among other

duties, it was Bob's job as chief to set the discussion agenda for the justices when the court was in term. "When you become a judge, you're immediately thrust into a hierarchy," he explained. "Associate judges are appointed by elected circuit justices; circuit justices aspire to be appellate justices; appellate justices aspire to be Supreme Court justices. There is a 'pecking order.' When your peers vote you in for a period of time as the chief justice, that hierarchy continues. As chief justice, you're looked upon as the face of the court, and it's your opportunity to try and make an improvement upon the system. The one which I really wanted to bring to the court—and I'm glad the court went along with it—was professionalism."

A few years earlier, Thomas participated in a conference in DuPage County, the Roger O'Reilly Symposium, which was named after a deceased attorney from Wheaton who long exemplified the virtues attorneys were expected to display. Among other presentations at the symposium, Bob participated on a panel discussion about courtroom professionalism. He and the other presenters noticed they were essentially "preaching to the choir" at the event, as the attendees were largely attorneys who were already displaying many of the desired qualities. Thomas and the rest of the group went back to the drawing board

> The outgrowth of the seminar was, "How do we get to the attorneys in the 'back row'—the ones who really need to be here? You hear a lot about how the practice of law is different now than in days past, when a lawyer's handshake meant something, and a lawyer's word was his bond. That may be an oversimplification, but in this age with competition in the profession for dollars and clients, activities sometimes degenerate into a win-at-all cost attitude by attorneys.
>
> I think things really regressed with some commercials and programs that started appearing on TV, in which lawyers would engage in "Rambo-style" tactics in the courtroom in representing clients. The public began thinking, "Hey, I need an attorney like *that*—where do I get one?" And from there, it turned into a profit motive for many attorneys, in which they try to be cantankerous and turn everything into a knock-down, drag-out fight. The client isn't there to serve the purposes of the attorney—it's the other way around.

What followed was the establishment of the Illinois Supreme Court Committee on Civility. Thomas's commitment to increased decorum in the courtroom was recognized by Debra Walker, a judge on the Cook County

Circuit Court who shares the same goal. "When a Supreme Court justice becomes chief justice, that person has the opportunity to move a project forward that is particularly important to him or her," Walker noted in 2018. "Justice Kilbride, for example, formed the Access to Justice Commission. Justice Garman established the Commission on Equality. And when Justice Thomas assumed the position of chief justice in 2005, he was able to help carry forward the work of the committee into the form of the Illinois Supreme Court Commission on Professionalism the following year."[2]

Thomas was empowered to appoint two individuals to the commission, as he, Walker, and the group enthusiastically began constructing an action plan. But as the work of the commission moved forward, Bob noticed it was being received cynically by the media. "I recall that, when we tried to implement the idea, the press would ask me, 'Why would you want to put a spotlight on a glaring weakness in the legal profession?' The question implied that we were just doing it for recognition and that it wouldn't have any tangible impact. Well, I told the press, and I continue to say, 'We're putting the spotlight on it because we intend to make a difference in the profession.'

"I think the two biggest initiatives during my term as chief have been mandatory minimal continuing legal education and professionalism," Bob stated proudly. "It's hard to believe that barbers have to go on for extra schooling, but lawyers did not."

The commission succeeded in having the state of Illinois mandate that attorneys complete six hours of continuing education credits every two years (known as mandatory continuing legal education, or MCLE). Additionally, first-year students at each of the nine law schools in Illinois were now required to take a "pledge of professionalism" administered by a Supreme Court justice or an appellate court judge. For those already in the field, a comprehensive lawyer-to-lawyer mentoring network was also established; and to ensure the conversation did not cease, the commission developed a website to complement the commission's activities, with a blog by attorneys on a variety of professionalism topics that continues to this day.

"I think we're one of fourteen states which has a professionalism commission," Thomas said in 2019. "The whole purpose was to make civility and professionalism the norm among attorneys in the state. Now, we have a widespread program, and I think the profession is in a better place for it having happened. But there was definitely a need for it to *get to* a better place."

With word of the commission's achievements surging beyond the state line, the new practices established in Illinois became a model for civility training as a part of legal education in other places. "Often, our commission is asked to speak at various conferences and meetings around the country, and has gained an international reputation as well," Walker said. "As one example, we once provided training on professionalism to a large group of Chinese lawyers who had visited Illinois."[3]

When his time in the chief justice chair was finished in September 2008, Bob made way for Thomas Fitzgerald in the position. Thomas's passion for courtroom civility, however, did not end there. Keeping the momentum going, Thomas agreed to continue serving as the court's liaison to the Professionalism Commission. "After someone has been chief justice or retires from the court, some of the projects remain a part of the court going forward, and some do not," Walker summarized. "This one did."[4]

The sustainability of Thomas's efforts doubtlessly had its underpinnings in the strong relationships he had formed with his colleagues on the Supreme Court, such as with Justice Anne Burke—who took a seat on the bench in 2006 during Thomas's run as chief. "Bob is a true collaborator," Burke said. "He's like a coach and a team player. Like any good team, none of us tries to steal the spotlight, but instead, we want the group to thrive. Bob is at the center of that effort, as he makes all our discussions so seamless. He and I have the ability to disagree, but we remain friends when it's all said and done. We have to look into some very dark things in our work, but Bob can bring a sense of humor to it all."[5] Justice Rita Garman also appreciates Bob's lighthearted yet professional approach:

> He's easy to tease, and part of that is because he loves to tease other people. Bob is delightful to be around. He is a very engaging fellow—the kind of person that as soon as you get to know him, you feel like you've known him for a very long time. He's also a very open person, a wonderful storyteller, and has a quick wit that is coupled with deep moral and religious convictions.
>
> Bob is really committed to collegiality, as he is friendly with all members of the court. As one might imagine, there are different personalities among the justices, but he can relate to everyone. We eat our meals together; and while we do so, he'll often tell a story from the Bears or something else— such as the time one of his children was getting married and he was having trouble getting his tux shirt cleaned. He always has something interesting and entertaining to share.[6]

Justice Thomas Kilbride, who joined the court on the very same day as Thomas on December 4, 2000, feels the same way. "Bob is a smart fellow— one of the best questioners and one of the most engaging members of the court." And while Kilbride echoed his colleagues' assessment of Thomas's collegiality, he added one qualifying remark. "But Bob can also be feisty like the football player he once was," he amended with a smile. "He is passionate about the points of law he tries to make on a given case, and sometimes— even after he's already convinced us—he keeps going. We'll try to stop him and say, 'Hey Bob—you've already won!' While I don't agree with him all the time, we agree more often than not. He's definitely the funniest member of the court. Bob has a great sense of humor, and like Justice Garman said, he has a real gift as a storyteller."[7]

The charisma and humor which Thomas has carried over from his years in the NFL, however, is not what has made the greatest impression on his coworkers. "What I've learned from Bob, in this very intense world of shared decision-making in which we discuss cases, and what stands out to me about him more than his history as a football player, is that he is incredibly intelligent," Justice Mary Jane Theis stated. "He is always thoroughly prepared; not only does he read all the materials which the lawyers present to him, but he listens very carefully at oral arguments and asks questions that are not just obvious ones. In other words, he is genuinely reacting to what's happening in the courtroom—he's very present."

Theis also values the reflective manner in which Thomas approaches the evidence the court entertains. "Bob is also a very *creative* legal thinker. In the cases that we hear, he has a great ability to think by analogy, and to think of the consequences of a decision. We're very fortunate to have someone of the depth of his legal mind on the Illinois Supreme Court."[8]

Justice Lloyd Karmeier, whose term as chief justice ended in the autumn of 2019, shares the sentiment of the other justices. "Bob is a true colleague and has been an immense help to me on the court. I try to keep up with him on the golf course, but it's tough. He's still a great competitor."[9] Thomas and several other justices hold a weekly Bible study when the Supreme Court is in term, a gathering that includes law librarians, marshals, clerks, and others around the courthouse in Springfield as well. "It's a very meaningful time for us," Garman made a point to say.

As he was preparing to pass the mantle of chief justice to Fitzgerald in 2008, Bob found time in June to return to Rochester and serve as the keynote speaker for the very first induction ceremony of the McQuaid High School Hall of Fame—which included him in the inaugural class. In addition to ten others, Thomas was honored alongside his unlikely high school coach, Tom Seymour, who gave Bob his first shot in organized football. Two years later, Seymour passed away at the age of eighty-three. "I was just very impressed how he coached with such professionalism and dignity and composure," Bob said in thinking of his second mentor after Augie on the gridiron. "He reminded me a little bit of a high school Tom Landry."[10]

In 2001, with son Rick practicing law in Illinois in addition to Bob serving on the bench, Augie and Anne decided to uproot the only home they had ever known in America and move from Rochester to the Chicago area, while Augie continued to tutor kickers on the soccer style. After his heart surgery in May 2003, he gradually lessened his coaching pace. But out of his love for teaching, he yearned to guide one more protégé in 2006.

Augie developed a close friendship with the surgeon who had performed his operation, Dr. John Grieco. Grieco had graduated from Loyola the same year Bob finished at Notre Dame and met the Thomases at a neighborhood yard party in Glen Ellyn, Illinois, in 1988 while Bob was running for circuit court judge and shortly after the Griecos had moved to the community. "Augie would sometimes say things to me in Italian that I could understand, and I really enjoyed that," the doctor recalled of their shared heritage.[11] Grieco became so endeared to the Thomas family that he was their sole choice to perform the operation when Augie's surgery became necessary—which occurred around the same time Grieco lost his own father. "I suggested they might want to look at Northwestern Hospital or somewhere in New York," Grieco said, "but they wanted me to do it."[12]

The procedure was a success, and the surgeon followed up regularly with Augie over the next few years to discuss his post-operative regimen. In doing so, Dr. Grieco had the opportunity to introduce Augie to his son, Mike, mentioning that Mike played soccer—which naturally grabbed Augie's attention. Augie took notice of Mike's skills on the pitch, prompting Augie to suggest the young man had the ability for another sport as Mike was finishing his sophomore year at St. Ignatius College Preparatory High School in Chicago in 2006. "Augie approached me and said, 'You should try kicking a football,' Mike remembered. "We talked a couple more times, and he and I started working out in a field near our home." From the beginning, the two struck up a kinship. "I think of myself of a low-key surgeon, and I don't ever expect favors from my patients," John said. "But Augie and Mike really hit it off, and they wanted to work together."[13]

Following Augie's guidance over the summer, Grieco became the starting St. Ignatius kicker that fall. The duo continued to practice regularly as Grieco prepared for his senior season. "A lot of his training methods were 'old-school,' but I think they were more effective," Mike said. "He had me doing a lot of box jumps, a lot of short sprints, kicking a soccer ball at first to develop form and consistency, and other basics like that. He would come over to my house, and my dad would set up a lawn chair for him—and he would coach me from there."

Augie provided Grieco with a handwritten note that summarized the fundamentals of a successful placement kick:

1. Keep your eyes on the ball.
2. Keep your head down.
3. Follow through.
4. Square with the target.
5. Don't go [cross] over your non-kicking foot.
6. Kick soccer-style [but] finish conventional.
7. Check wind and control it.
8. All mechanics should be the same.

Just as Bob had done over the years, Grieco thrived on every morsel of advice he could glean. "One of his famous quotes was, 'If your technique is great you'll never miss; and if you're technique is good you'll rarely miss,'" Mike recalled fondly. "I could always tell he loved coaching kickers and was extremely passionate about it." By the time he graduated from St. Ignatius in 2008, Grieco had improved so dramatically that he was considering the extension of his football career beyond high school. And his deliberations were eerily similar to those of Augie's first student: "I was planning on going to a small Division Three school, either Illinois Wesleyan or Case Western Reserve, but I had always loved Notre Dame since I was in the fourth grade."

Thomas's inspiration had Grieco ultimately shooting for the highest target. "Augie encouraged me to chase my dream. He kept saying to me, 'You're going to kick at Notre Dame,' even though it was unrealistic, for I was not a big-time prospect making sixty-yard field goals. I was mostly hitting only thirty-five-yarders."[14] But Mike listened, and decided to take a leap of faith.

As in the plot from the movie *Rudy* from fifteen years earlier, Mike headed to South Bend in the fall of 2008 without admission to Notre Dame and instead began his postsecondary studies at Holy Cross College across the street. During his first semester of classes, he headed back home to the west suburbs as often as possible to work with Augie and talked with him over the telephone at other times when Mike had to remain on campus.

Shortly after Christmas, however, Mike noticed that his mentor was suddenly unable to spend as much time with him. Augie was starting to suffer the ravages of lung cancer, a disease that would advance on him quickly. By late January 2009, he moved into the Wynscape Rehabilitation Center in Wheaton, where he was visited by numerous friends—including members of the Italian-American Sports Club from Rochester who had made the long journey west. Among them was Tito Laurini, one of the many whom Thomas had helped both to assimilate into American life and to learn how to kick an American football.

Within a few weeks, Augie was moved into hospice. In the early hours of February 13 he passed away, one month shy of his eighty-ninth birthday. When Augie was remembered at a funeral mass at St. Michael's Catholic Church in Wheaton two days later, Bob requested a special favor of Mike. "He asked me to be a pall bearer, and that was a very touching experience for me," Grieco said. "I was pretty beat up at the funeral because I thought of Augie as another grandfather."

The many loved ones said their goodbyes and comforted Bob, Rick, and Anne. Among them was Joe Power—who relayed his favorite story of Mr. Thomas. "Bob was a good kicker," he once told Joe, "but if *I* had been a kicker, I would *never* have missed." Bob nodded and grinned whenever he thinks of it. "My dad truly believed that about himself."

Through it all, August and Anne Thomas were eminently proud of their *sons'* special gifts, as Bob remembered:

> To my dad, I was always the best kicker who ever kicked in the NFL—whether I was or not. He was continuously showing his confidence in me, which allowed me to develop confidence in myself. For him and my mom, I think it was all part of being immigrants, with the mindset that "there is nothing you can't do." They wanted a better life for me than the one they had, which had some discrimination attached to it. But they felt that, in America, with hard work and effort, you could do anything—and I trusted

in that attitude throughout my life as I proceeded in football and the law. They felt they always had to prove themselves; they knew that life was better here, and that it could be even greater for their kids who were completely assimilated into the culture.

In the spirit and memory of his father, Bob picked up the baton for Augie's final student and made certain Grieco kept his eyes on the prize. "That's when Bob started working with me more," Mike remembered, "because I think he wanted to see it through."

With Bob now overseeing his kicking program, Mike posted a strong academic performance at Holy Cross and was able to transfer into Notre Dame as a sophomore. He attempted to join the football team that summer; but Charlie Weis, the head coach who had arrived in 2005 with much fanfare, told Grieco at walk-on tryouts that he was not needed. Mike refused to surrender and kept working. By the time Weis was fired and Brian Kelly was brought aboard to coach the Irish in 2010, Grieco was ready to give it another shot. That year, he found a spot on the roster—thus making Augie's very *first* pupil and his very *last* pupil both Notre Dame kickers, separated by forty years and each of them having begun his career as a non-scholarship player.

Grieco spent his junior season of 2010 watching from the bench as David Ruffer, another walk-on who had never played high school football, handled the kicking chores. Making certain he was always ready for the call, Grieco waited through the first half of his senior season as well. In the early fall of 2011, his opportunity came. On a warm eighty-degree afternoon under clear blue skies on October 8, the Irish were playing Air Force at Notre Dame Stadium in front of 81,000 spectators. Midway through the fourth quarter, Kelly's team was throttling the Falcons, 52–19 when running back George Atkinson leapt over from the one-yard line for another Notre Dame touchdown. Rather than trotting out to the field for his eighth extra point of the day, Ruffer instead hurried over to Kelly on the sidelines. In Rudy-esque fashion, he convinced the coach that his backup should have a chance. With Kelly tilting his head approvingly and waving Grieco onto the sacred field, Mike took his place in between the hashmarks and stared up at the goalposts at the south end, a stiff oncoming breeze meeting his face. With the habits of Augie's eight-point list automatically part of his routine, he lined up, began his steps as the ball met the holder's hands, and confidently drilled the conversion through the uprights—leaving himself a perfect one-for-one in his Irish career.

Shortly after graduating the following spring, Grieco received a letter of recommendation from Bob for his application to the Loyola University School of Law—another goal Mike successfully conquered before passing the bar exam in the spring of 2018. "What other kind of mentor could you want than Justice Thomas as you're going through college and getting ready for life?" he offered. "Notre Dame was the culmination of a great dream and goal, in which people like the Thomases helped me along the way. Bob's a humble guy, and he and his dad showed that to me in taking me under their wings."[15] Mike's dad agreed. "Bob is the consummate Italian gentleman," Dr. John Grieco said, "just like his father."[16]

With his reputation having grown around Illinois since becoming a judge, Bob was periodically approached with new opportunities. In March 2009, Thomas was mentioned as a potential GOP candidate for governor in the wake of the Rod Blagojevich scandal. "I'm happy where I'm at," he told the *Sun-Times*.[17] Instead of pursuing the gubernatorial office, Thomas remained in his position on the Supreme Court. That November, Thomas was retained for a second ten-year term on the court with 81 percent of the vote—the highest of any judge in that round of elections—as he became the first DuPage County resident to serve a full decade on Illinois's highest bench.

While the courtroom still commands Thomas's attention as of this writing, he also finds time to feed his competitive and recreational side. Golf remains a favorite leisure activity and also serves as a further bonding opportunity with Jonathan. Like her brothers, Jessica values the time she shares with her father: "I think he just enjoys being a grandpa. I love seeing him with my kids—and seeing how much he loves my kids."[18]

A new solitary activity combining both adventure and recreation for Thomas is learning the guitar, as he reboots a musical pursuit from his grade-school days back in Rochester. As a cousin of the late Jim Croce, Bob figures there must be *some* semblance of talent within him. "He brings the guitar with him when we're in Springfield," revealed Justice Garman. "We all live together in the court building when we're in term, and my suite is directly across from his. I hear him practicing sometimes, which of course doesn't go unnoticed. I'm quick to tell him that he should not give up his day job. We kid him sometimes that we're going to have a 'Supreme Court Talent Show' and put him on there."[19] While Garman is afforded the slight buffer zone of the hallway, Kilbride is spared nothing. He has an adjoining suite to Thomas where the sound is amplified. "We share a wall, and I can hear the playing and singing," he stated with a laugh. "But it's all OK. That's part of who Bob is, and we enjoy it."[20]

The largest part of who Bob Thomas is, however, continues to thrive at home—where unbounded love, care, and respect remain at the heart of a blessed union of souls that passed its fortieth anniversary in June 2019. "We have a friendship that I wouldn't say is necessarily unique, but it's long-lasting," Maggie reflected on their marriage. "We have fun, we joke, and can tease each other and just laugh. What I love is that I make him laugh every day. If I need to call him out on something, I do it through humor—he can laugh about it and not be defensive."

Bob agrees: "Our faith journey was solidified very early in our marriage. Maggie really became the leader; not only with our kids in molding them and sharing faith with them, but also in keeping me grounded as we went through various trials—whether it was being cut from the Bears, going to work at my first law firm, or the many other times in our lives. She was always there, and I have always relied upon her. We truly have had, and continue to have, a very strong relationship based upon respect for one another and upon faith."

The couple's reliance on faith—and on one another—supported them in 2010, as Bob and Maggie confronted a frightening battle side-by-side and hand-in-hand. The two had been looking forward to a trip to Italy that year, which was to be their first excursion overseas. The vacation was called off, however, as Maggie suddenly had an unexplainable drop in weight. "The trip had to be postponed, because you don't want to go to Italy with someone who is having trouble eating," Bob recalled with a nervous laugh.

While the main symptom of her condition was a recurring bout of severe acid reflux, the most disturbing result was the weight loss, gradually taking its toll until Maggie was down to around 80 percent of her normal body makeup. Upon seeing a gastroenterologist, a scope taken of her system proved negative, and she was prescribed a simple proton-pump inhibitor (PPI). Yet, the weight loss persisted, and because of the discomfort Maggie was able to sleep only one or two hours a night. "The doctors kept changing the PPI pre-scription, and at one point they doubled the amount she was taking," Bob continued. "I was getting very concerned."

While in Springfield for the Supreme Court term, Bob decided to call Dr. Steven Armbrust, a specialist in hard-to-solve cases. Armbrust spent forty-five minutes listening on the phone and then presented his advice. "The first thing we have to do is get her to sleep," he told Bob. "She can't exist on the one or two hours a night that she's getting." After being issued a new prescription, Maggie was finally able to get some extended rest.

One afternoon after getting Maggie settled in, Bob played a round of golf. There was a doctor in the foursome whom Bob approached about his wife's situation. But as the group moved from hole to hole, it was instead an attorney in the foursome who overheard the conversation and recommended another highly regarded gastroenterologist. When Bob returned home, he phoned Dr. Donald Hoscheit. "Well, I'm sure that Maggie has had ultrasounds and CT scans . . ." Hoscheit began. To Bob's dismay, he had to report that she had not had any such tests. He was worried that a critical component in Maggie's diagnosis had been missed, with her condition perhaps now worsening to a point beyond curability.

Maggie never lost her trust in God in her suffering; nonetheless, the Thomas family needed a new guiding force to step up in the throes of the difficulty. "I was forced into a spiritual leadership role in the home in which I hadn't been in the past," Bob realized. "I prayed with her and read Scripture to her. I put together hymns and worship songs for her to listen to when she was having trouble sleeping."

But as the days went on, there were virtually no signs of improvement. The prospect of what lay ahead was overwhelming to Bob. "I remember sitting in a chair in our family room, and I was really scared. As I sat there, I wept—thinking not only about the fact that I might lose my wife, but that God may have been allowing this to happen because that, for years, I had been shirking my responsibility as the spiritual head of the home—and *that* was even harder for me to take. It was not that I *caused* what was happening to Maggie, but that God was allowing it to occur in order to change me."

With the couple was still seeking answers for the illness, Bob was scheduled to make a speech to the men's group of his local church. "I had prepared some remarks. I remember getting there, and just throwing aside the paper version of my speech. Instead, I shared the story of Maggie's sickness and the impact it had on me." Bob delivered a heart-filled address on how his wife's situation was tormenting him. When finished, he offered to take questions from the audience. "I still remember this one guy getting up in the back of the room, who had probably come there expecting to hear stories from my years with the Bears or whatever. He didn't have a question for me; instead, with tears in his eyes, he just stood up and said, 'I need to go home and reconcile with my wife.' That was a powerful moment."

Shortly thereafter, news returned from the ultrasound and computed tomography scan. The results were negative. A blood test revealed Maggie was suffering from a bacterial infection, and the gastroenterologist prescribed a new PPI that also contained an antibiotic. Before long, a fully healthy Maggie was bounding down the stairs at the family home while announcing, "I put on a pound!" And then: "I put on two pounds!" Two years later in 2012, Bob and Maggie completed their postponed trip to Italy—and were finally able to eat their fill of pasta.

Over the long road of their years together—through all of the freezing Bears games on the lakefront at Soldier Field, through the long nights of Bob studying for the bar exam and attending the endless campaign events, Maggie was there behind the scenes. She kept the Thomas family moving by organizing the daily activities and getting the kids where they needed to go. "I've always enjoyed the adventure of each new thing with Bob," she said in reflection. "I didn't think I was that kind of person, but I am. I rolled with all the changes, and I liked it. Regardless of whatever the new challenge was, it was always just a matter of believing in him."[21]

Thomas's fellow erstwhile bachelor Bob Avellini fondly remembered Bob and Maggie's initial courtship back in 1979. "Maggie lived way on the south side of the city—but Bob was the type of guy who could pursue," the former quarterback said with a smile in thinking of those days. "That's always the way Bob has been with everything—if he wanted something, he could go after it. And that's probably why he is where he is right now."[22]

Mike Ditka agreed. "Bob is a go-getter; he is just an outstanding person and a class act," the coach said in 2018. "I have always appreciated what he did for the Bears, and I knew he would be a success in whatever he chose to do after football."[23]

On top of everything else, Bob also remains a caring sibling. "He's a good older brother," added Rick, a former college professor who in 2019 launched Ethical Presence Consulting, a firm that combines his skills in teaching, law, and improvisational theater to help companies and individuals attain their goals. "We were always close, and we were always each other's biggest fan. I loved watching him kick field goals, and he loved laughing at my jokes. If he missed a kick, I tried to make him feel better; and if no one laughed at my jokes, he tried to make me feel better. Bob is a character guy, and he got his character from our parents."[24]

Before Bob Thomas arrived, Mirro Roder was the last placekicker for the Chicago Bears in a game at RFK Stadium on December 15, 1974, against the Washington Redskins—the other team that had selected Thomas on the waiver wire that winter before he was awarded to Chicago. A decade later, the last field goal Bob would make in a Chicago uniform occurred in the Bears' playoff game in RFK Stadium against the Redskins almost ten years to the day—on December 30, 1984.

When Thomas finally departed the game in 1986, his 756 career points tied him with his boyhood football idol, Jim Brown, landing the pair just outside the top twenty all-time in the NFL and just ahead of Payton's 750. Heading into the 2019 season, Thomas and Brown stood at number 101 on the career list, while Bob still ranks fourth among Bears' scorers—behind Robbie Gould, Butler, and Payton—and third in team history in field goals made (128) and attempted (205). His fifty-five-yard field goal in 1975 was the Bears' longest until Butler matched it in 1993.

Regardless of what he decides to do next in life, Bob Thomas has achieved the rarity of reaching the pinnacle of two separate and distinct professions, for which he expressed gratitude in 2019.

> I've had two great careers. Every kid that plays youth football dreams of playing in the NFL, and I played professional football for twelve years. Every judge—and many attorneys—dream of being Supreme Court justices. I've been really blessed. But still, I think there may be something more. Even in retirement, I just don't see myself being a snowbird and playing golf six months out of the year. It's another aspect of faith. I want to make sure I say, "Lord, if You have something for me, make it clear; if You have something else, make it clear, and open my eyes to it, if it's what you'd have me do next." Instead of making my own plans—telling myself I'm going to do this and going to do that'—I just want to follow *His* plan.

> "For I know the plans I have for you," declares the Lord, "plans to prosper you and not to harm you, plans to give you hope and a future."
> *(Jeremiah 29:11 NIV)*

Thomas thus knows that, wherever the path leads, an omnipresent guiding force will show the way. "Faith helps you to prioritize. I certainly enjoy being a Supreme Court justice. Whatever I do next, I would imagine the same type of decisions I've made in the past will still apply. I want to make sure I have time with my wife and kids—and now it's my wife and my kids and my grandkids. So, that's still a priority, and based on an outgrowth of my faith. I've had time to be involved in ministry opportunities at my church and do speaking about my faith. I'd like to do more of that and talk about what a difference the Lord has made in my life. And maybe, when this job is through, I'll have even more time for that."

As usual, Maggie is up for anything he wants to try—and Bob appreciates her for it. "He really likes what he's doing," she noticed about his career in the law. "But he asks himself, 'Is there something else beyond this?' There's no answer yet. The question just pops into his head once in a while. For now, our kids and our grandkids are everything."[25]

To Pierson, the man who wrote about him for many years, Bob embodied a "me-second" servanthood all the way. "He was one of my favorite players because he had such a great attitude, sense of humor, and perspective on life—he could talk about more than just kicking," the *Tribune* scribe concluded in 2018.[26] The legendary Ara Parseghian agreed. "He had the skill as a kicker—good distance, good range," Parseghian said in early 2017 shortly before his death. "But it is Bob's quality as a person that I most remember."[27] At Ara's funeral in South Bend a few months later, teammate Jim Zloch stopped Thomas and several of his Notre Dame teammates while they were all walking back to the hotel, with the golden dome shining off in the distance. "We need to remember that we are part of Notre Dame history," Zloch told his friends. "We have gone on to do all sort of things in life, but this one moment that connects all of us." The good times were resurrected at Parseghian's ninetieth birthday party in 2013. "Doherty and I did another jingle," Thomas said of the event, "and we included Ara in the song."

Shortly after he was inducted into the Chicagoland Sports Hall of Fame in 2012 (joining Payton, Ditka, Bobby Hull, Ryne Sandberg, Harry Caray, and other notable figures), Bob received the Distinguished American Award from the National Football Foundation in February 2013. On hand to help honor his friend at the event was Brian Baschnagel, yet another ex-Bear who became successful in a second career as an executive for a large commercial distributor in the north suburbs of Chicago. While perhaps fighting the inclination to do so, the longtime holder refrained from pointing his fingers in the air in triumph when Bob was handed his plaque. "We were a great tandem for such a long time," Brian said of Bob. "It was a great privilege to be part of all those kicks he made. Bob was always very protective of me. He would ask me, 'Why do you have to play wide receiver and special teams? Why can't you just hold?'"[28]

Like anyone else, Thomas has endured times of uncertainty, such as when he wondered whether he was good enough to play at Notre Dame . . . whether he would get a chance in the NFL . . . whether he could balance the NFL and law school . . . whether he could return to the NFL . . . whether he would ever get a chance at being on a Super Bowl team . . . whether he could become a judge . . . and whether he could clear his good name in the most personal and public affront he could have ever imagined. But with every hurdle that arose, faith brought Bob through the valleys of life and back up to the sunlight. As bad times struck him down, it was his trust in God that kept him going, whispering into his ear that things can—and *will*—always change.

"I am fortunate because I have pulpit in being a judge and having played twelve years in the NFL. When I speak to people, I often tell them that 'I doubt that anyone is this room has missed out on being in a Super Bowl, but I definitely don't have a monopoly on disappointment.' As human beings, we think in terms of justice and fairness. But, in the end, it is really about trust in God's mercy. Our self-esteem isn't based on winning Super Bowls but on being children of God. That whole thing played out for me in 1985. That experience solidified faith for me. Regardless of who we are, where we go, what we do, or what we're forced to overcome, if we put our faith in the Lord, He is always looking out for us."

> Trust in the Lord with all your heart, and do not lean on your own
>   understanding.
> In all your ways acknowledge Him, and He will make straight your paths.
>   *(Proverbs 3:5–6 ESV)*

NOTES

1. A Ride to Freedom

1. Rick Thomas, interview with author, March 23, 2017.
2. Rick Thomas interview.
3. Rick Thomas interview.
4. Rolf Benirschke, interview with author, October 23, 2017.
5. Gary Gianforti, interview with author, March 21, 2017.
6. Scott Pitoniak, "Ex-NFL Kicker Recalls Hectic McQuaid Career," *Rochester Democrat and Chronicle*, June 17, 2008.
7. Steve Klein, "Thomas Kicks his Way toward Irish Record Book," *South Bend Tribune*, October 11, 1972.
8. Gianforti interview.
9. John Doser, "Excelling in Two Sports," *Rochester Democrat and Chronicle*, October 23, 1969.

2. South Bend

1. Brian Doherty, interview with author, February 12, 2017.
2. Tom Gora, "Four Years Later," *Scholastic 1973 Irish Football Review*, February 1, 1974, 16.

3. Gora, "Four Years Later."

4. Doherty interview.

5. Doherty interview.

6. Joe Doyle, "Irish Defense Snuffs Cats," *South Bend* (IN) *Tribune*, September 19, 1971.

7. Steve Klein, "Thomas Duels Dorais," *South Bend* (IN) *Tribune*, October 11, 1972.

8. Ara Parseghian, interview with author, February 8, 2017.

9. Joe Doyle, "Spartans Tough, N.D. Tougher," *South Bend* (IN) *Tribune*, October 8, 1972.

10. Paul Hornung, "The Midwest," *Sporting News*, October 21, 1972.

11. Parseghian interview.

12. Michael Haggerty, "Bob Thomas," *Go Irish!* February 21, 1983, 24.

13. Tom Gora, "I Get a Kick out of Life," *Scholastic 1973 Irish Football Review*, February 1, 1974, 23.

14. Gora, "I Get a Kick out of Life."

15. Gora, "I Get a Kick out of Life."

16. Brian Doherty, interview with author, February 12, 2017.

17. Doherty interview.

18. Doherty interview.

19. Parseghian interview.

20. Doherty interview.

21. Ray Sons, "Ex-Bear Judges Butler Problem," *Chicago Sun-Times*, September 8, 1981.

22. Doherty interview.

23. Dave Casper, interview with author, February 8, 2017.

24. Casper interview.

25. Casper interview.

26. Peter Finney, "Irish Ride Tide to Crest in Sugar Spectacular," *Sporting News*, January 19, 1974.

27. Parseghian interview.

3. Claimed on Waivers

1. Joe Hendrickson, "The Kicking Game," *Pasadena Star-News*, August 4, 1974.

2. Jim Murray, "The One Footman," *Los Angeles Times*, July 31, 1974.

3. Murray, "The One Footman."

4. Hendrickson, "The Kicking Game."

5. Michael Lewis, "Thomas: Right Now I'm No. 1," *Rochester Democrat and Chronicle*, August 7, 1974.

6. John Smith, "WFL Castoff Alive, Kicking," *Florida Today*, August 4, 1974.

7. Smith, "WFL Castoff."

8. Ron Martz, "Father Is No Doubting Thomas," *St. Petersburg Times*, September 27, 1974.

9. Martz, "Father Is No Doubting Thomas."

10. Charles Leroux, "A Time to Sweat," *Chicago Tribune*, August 31, 1975.

11. Brian Doherty, interview with author, May 13, 2017.

12. Bob Avellini, interview with author, September 28, 2017.

13. Peter Pascarelli, "Thomas's Kicking Makes His Points," *Rochester Democrat and Chronicle*, August 13, 1975.

14. Don Pierson, interview with author, December 5, 2018.

15. Avellini interview.

16. Doug Plank, interview with author, January 18, 2017.

17. Plank interview.

18. Don Pierson, "Unbearably Colt (35–7) NFL Debut," *Chicago Tribune*, September 22, 1975.

19. Pierson, "Unbearably Colt."

20. Jeff Pearlman, *Sweetness: The Enigmatic Life of Walter Payton* (New York: Gotham Books, 2011), 58.

21. *Pro Football Weekly*, "NFC Review," October 7, 1975.

22. Gary Huff, interview with author, May 1, 2017.

23. Bob Oates, "Knox Philosophy Tested," *Los Angeles Times*, October 2, 1975.

24. Steve Schubert, interview with author, February 15, 2017.

25. Plank interview.

26. Terry Schmidt, interview with author, January 25, 2017.

4. The Meadowlands

1. Brian Baschnagel, interview with author, February 15, 2017.

2. Don Pierson, "Bear Hopeful Sells Kicks, or Insurance," *Chicago Tribune*, July 14, 1976.

3. Pierson, "Bear Hopeful."

4. Pierson, "Bear Hopeful."

5. Jim Selman, "'Luck of the Irish' Beats Bucs," *Tampa Tribune*, August 29, 1976.

6. Dan Stoneking, "Bear Could Kick Himself," *Minneapolis Star*, October 11, 1976.

7. Stoneking, "Bear Could Kick Himself."

8. Don Pierson, "Referee's Whistle Blows Bears Dead," *Chicago Tribune*, November 8, 1976.

9. Pierson, "Referee's Whistle."

10. Kevin Lamb, "Bears Fall to Raiders," *Chicago Daily News*, November 8, 1976.

11. Pierson, "Referee's Whistle."

12. Pierson, "Referee's Whistle."

13. Don Pierson, interview with author, December 5, 2018.

14. John Czarnecki, "Thomas Stays the Course," *Rochester Times-Union*, November 11, 1976.

15. Don Pierson, "Thomas Eager for Next Kick," *Chicago Tribune*, November 10, 1976.

16. Czarnecki, "Thomas Stays the Course."

17. Kevin Lamb, "Shaking Off the Shanks," *Chicago Daily News*, August 3, 1977.

18. Doug Plank, interview with author, January 18, 2017.

19. John Husar, "New Style Gives Thomas Big Kick," *Chicago Tribune*, August 28, 1977.

20. Husar, "New Style."

21. Lamb, "Shaking Off the Shanks."

22. Ray Buck, "Better Days Ahead," *Rochester Times-Union*, September 16, 1977.

23. Buck, "Better Days."

24. Terry Schmidt, interview with author, January 25, 2017.

25. Baschnagel interview.

26. Bob Avellini, interview with author, September 28, 2017

27. Ray Buck, "Bears Make Playoffs with Overtime Win," *Rochester Democrat and Chronicle*, December 19, 1977.

28. Don Pierson, "Bears Reach Playoffs—Miraculously," *Chicago Tribune*, December 19, 1977.

29. Pierson, "Bears Reach Playoffs."

30. Jerry Izenberg, "An Unlikely Hero," *Newark Star-Ledger*, December 19, 1977.

31. Bob Parsons, interview with author, May 5, 2017.

32. Dan Neal, interview with author, May 18, 2017.

33. John Schulian, "Bears Basking in Thrilling Win," *Chicago Daily News*, December 20, 1977.

34. Don Pierson and Dan Pompei, *Chicago Bears Centennial Scrapbook* (Winnetka, IL: Rare Air Media), 14.

35. Dan Bickley, "Thanks for the Memories," *Chicago Sun-Times*, July 7, 1993.

36. Pierson, "Bears Reach Playoffs."

37. Pierson, "Bears Reach Playoffs."

38. Pierson, "Bears Reach Playoffs."

39. Avellini interview.

40. Don Pierson, "Don't Hassle Bob Thomas, He Can Cope," *Chicago Tribune*, December 24, 1977.

5. Maggie

1. Don Pierson, "Bears Name Viking Aide Head Coach," *Chicago Tribune*, February 17, 1978.

2. Pierson, "Bears Name Viking Aide."

3. Maggie Thomas, interview with author, May 16, 2017.

4. Maggie Thomas interview.

5. Brian Doherty, interview with author, May 13, 2017.

6. Don Pierson, "Thomas Can't Kick about Attention," *Chicago Tribune*, July 27, 1978.

7. Pierson, "Thomas Can't Kick about Attention."

8. Pierson, "Thomas Can't Kick about Attention."

9. Pierson, "Thomas Can't Kick about Attention."

10. John Skibinski, interview with author, December 2, 2017.

11. Ralph Reeve, "Vikings Notes," *St. Paul* (MN) *Evening Dispatch*, November 9, 1979.

12. Kevin Lamb, "Thomas Shoots for New Heights," *Chicago Sun-Times*, November 26, 1978.

13. Don Pierson, "Are Eight Enough for Skidding Bears?" *Chicago Tribune*, November 13, 1978.

14. Lamb, "Thomas Shoots for New Heights."

15. Pierson, "Are Eight Enough."

16. Pierson, "Are Eight Enough."

17. Rick Woodson, "Thomas Takes the Pressure in Stride," *Rochester Times-Union*, October 4, 1979.

18. Jeff Pearlman, *Sweetness: The Enigmatic Life of Walter Payton* (New York: Gotham Books, 2011), 233.

19. Larry Bump, "Bears' Hopes Against Cardinals Riding on Thomas," *Rochester Democrat and Chronicle*, December 14, 1979.

20. Robin Earl, interview with author, March 9, 2017.

21. Don Pierson, "Incredible Day for the Bears," *Chicago Tribune*, December 17, 1979.

22. Earl interview.

23. Earl interview.

24. Skibinski interview.

6. Cut

1. Don Pierson, "Bears Sputter after One Long Drive, Lose to Giants," *Chicago Tribune*, August 9, 1981.

2. Don Pierson, "Bears Figure Two Top Rookies Look Good for Starters," *Chicago Tribune*, July 26, 1981.

3. Pierson, "Bears Sputter."

4. Larry Casey, "Sports Log," *Chicago Tribune*, August 20, 1981.

5. Mike Kiley, "Hans Becomes Hero by Accident," *Chicago Tribune*, August 23, 1981.

6. Kevin Lamb, "NFC Central," *Sporting News*, October 10, 1981.

7. Kiley, "Hans Becomes Hero."

8. Don Pierson, "Our Spotty Bears are on the Spot," *Chicago Tribune*, August 30, 1981.

9. Don Pierson, "Bears Recall Nielsen; Thomas Out," *Chicago Tribune*, September 17, 1981.

10. Pierson, "Bears Recall Nielsen."

11. Pierson, "Bears Recall Nielsen."

12. Don Pierson, "Bears Give Kicker Hans Nielsen Another Boot," *Chicago Tribune*, October 7, 1981.

13. Don Pierson, "Fans Growl as Rams Maul Wounded Bears," *Chicago Tribune*, September 29, 1981.

14. Don Pierson, "An Annual Event: The Bears Swoon in Vikingland," *Chicago Tribune*, October 5, 1981.

15. Steve Daley, "Some Moments Worth Reliving," *Chicago Tribune*, December 25, 1981.

16. Pierson, "An Annual Event."

17. Pierson, "Bears Give Kicker."

18. Pierson, "Bears Give Kicker."

19. Pierson, "Bears Give Kicker."

20. Pierson, "Bears Give Kicker."

21. Pierson, "Bears Give Kicker."

22. Howard Balzer, "Pro Football Focus," *Sporting News*, November 7, 1981.

23. Mike Kiley, "Reject Aches to Boot Bucs for Bears," *Chicago Tribune*, October 28, 1981.

24. Kiley, "Reject Aches."

25. Don Pierson, "Ditka Remains at the Top of Halas's Shopping List," *Chicago Tribune*, January 5, 1982.

26. Jeff Pearlman, *Sweetness: The Enigmatic Life of Walter Payton* (New York: Gotham Books, 2011), 272.

27. Lyle Rolfe, "Thomas Kicking at New Career," *Aurora* (IL) *Beacon-News*, April 24, 1982.

28. Rolfe, "Thomas Kicking."

29. John Fineran, "New Bears' Regime Has Thomas Enthused," *South Bend Tribune*, April 14, 1982.

30. Fineran, "New Bears' Regime."

31. Frank LaGrotta, "Former McQuaid Star Looking to Compete," *Rochester Times-Union*, July 20, 1982.

32. LaGrotta, "Former McQuaid Star."

33. Don Pierson, "Bears' Cut a Shocker to Thomas," *Chicago Tribune*, September 7, 1982.

34. Pierson, "Bears' Cut."

35. Pierson, "Bears' Cut."

36. Pierson, "Bears' Cut."

37. Kevin Lamb, "NFC Central," *Sporting News*, September 13, 1982.

38. Lamb, "NFC Central," September 13, 1982.

39. Lamb, "NFC Central," September 13, 1982.

40. Lamb, "NFC Central," September 13, 1982.

41. Pierson, "Bears' Cut."

42. Doug Plank, interview with author, January 18, 2017.

7. Resilience

1. Eddie Murray, interview with author, September 7, 2017.

2. Don Pierson, "Lions Give Thomas a Tryout," *Chicago Tribune*, September 9, 1982.

3. Pierson, "Lions Give."

4. Mike Kiley, "Thomas will Get his Kicks Sunday," *Chicago Tribune*, September 10, 1982.

5. Mike Downey, "With Kickers Gone, Lions Can't Be Doubting Thomas," *Detroit Free Press*, September 8, 1982.

6. John James, interview with author, December 11, 2017.

7. Mike Thomas, "How Chicago Shaped Stephen Colbert," *Chicago Reader*, September 3, 2015.

8. Mike Kiley, "Lions Can't Figure Bears, Either," *Chicago Tribune*, September 13, 1982.

9. Kiley, "Lions Can't Figure."

10. James interview.

11. Tom Skladany, interview with author, September 5, 2017.

12. Don Pierson, "Bears Tackle Sore Spot," *Chicago Tribune*, September 14, 1982.

13. Kevin Lamb, "NFC Central," *Sporting News*, September 20, 1982.

14. James interview.

15. Don Pierson, "Thomas Suffers the Unkindest Cut of All," *Chicago Tribune*, November 21, 1982.

16. Pierson, "Thomas Suffers."

17. James interview.

18. Brian Hewitt, "Mistakes Doom Bears Again," *Chicago Sun-Times*, November 29, 1982.

19. Curt Sylvester, "Pro Football," *Detroit Free Press*, December 9, 1982.

20. Kevin Lamb, "NFC Central," *Sporting News*, December 27, 1982.

21. Lamb, "NFC Central," December 27, 1982.

22. Joe Distelheim, "Bears Have Their Old Boot Back," *Detroit Free Press*, December 22, 1982.

23. Don Pierson, "Bears Gasp, but Stay Alive," *Chicago Tribune*, December 27, 1982.

24. Steve Daley, "Chicago Finally Sporting a Winner," *Chicago Tribune*, December 26, 1982.

25. Pierson, "Bears Gasp."

26. Pierson, "Bears Gasp."

8. Comeback

1. Michael Haggerty, "Bob Thomas," *Go Irish!* February 21, 1983, 24.

2. Mitch Lawrence, "Bears' Thomas Is Taking NFL Experiences into Courtroom," *Rochester Democrat and Chronicle*, February 5, 1985.

3. Don Pierson, "While Ditka Burns, Bears' Players Fidget," *Chicago Tribune*, October 16, 1983.

4. Don Pierson, "Roasters Only Singe Big Bear," *Chicago Tribune*, March 13, 1984.

5. John Husar, "Ditka's Way: Make 'em Pay," *Chicago Tribune*, October 17, 1983.

6. Eddie Murray, interview with author, September 7, 2017.

7. Don Pierson, "Bears Bumble, Stumble," *Chicago Tribune*, October 17, 1983.

8. Pierson, "Bears Bumble."

9. Husar, "Ditka's Way."

10. Husar, "Ditka's Way."

11. Murray interview.

12. Husar, "Ditka's Way."

13. Don Pierson, "Bears-Lions: A Series of Broken Bones," *Chicago Tribune*, October 30, 1983.

14. Pierson, "Bears-Lions."

15. Pierson, "Bears-Lions."

16. Don Pierson, "Bears' 2nd Season Looks Awfully Familiar," *Chicago Tribune*, October 31, 1983.

17. Murray interview.

18. Greg Couch, "No Easy Feet," *Chicago Sun-Times*, November 16, 1999.

19. Murray interview.

20. Bob Parsons, interview with author, May 2, 2017.

21. Steve Daley, "Just a Bit of Parting Warmth," *Chicago Tribune*, December 19, 1983.

22. Kevin Lamb, "NFC Central," *Sporting News*, December 26, 1983.

23. Bill Jauss, "'A Bitter Defeat,'" *Chicago Tribune*, December 19, 1983.

24. Bob Logan, "Ditka Sees Offensive Line as Key to Bears," *Chicago Tribune*, July 27, 1984.

25. Daley, "Just a Bit."

26. Brian Baschnagel, interview with author, February 15, 2017.

27. Baschnagel interview.

28. Bob McCoy, "Keeping Score," *Sporting News*, January 30, 1984.

29. Daley, "Just a Bit."

9. Hitting New Heights

1. Steve Daley, "Just a Bit of Parting Warmth," *Chicago Tribune*, December 19, 1983.

2. Daley, "Just a Bit."

3. Cooper Rollow, "Slow Start Unbearable," *Chicago Tribune*, August 22, 1984.

4. Cooper Rollow, "Bears Restore Lost Emotion," *Chicago Tribune*, September 10, 1984.

5. Rollow, "Bears Restore."

6. *Chicago Sun-Times* (no author), September 10, 1984.

7. *Chicago Sun-Times*, September 10, 1984.

8. Brian Baschnagel, interview with author, February 15, 2017.

9. Kevin Lamb, "Under the Pressure, Chicago Bears Up," *The Sporting News*, December 10, 1984.

10. Terry Schmidt, interview with author, January 25, 2017.

11. Schmidt interview.

12. Don Pierson, "Bears' Schmidt Quits after 11 Pro Seasons," *Chicago Tribune*, April 18, 1985.

13. Schmidt interview.

10. Faith Rewarded

1. Don Pierson, "Bears Pull Big Surprise," *Chicago Tribune*, May 1, 1985.

2. Don Pierson, "Thomas Now in Step with Bears' Decision," *Chicago Tribune*, May 5, 1985.

3. Ray Sons, "Camp Competition for Thomas," *Chicago Sun-Times*, August 11, 1985.

4. Sons, "Camp Competition."

5. Sons, "Camp Competition."

6. Sons, "Camp Competition."

7. Ed Sherman, "Wrightman Impresses Ditka," *Chicago Tribune*, August 18, 1985.

8. Don Pierson, "Bears Out to Deal a Few Telling Blows," *Chicago Tribune*, August 26, 1985.

9. Don Pierson, "Bear Offense Receives a Much-Needed Lift," *Chicago Tribune*, August 31, 1985.

10. Ed Sherman, "Some Bears to Lose Jobs on Labor Day," *Chicago Tribune*, September 2, 1985.

11. Bob Verdi, "Thomas's Emotions Getting Kicked Around," *Chicago Tribune*, September 2, 1985.

12. Verdi, "Thomas's Emotions."

13. Verdi, "Thomas's Emotions."

14. Don Pierson, "Thomas Gets the Ax," *Chicago Tribune*, September 3, 1985.

15. Kevin Lamb, "Thomas Left on the Outside," *Chicago Sun-Times*, September 3, 1985.

16. Pierson, "Thomas Gets the Ax."

17. Pierson, "Thomas Gets the Ax."

18. Lamb, "Thomas Left."

19. Skip Myslenski and Linda Kay, "Odds and Ins," *Chicago Tribune*, September 4, 1985.

20. Myslenski and Kay, "Odds and Ins."

21. Rich Lorenz, "Thomas Signs with Chargers," *Chicago Tribune*, September 13, 1985.

22. Rolf Benirschke, interview with author, October 23, 2017.

23. Benirschke interview.

24. Chris Cobbs, "Chargers Notes," *North County* (San Diego, CA) *Times*, September 16, 1985.

25. Dave Distel, "Former Bear Finds Super Bowl Absence Bearable After All," *Los Angeles Times*, January 25, 1986.

26. Cobbs, "Chargers Notes," *North County* (San Diego, CA) *Times*, September 23, 1985.

27. Rich Lorenz, "Thomas Has Starring Role in Charger Victory," *Chicago Tribune*, September 23, 1985.

28. Clark Judge, "Convinced Rolf's Ready, Thomas Requests Release," *San Diego Tribune*, April 5, 1986.

29. Kevin Oklobzija, "Thomas's Faith Is Unshaken," *Rochester Democrat and Chronicle*, November 21, 1985.

30. Dave Distel, "Former Bear Finds Super Bowl Absence Bearable After All," *Los Angeles Times*, January 25, 1986.

31. Bob Verdi, "Butler Knows His Job Cold," *Chicago Tribune*, January 7, 1986.

32. Verdi, "Butler Knows."

33. Skip Myslenski and Linda Kay, "Odds and Ins," *Chicago Tribune*, January 7, 1986.

34. Scott Pitoniak, "Former McQuaid Star Counts Blessings," *Rochester Democrat and Chronicle*, January 21, 1986.

11. Boot Camp—and Moving On

1. Scott Pitoniak, "Former McQuaid Star Counts Blessings," *Rochester Democrat and Chronicle*, January 21, 1986.

2. Clark Judge, "Convinced Rolf's Ready, Thomas Requests Release," *San Diego Tribune*, April 5, 1986.

3. Rolf Benirschke, interview with author, October 23, 2017.

4. Herb Gould, "It's Boot Camp for Ex-Bear Thomas," *Chicago Sun-Times*, August 5, 1986.

5. Gould, "It's Boot Camp."

6. Gould, "It's Boot Camp."

7. Scott Pitoniak, "More Than Just an Ex-Jock," *Rochester Democrat and Chronicle*, March 5, 1993.

8. Robin Earl, interview with author, March 9, 2017.

9. Skip Myslenski and Linda Kay, "Odds and Ins," *Chicago Tribune*, May 21, 1987.

10. Thomas Frisbie, "Former Bear Bob Thomas Wins Court Nomination," *Chicago Sun-Times*, March 16, 1988.

11. Jan Crawford, "Ex-Bear Wins Race for Judge," *Chicago Tribune*, November 9, 1988.

12. Crawford, "Ex-Bear Wins."

13. Jan Crawford, "New Judge will Hear Civil Cases," *Chicago Tribune*, November 10, 1988.

14. Kevin Schmit, "Fresh Talent Keys Naperville Soccer Squads," *Daily Herald*, September 8, 1995.

15. Jonathan Thomas, interview with author, November 21, 2017.

16. Pitoniak, "More Than Just an Ex-Jock."

17. Dr. Charlie Ireland, interview with author, July 17, 2018.

18. John Skibinski, interview with author, December 2, 2017.

19. Brendan Thomas, interview with author, November 17, 2017.

20. Kevin Schmit, "Fresh Talent Keys Naperville Soccer Squads," *Daily Herald* (Arlington Heights, IL), September 8, 1995.

21. Schmit, "Fresh Talent."

22. John McCarthy, "Now, Judge Bob Thomas Bears Down as a Coach," *Chicago Tribune*, October 22, 1995.

23. Rev. Patrick King, interview with author, January 11, 2019.

12. Justice Tempered with Civility

1. Janan Hanna, "State High Court Vacancy May Affect DuPage County," *Chicago Tribune*, December 15, 1998.
2. Ted Gregory, "Thomas Kicks Off Run for High Court," *Chicago Tribune*, September 14, 1999.
3. Jessica Thomas, interview with author, October 1, 2017.
4. Janan Hanna, "Supreme Court Shuffle?" *Chicago Tribune*, March 15, 2000.
5. Janan Hanna, "Da Coach Stumps for Judge Thomas," *Chicago Tribune*, March 3, 2000.
6. Hanna, "Da Coach."
7. Michael Sneed, "Sneed," *Chicago Sun-Times*, March 3, 2000.
8. Jeff Coen, "Atty. Gen. Ryan Gives Backing to Rathje for State High Court," *Chicago Tribune*, February 8, 2000.
9. Janan Hanna, "High Court Hopefuls Shift into High Gear," *Chicago Tribune*, March 9, 2000.
10. Hanna, "Supreme Court Shuffle?"
11. N. Don Wycliff, "Thomas, Hawkinson for High Court," *Chicago Tribune*, March 5, 2000.
12. N. Don Wycliff, "A Small Lesson in Big-Money Politics," *Chicago Tribune*, March 23, 2000.
13. R. Bruce Dold, "For the Illinois Supreme Court," *Chicago Tribune*, October 25, 2000.
14. Carol Ritter, "Ex-Football Player Warms New Bench—as a Judge," *Rochester Democrat and Chronicle*, November 9, 2000.

13. Integrity

1. James Kimberly, "Judge Wins $7 Million in Libel Trial," *Chicago Tribune*, November 15, 2006.
2. Report of Proceedings, Circuit Court for the Sixteenth Judicial District of Illinois, Thomas v. Page, et al., 3544–3545, November 13, 2006.
3. Dan Rozek, "Libel Trial Kicks Chief Justice to Other Side of Bench," *Chicago Sun-Times*, October 22, 2006.
4. "Metro Briefs," *Chicago Sun-Times* (no author), January 16, 2004.
5. Joe Power, interview with author, February 28, 2018.
6. Maggie Thomas, interview with author, March 27, 2018.
7. Power interview.
8. Power interview.
9. Dan Rozek, "'Making Up Facts' Alleged in Libel Case," *Chicago Sun-Times*, November 7, 2006.
10. Dan Rozek, "Justices Support Chief in Libel Lawsuit," *Chicago Sun-Times*, November 1, 2006.

11. Russell Working, "Justices Stand by Colleague in Defamation Trial in Kane," *Chicago Tribune*, November 1, 2006.

12. Justice Rita Garman, interview with author, March 23, 2018.

13. Matt Hanley, "Chief Judge Says He Was Humiliated by Accusations Made by Columnist," *Aurora* (IL) *Beacon-News*, November 8, 2006.

14. Report of Proceedings, Circuit Court for the Sixteenth Judicial District of Illinois, Thomas v. Page, et al., 2424, November 7, 2006.

15. Report of Proceedings, Circuit Court for the Sixteenth Judicial District of Illinois, Thomas v. Page, et al., 3539, November 13, 2006.

16. Dan Rozek, "I Never Witnessed Thomas Bias," *Chicago Sun-Times*, November 2, 2006.

17. Russell Working, "Ex-Columnist Didn't Seek Justice's Side, He Testifies," *Chicago Tribune*, November 2, 2006.

18. Eric Herman, "Justice's Libel Suit Figures His Losses," *Chicago Sun-Times*, July 10, 2006.

19. Russell Working, "Writer Defends Stories on Judge," *Chicago Tribune*, November 3, 2006.

20. Report of Proceedings, Circuit Court for the Sixteenth Judicial District of Illinois, Thomas v. Page, et al., 3544–3537, November 13, 2006.

21. Matt Hanley, "Justices, Columnist Expected to Testify in Thomas Lawsuit," *Aurora* (IL) *Beacon-News*, October 31, 2006.

22. Matt Hanley, "Justice Thomas's Libel Suit Goes to the Jury," *Aurora* (IL) *Beacon-News*, November 14, 2006.

23. Dan Rozek and Abdon Pallasch, "Top Judge Gets $7 Million," *Chicago Sun-Times*, November 15, 2006.

24. Rozek and Pallasch, "Top Judge."

25. Rozek and Pallasch, "Top Judge."

26. Adam Liptak, "A Judge at the Plaintiff's Table Tips the Scales," *New York Times*, June 25, 2007.

27. Russell Working, "Newspaper Rejects Reduced Libel Award," *Chicago Tribune*, November 28, 2006.

14. Looking Ahead

1. Melissa Jenco, "Son Follows Footsteps of Supreme Court Justice Father," *Chicago Tribune*, November 17, 2011.

2. Judge Debra Walker, interview with author, January 23, 2018.

3. Walker interview.

4. Walker interview.

5. Justice Anne Burke, interview with author, March 21, 2018.

6. Justice Rita Garman, interview with author, March 22, 2018.

7. Justice Thomas Kilbride, interview with author, March 27, 2018.

8. Justice Mary Jane Theis, interview with author, April 4, 2018.

9. Justice Lloyd Karmeier, interview with author, March 23, 2018.

10. Jeff Diveronica, "Ex-McQuaid Coach Dies," *Rochester Democrat and Chronicle*, July 28, 2010.

11. Dr. John Grieco, interview with author, April 24, 2018.

12. Dr. John Grieco interview.

13. Dr. John Grieco interview.

14. Mike Grieco, interview with author, April 3, 2018.

15. Mike Grieco interview.

16. Dr. John Grieco interview.

17. Steve Huntley, "GOP Looks to Unusual Suspects for Gov Race," *Chicago Sun-Times*, March 17, 2009.

18. Jessica Thomas, interview with author, April 7, 2018.

19. Justice Rita Garman, interview with author, March 23, 2018.

20. Justice Thomas Kilbride, interview with author, March 28, 2018.

21. Kilbride interview.

22. Bob Avellini, interview with author, September 28, 2017.

23. Mike Ditka, interview with author, March 22, 2018.

24. Rick Thomas, interview with author, March 23, 2017.

25. Maggie Thomas, interview with author, March 27, 2018.

26. Don Pierson, interview with author, December 5, 2018.

27. Ara Parseghian, interview with author, February 8, 2017.

28. Brian Baschnagel, interview with author, February 15, 2017.

INDEX